FAMILY ENVIRONMENT
AND DELINQUENCY

FAMILY ENVIRONMENT
AND
DELINQUENCY

by

SHELDON AND ELEANOR GLUECK

Harvard Law School

With the Statistical Assistance of Rose W. Kneznek
Director of Research Services, United Research Inc.
Cambridge, Massachusetts

HOUGHTON MIFFLIN COMPANY
BOSTON

First published 1962
Printed in Great Britain

To Our Valued Friend and Colleague
the late
SAMUEL ANDREW STOUFFER
Fearless Architect of the Social Sciences

CONTENTS

Contents

PREFACE

THIS is not a 'how to' book; nor is it one that can be sketchily read. Its content needs to be thoroughly mastered by the earnest reader who already has some familiarity with the parent volume, *Unraveling Juvenile Delinquency*, and with *Physique and Delinquency*. We point this out in order not to disappoint those who may be attracted to this work by its title, *Family Environment and Delinquency*. Knowledge is not gained without effort, and we, the authors, who have labored over the course of five years to bring this work to fruition in the hope that it will provide new insights into the etiology of juvenile delinquency, are still in process of digesting the findings.

If the reader is a criminologist, he should find some light on the bewildering question of why it is that not *all* children in a given family or in a given neighborhood become delinquent, despite similarity in their 'subculture'; if he is a psychologist, he may find himself in the midst of the age-old controversy about the relative impact of Nature and Nurture on the formation of character and personality. The facts and inferences of this book may not be to his liking; but before he adopts a destructively critical attitude, we hope he will master the analysis of the probable orientation of traits which comprises Part I of this work.

If the reader is a clinician facing the daily problem of treating antisocial children, his major focus should be on Part II of this volume, where the differential impact of various aspects of the home environment on the delinquency of children possessing certain traits has emerged as the basic finding. His imagination may be quickened by the implications of this discovery for his task of rehabilitating such children. He might even gain comfort from the fact that there are unfortunately inescapable limits to his success in the treatment of certain delinquents as suggested by the study. And if the reader is an educator, or a social worker, or a clergyman, he may glean hints on how to modify some of the time-worn procedures that have guided his re-educative and preventive efforts.

In the achievement of this work, as in our previous inquiries, we are indebted to the Harvard Law School and to Dean Erwin N. Griswold for sponsorship of our continuing researches; and to the

ix

Ford Foundation which, since 1952, has been providing the major financial support to our work.

We wish also to thank our statistical consultant, Dr. Jane Worcester, Associate Professor of Biostatistics, Harvard School of Public Health, with whose aid we were able to clarify certain knotty problems concerning the management of the data during the early stages of this research.

Our debt is great to Mrs. Rose Kneznek, formerly Executive Secretary of the Bureau of Business Research of the Harvard Graduate School of Business Administration, and more recently Director of Research Services of United Research Inc., Cambridge, Mass. Her technical understanding of our basic materials and the meticulous care with which she has supervised every detail involved in key-punching, sorting, and tabulating the data, setting up tables and exhibits, and carrying out certain editorial tasks, has been of inestimable aid to us. We wish also to thank Mrs. Bonnie Winberg of United Research Inc. for her considerable contribution in the typing and retyping of the many exhibits.

We must also express our appreciation to the members of our small staff—Mildred P. Cunningham and George F. McGrath (now Massachusetts Commissioner of Correction)—for the preparation in 1949 of 'The Case of Henry W' which constitutes Appendix A of this volume; to Mrs. Sheila Murphrey, for her quiet attention to numerous matters pertaining to the functioning of our research program; and to Dorothea Munro, for frequent retypings of the manuscript (which has gone through several revisions).

And, finally, to readers in different lands we would like to say that their continuing interest in our researches is most encouraging and gratifying, and their perceptive criticisms are challenging. After long effort and much questioning of the materials, we are ready to release this volume. We shall await the reactions of our readers with great interest.

SHELDON AND ELEANOR GLUECK

Harvard Law School
March 24, 1961

'Up to the present, all the systems in terms of which men have attempted to think about human differences have been unsatisfactory. Some, for example, have conspicuously failed to cover more than a part of the relevant facts. This is especially true of psychology and sociology as commonly taught and practiced at the present time. How many of even the best of our psychologists talk, write, think, and act as though the human body, with its innate constitution and its acquired habits, were something that, in an analysis of mental states, could safely be ignored. And even when they do admit, rather reluctantly, that the mind always trails its carcass behind it, they have little or nothing to tell us about the ways in which mental and physical characteristics are related.

'Sociologists deal with abstractions even more phantasmally bodiless. For example, they will carry out laborious researches into the problems of marriage. But when we read the results, we are flabbergasted to find that the one factor never taken into account by the researchers is who the men and women under investigation actually *are*. We are told every detail about their social and economic background; nothing at all about their inherited psycho-physical constitution.

'There are other classificatory systems which claim to be comprehensive, but in which the indispensable process of simplification has been carried so far that they are no longer true to the facts. The interpretation of all human activity in terms of economics is a case in point. Another type of oversimplification is to be found in such theories as those of Helvetius in the eighteenth century and of certain Behaviorists in the twentieth—theories which profess to account for everything that men do or are in terms of environment, education, or conditioned reflexes. At the other extreme of oversimplification we find some of the more rabid Eugenists, who attribute all the observable differences between human beings to hereditary factors, and refuse to admit that environmental influences may also play a part.'

—ALDOUS HUXLEY, 'Who Are You?' in
Gentlemen, Scholars and Scoundrels

'Science advances one step, then another, and then draws back and meditates before taking a third. Does the impossibility of taking that last step suppress the success acquired by the two others? Would you say to an infant who hesitated before a third step, having ventured on two previous ones: "Thy former efforts are of no avail; never shalt thou walk"?'

—LOUIS PASTEUR

INTRODUCTION

I

BACKGROUND OF INQUIRY

ONE of the most crucial weaknesses in pre-existing analyses of delinquency causation has been the failure to ascertain the specific psychologic and physiologic traits and the specific factors in the environment which occur more frequently among delinquents than among nondelinquents. In addition, there has been little attempt to determine which traits, reasonably inferred by such comparison to be associated with delinquency, are essentially hereditary and which are essentially environmental.

In *Unraveling Juvenile Delinquency*[1] a contribution was made toward filling the first gap—the determination of statistically significant differences between a representative sample of true delinquents and a matched sample of true nondelinquents. In *Physique and Delinquency*[2] a second step was taken—that of isolating those traits for which reasonable grounds exist to assume that they are essentially *constitutional* in orientation. In the present work our aim is to take a third step—to ascertain the involvement of sociocultural influences (largely in the most intimate *environmental* circle, the home with its under-the-roof culture) in the laying down and moulding of delinquency-related traits both in general and with respect to boys of various physique types. Only then are we in a position to take the fourth step—to learn something definitive about the relationship of delinquency-related factors and traits to the genesis of delinquency and thereby to define more specifically the targets of preventive effort.

In *Physique and Delinquency*[3] we focused attention on one important aspect of the causal complex in delinquent behavior—bodily morphology and certain of its accompanying traits. It was pointed out that preoccupation with the constitutional matrix in criminogenesis does not necessarily imply that we regard genetic influence

---

[1] Sheldon and Eleanor Glueck, *Unraveling Juvenile Delinquency*, New York, The Commonwealth Fund, 1950.
[2] Sheldon and Eleanor Glueck, *Physique and Delinquency*, New York, Harper & Brothers, 1956.
[3] S. and E. T. Glueck, *op. cit.*

3

as the weightiest of the forces making for delinquency. The inquiry into the relationship between body structure and delinquency was merely one avenue of exploration.

The present volume is the second of these intensive analyses. It examines in detail the opposite side of the presentation in *Physique and Delinquency*, by focusing upon certain sociocultural influences involved in the development of traits (in general and differentially among various body types) and, in turn, in the criminogenic dynamism.

It is helpful, at the outset, to review the plan of the basic research from which both the present volume and the preceding one derive, as in these two works we continue the quest begun in *Unraveling Juvenile Delinquency* (published in 1950), a wide-ranging first inquiry into the etiologic involvements in juvenile crime. In it were compared, in respect to the presence or absence of some 400 traits and factors, 500 true delinquents and 500 proven nondelinquents. It should be mentioned that relatively persistent delinquents were chosen because these are representative of true rather than of pseudo-offenders (the latter being those who once or twice steal a toy, sneak into a motion picture theater, or truant—prohibited behavior that many children not infrequently indulge in by way of experimental deviation from legally dictated norms). Delinquents, as used in *Unraveling*, are children between seven and seventeen years of age who commit repeated acts of a kind which, when carried out by persons beyond the statutory juvenile court age of sixteen, are punishable as crimes (either felonies or misdemeanors).

The 500 delinquents were drawn from the two correctional schools of Massachusetts—Lyman and Shirley. Much effort and care was devoted to matching them with 500 proven nondelinquents in terms of age, general intelligence (I.Q.), ethnico-racial derivation and residence in depressed areas of Greater Boston.[1] This was a prerequisite to the intensive comparison of the delinquent with the nondelinquent group.

As is true of all research of this kind, general conclusions must be interpreted in the light of the major aspects and limitations of the two samples compared. However, widespread experience with a prediction table emerging from this comparison, based on five factors of family life that were found most markedly to differentiate de-

---

[1] S. and E. T. Glueck, *Unraveling Juvenile Delinquency*, Chapter IV, pp. 27 *et seq.*, 'Selecting and Matching Delinquents and Non-Delinquents.' See also, S. Glueck, 'Ten Years of Unraveling Juvenile Delinquency, An Examination of Criticisms,' *Journal of Criminal Law, Criminology and Police Science*, Vol. 51, No. 3, September–October 1960, pp. 283–308.

linquents from nondelinquents,[1] together with other evidence derived from *Unraveling Juvenile Delinquency*, would seem to indicate that the samples in question are more typical of true juvenile offenders in general than might offhand be assumed.[2]

Basic data for comparison of the delinquents with the control group were derived from intensive exploration of various aspects of the family structure and psychology of the two groups of boys, their physique, their health, certain aspects of their intelligence, their temperament, and their personality and character.

As pointed out in *Physique and Delinquency*, the matching of the delinquents and nondelinquents in respect to ethnico-racial derivation (an Irish delinquent with an Irish nondelinquent, an Italian with an Italian, and so on) enhances the reliability of the morphologic findings in that the differences shown to exist in the general body structure of delinquents and nondelinquents, and among boys of the four major physique types (mesomorphic, endomorphic, ecto-morphic and balanced) can be considered roughly (albeit not completely) independent of the influence of ethnic origin. Apart from this, the verification and extensive collation of the raw materials of the original research[3] give promise of enhanced reliability of the association tables in the analyses encompassed in the present volume which are in a sense correlative to the findings in *Physique and Delinquency*.

Apart from the careful matching of delinquents and nondelinquents, the intensive verification of the raw materials, and the employment of a wide and varied range of explorations (including not only social data but also psychiatric assessments and Rorschach tests), there is another highly significant methodologic aspect of the basic research from which the present volume derives. At the onset of the inquiry made in connection with *Unraveling Juvenile Delinquency*, the authors, in planning and directing the investigation, insisted that each segment—anthropologic, intellectual, characterial (Rorschach), temperamental-affective (psychiatric), and socio-cultural—be explored independently of every other. No investigator (and there were 23 such during the course of the project) in any of the areas was given access to the findings of the other segments of

---

[1] S. and E. T. Glueck, *Unraveling Juvenile Delinquency*, pp. 260 *et seq.*
[2] E. T. Glueck, 'Role of the Family in the Etiology of Delinquency,' *Bulletin* de Societé Internationale de Criminologie, 1er Semestre, 1960, pp. 13 *et seq.* (in English); also reprinted in the *Alabama Correctional Journal*, Vol. 7, No. 1, June 1960, pp. 63 *et seq.*
[3] S. and E. T. Glueck, *Unraveling Juvenile Delinquency*, Chapters V, VI, and VII. See also Appendix A of the present volume, G. McGrath and M. Cunningham, 'The Case of Henry W.'

the research. Thus, there was no 'reading in' or 'tainting' of the materials of any one area through the information obtained from any other line of inquiry.

The reliability of the facts thus obtained from independent and insulated sources, by various methods and by different staff members, revealed an essential harmony, reflected for example in consistency between the psychiatric and Rorschach diagnoses[1] and in the finding that the three diagnostic-prognostic (predictive) tables prepared by the authors from the most differentiative social, Rorschach and psychiatric data were found to have high potential power to distinguish delinquents from nondelinquents.[2]

Evidence of the internal consistency of the basic data from which the tentative conclusions in *Unraveling Juvenile Delinquency* were derived fortifies the reliability of the already completed somatotype study (*Physique and Deliquency*) published in 1956.

As previously stated, over 400 traits and factors comparing delinquents and nondelinquents were included in *Unraveling Juvenile Delinquency*. These comparisons yielded some fundamental insights into the forces at play in the etiologic dynamics of true delinquency (as opposed to accidental or fleeting maladjustment). The summation of the major resemblances and dissimilarities emerging from the comparison of the experimental group with the control group indicated that the separate findings, independently arrived at, integrate into a dynamic pattern which is neither exclusively biologic nor exclusively sociocultural, but which derives from an interplay of certain somatic, temperamental, psychologic and social influences, described in *Unraveling Juvenile Delinquency* in the following terms:

> The delinquents as a group [were found to be] distinguishable from the non-delinquents: (1) *physically*, in being essentially mesomorphic in constitution (solid, closely knit, muscular); (2) *temperamentally*, in being restlessly energetic, impulsive, extroverted, aggressive, destructive (often sadistic) . . .; (3) *in attitude*, by being hostile, defiant, resentful, suspicious, stubborn, socially assertive, adventurous, unconventional, nonsubmissive to authority; (4) *psychologically*, in tending to direct and concrete, rather than symbolic, intellectual expression, and in being less methodical in their approach to problems; (5) *socioculturally*, in having been reared to a far greater extent than the control group in homes of little understanding, affection, stability, or moral fibre by parents usually unfit to be effective guides and protectors or . . . desirable sources for emulation and the construction of a consistent, well-balanced, and

---

[1] S. and E. T. Glueck, *Unraveling Juvenile Delinquency*, p. 242, Note 8.
[2] S. and E. T. Glueck, 'Early Detection of Future Delinquents,' *The Journal of Criminal Law, Criminology and Police Science*, Vol. 47, No. 2, July–August 1956.

socially normal superego during the early stages of character develop-ment. While in individual cases the stresses contributed by any one of the above pressure-areas of dissocial-behavior tendency may adequately account for persistence in delinquency, in general the high probability is dependent upon the interplay of the conditions and forces from all these areas.

In the exciting, stimulating, but little-controlled and culturally incon-sistent environment of the underprivileged area, such boys readily give expression to their untamed impulses and their self-centered desires by means of various forms of delinquent behavior. Their tendencies toward uninhibited energy-expression are deeply anchored in soma and psyche and in the malformations of character during the first few years of life.[1]

In *Unraveling Juvenile Delinquency* we anticipated need of a more intensive exploration of each of the major areas of the inquiry on the basis of a series of 'breakdowns' of the general criminogenic field.

Some of the more important questions that will concern us in further, more detailed explorations of our materials are:

What causal syndromes can be inductively arrived at and defined by means of correlation of the various factors within each level of the inquiry? What syndromes will emerge from a comparison of delinquents and non-delinquents on the basis of a breakdown into ethnico-racial groupings? Into somatotypes? . . .

Further, what somatopsychic types will emerge from detailed cross-correlations between somatotypes and various characterial and person-ality traits? A more exact appreciation of the significance of constitu-tional typology in the causation of persistent delinquency than has yet been established awaits the result of such correlations.[2] . . .

Physique and Delinquency brought out the relationships of various traits to the four major physique types (mesomorphic, ectomorphic, endomorphic and balanced)[3] within which the boys embraced in *Unraveling Juvenile Delinquency* had been classified on the basis of

---

[1] S. and E. T. Glueck, *Unraveling Juvenile Delinquency*, pp. 281–282.

[2] *Ibid.*, p. 285.

[3] '*Endomorphy* means relative predominance of soft roundness throughout the various regions of the body. When endomorphy is dominant the digestive viscera are massive and tend relatively to dominate the bodily economy. The digestive viscera are derived principally from the *endodermal* embryonic layer.

'*Mesomorphy* means relative predominance of muscle, bone and connective tissue. The mesomorphic physique is normally heavy, hard, and rectangular in outline. Bone and muscle are prominent and the skin is made thick by a heavy underlying connective tissue. The entire bodily economy is dominated, relatively, by tissues derived from the *mesodermal* embryonic layer.

'*Ectomorphy* means relative predominance of linearity and fragility. In proportion to his mass, the ectomorph has the greatest surface area and hence relatively the greatest sensory exposure to the outside world. Relative to his mass he also has the largest brain and central nervous system. In a sense, therefore, his bodily economy is relatively dominated by tissues derived from the *ectodermal* embryonic layer.'

anthropometric measurements and informed judgment by trained anthropologists (Drs. Carl C. Seltzer and Ashton M. Tenney). With certain modifications of methodology, the body type assessments followed the classification advanced by William Sheldon in his two basic works, *The Varieties of Human Physique*[1] and *Atlas of Men*.[2]

In *Physique and Delinquency*, it was established that certain traits are more closely referable to the constitutional (essentially genetic) end of a postulated *biosocial continuum* than to the sociocultural. This conclusion was derived from statistically significant variation in the incidence of the traits among the body types. The assumption was made that if a trait is in large measure constitutionally oriented this fact ought to be reflected in such variation. It is reasonable to suppose that a psychologic trait, if focused genetically, would occur in differing incidence among such contrasting body types as the thin, fragile ectomorphic and the muscular, compact mesomorphic, or the round, fat endomorphic. In this connection, it is of value to quote from a statement by William Sheldon which was reproduced in *Physique and Delinquency*:[3]

> . . . Constitution refers to those aspects of the individual which are relatively more fixed and unchanging—morphology, physiology, endocrine function, etc.—and may be contrasted with those aspects which are relatively more labile and susceptible to modification by environmental pressures, *i.e.*, habits, social attitudes, education, etc. . . . Although by constitution we refer to the relatively stable aspects of a person's endowment, we do not mean to insist, and indeed do not believe, that the human constitution is an altogether fixed and unalterable hereditary entity. We mean by constitution the basic, underlying pattern of the living individual, as it is at the time when the individual is studied. *That constitution is closely determined by heredity is highly probable, but we do not know that it is entirely so determined.* [Italics ours.][4]

---

[1] W. H. Sheldon, with the collaboration of S. S. Stevens and W. B. Tucker, New York, Harper & Brothers, 1940.

[2] W. H. Sheldon, with the collaboration of C. W. Dupertuis and E. McDermott, New York, Harper & Brothers, 1954.

[3] S. and E. T. Glueck, *op. cit.*, p. 11.

[4] *The Varieties of Human Physique*, *op. cit.*, pp. 1–2, Note 1. In his later work, Sheldon emphasizes the genetic core of the somatotype although assigning importance also to the role of nutrition: 'The phenotype (literally, the form now appearing) is of course an expression of the state of nutrition, and it is also an expression of an underlying genetic influence which is carried in all of the bodily cells and may be referred to as the genotype of the individual. The genotype is at work throughout the life of a living organism, transmitting its own individual stamp to the new material used for replacement, as it did originally in the first emergence of the organism into characteristic structure. The life of an organism is an expression of a reciprocal relationship going on continuously from conception to death, between the genotype and the flow of nourishing substance yielded to the organism by the environment.' *Atlas of Men, op. cit.*, p. 19.

What, now, of the derivation of traits?[1] The concept of somatotype, and the fourfold body type classification according to constitutional component-dominance that we derived therefrom, is of value in the formulation of views regarding the probable orientation of certain traits toward the genetic side of the heredity-environment continuum. We assume that the respective degrees of participation of hereditary and environmental influences in the laying down of a trait can be ordered along such a bipolar biosocial continuum. At one extreme are traits which are rooted directly in a complex of specific genes or are more indirectly hereditary (as through the mediating operation of the glandular system); at the other extreme are traits in which there is only a low degree of hereditary determination and which are in large measure socioculturally conditioned. In the present state of knowledge it is impossible to determine exact degrees of participation of the innate and the acquired in the structuring of different traits. Yet a reasonable induction is possible from our data. Where significant variation in trait incidence occurs among the body types of the *nondelinquents* (uncomplicated, that is, by its association with delinquency), it seems appropriate to infer that the trait is probably oriented toward the constitutional border of the postulated biosocial spectrum. For it does not seem probable that body structures of such contrasting embryonic influences and physical characteristics as the muscular, athletic mesomorphic and the thin, fragile ectomorphic would possess in equal incidence a trait such as sensitivity, for example. And, indeed, an examination of the relevant table[2] shows that the mesomorphs as a group (whether nondelinquent or delinquent) are, as might be expected, least sensitive, while the ectomorphs are most sensitive. From findings of this kind, plus the fact

[1] G. Allport has shown how confused are the concept and name 'trait' in the writings of psychologists, psychiatrists, and others; and he has done yeoman service in trying to bring some tangible order out of the chaos. Both in *Unraveling* and in the present work we have not attempted to be strictly technical in the use of the term; we have employed 'trait' in a general sense, to include even some data derived from medical examinations and from intelligence tests. But it would appear that most of the temperamental and emotional traits of personality and character derived from the psychiatric and Rorschach examinations employed in our research fulfill the more basic identifying criteria presented by Allport; namely, greater generalization of a trait than is true of an ordinary habit, and the dynamic or 'determinative' nature of a trait in the following sense: 'It is not the stimulus that is the crucial determinant in behavior that expresses personality; it is the trait itself that is decisive. Once formed, a trait seems to have the capacity of directing responses to stimuli into characteristic channels. This emphasis upon the dynamic nature of traits, ascribing to them a capacity for guiding the specific response, is variously recognized by many writers.' G. W. Allport, 'The Personality Trait,' *Psychological Theory*, M. H. Marx (ed.), New York, The Macmillan Co., 1952. See also: G. W. Allport, *Personality: A Psychological Interpretation*, New York, Henry Holt and Company, 1937, 1948, Chapter XI, 'The Theory of Traits'; and R. B. Cattell, *Description and Measurement of Personality*, Yonkers, New York, 1946, pp. 59–91.

[2] S. and E. T. Glueck, *Physique and Delinquency*, p. 124, Table 51.

that correlation of the *sociocultural* factors with physique types *did not disclose any significant variation in incidence among nondelinquents*, it seems reasonable to conclude that those traits in our series which vary significantly in incidence among the physique types of the nondelinquents somehow owe their formation more to constitutional than to sociocultural influences. We say 'somehow' because our research materials have not yet permitted us to say whether such traits are directly genetic, or are largely the indirect result of the differential *responses* to the conditioning influences exerted by the environment on physiques of such varying constitutional composition as the mesomorphic, ectomorphic and endomorphic. A trait can be either directly and specifically attributable to certain genes, or indirectly laid down in the personality structure by the *general* inherited inclinations of the various physique types to respond selectively to environmental influences.[1] In this indirect line of heredity we are, to be sure, dealing in large measure with sociocultural influences; but such traits are conditioned originally and fundamentally by the inherited anatomic and physiologic-endocrinologic structure of the particular physique type, which inclines it to respond to sociocultural stimuli in a certain way.[2]

[1] 'Is it the type of metabolism or biochemical relationships associated with given body builds that provides the physiologic substratum for defective functioning? Or is the relation due rather to the sort of reactions to life experiences that are most suitable to these people by virtue of their constitutional equipment? Or is it the constitutional equipment itself that predisposes the person to certain sensitivities to environmental influences and to certain types of experiences? As a concrete example, is it the possible superior physiologic functioning of the mesomorph compared to the ectomorph that provides him with greater psychosomatic resistiveness to developing schizophrenia or once having developed it to recover from it? Or could it be his greater capacity to fight —the type of reaction he finds most rewarding with his particular equipment? Or is it that people of athletic build are more favored in our society, are more accepted and admired, find greater opportunity for satisfaction and security? The same questions, *mutatis mutandis*, may be applied to the other extremes of body type—for instance, the greater nervous sensitivity of the ectomorph to outer stimulation that has been pointed out by Sheldon, Draper and others.' L. Alexander, *Treatment of Mental Disorder*, Philadelphia, Saunders Co., 1953, p. 22.

[2] It would not seem probable that with reference to most of the traits included in this research—complex and only fairly definable as they are—there is a direct and specific line of hereditary linkage between any identifiable gene or set of genes and some particular trait, for example, as physiologic sensitivity. 'Specialized traits, such as musical or mathematical ability, lend themselves most easily to studies in heredity . . . The study of the role of heredity in the development of individual differences in generalized traits presents difficult problems. Evidently such traits are affected by many genes whose descent cannot be traced in any simple or Mendelian way. It is difficult to study the inheritance of generalized qualities through the science of genetics.' F. Osborn, *Preface to Eugenics* (rev. ed.), New York, Harper & Brothers, 1951, p. 83.

'*No simple connection exists between most observable characters of the developed human being and a single gene;* and . . . *a single gene*, by being part of the network of developmental reactions, *will often influence more than a single character.*' C. Stern, *Principles of Human Genetics*, San Francisco, W. H. Freeman and Co., 1949, p. 36.

Even in the most carefully designed research into the highly complex Nature–Nurture problem it would be difficult to disentangle the genetic roots from the interacting environmental influences. Indeed, even before a child is born, both genetic and nongenetic influences are operative: not only the unfolding of the potentialities of the genes but also the operation of various intra-uterine environmental influences. But apart from this permeative difficulty, it is impossible to arrive at anything more than a very indirect and imperfect inference regarding the operation of hereditary influences in the affinity of various traits to one or another of the structurally differentiated physique types. For want of the kind of genetic records of several generations which are indispensable to a more definitive study of heredity, we must be content with the rough substitute of determining the significantly differentiative incidence of the traits within the body types of the nondelinquent group who serve as our norm.

We proceed on the assumption, then, that when significant variation is present in trait-incidence among body types of nondelinquents, it is reasonable to infer that the trait is essentially oriented in constitution, although removed from the genes by one or more steps. It should be pointed out, however, that we can not be certain that *absence* of variation means that the trait is largely attributable to sociocultural conditioning, because there may well be traits which are essentially hereditary although not varying among the body types (eye color, for example).[1] Thus, in the analysis of the traits in *Physique and Delinquency* and their relationship to body structure, we could speak with some assurance only about those in which significant variation in incidence was found in the four dominant physique types among the nondelinquents. Where such variation was not found, we could not be certain that the trait is largely attributable to sociocultural conditioning. The present inquiry leads us in this direction, however.

When we speak of the 'constitutional orientation' of a trait, then, we mean that it is significantly associated with physique type, although we are unable to say whether it is *directly* constitutional (*i.e.*, genetically linked) or *indirectly* so (*i.e.*, because of the varied fundamental structure of the body types and their differential response to stimuli). On the one hand, the science of genetics has not yet conclusively demonstrated which traits of temperament, personality and character are determined in the genes, and, on the

[1] See F. Osborn, *op. cit.*, pp. 13–14. Considering the nature and complexity of the traits analyzed in our work, such a possibility would seem to be remote; but if it does exist, our data and method do not enable us to isolate such uniformly hereditary traits.

other, reasoning in respect to constitutional influence must perforce deal with broad body *types* which result from varying degrees of participation of the primary constitutional elements, rather than with specific sharply-defined entities. Therefore, in using the device of determining whether a trait varies significantly with physique, we can at best speak only of a *reasonable probability that in the production of certain traits there is more involvement of innately determined constitution than of environmental conditioning.*[1]

It should be emphasized that while we assume that fundamental variations in body structure probably reflect basic differences in the physiologic-endocrinologic apparatus which mediates between body build and psychologic traits, we of course realize that as far as behavior is concerned even genetically anchored traits are not fixed in their ultimate development but are more in the nature of potentials.[2]

[1] Compare the titles 'Some Dominant Hereditary Defects in Which Environment Plays Practically No Part' and 'Recessive Defects Little Affected by the Environment,' in Osborn, *op. cit.*, pp. 10 and 13.

[2] 'Biological inheritance provides the stuff from which personality is fashioned and, as manifested in the physique at a given time-point, determines trends and sets limits within which variation is constrained. There are substantial reasons for believing that different genetic structures carry with them varying potentialities for learning, for reaction time, for energy level, for frustration tolerance. Different people appear to have different biological rhythms: of growth, of menstrual cycle, of activity, of depression and exultation . . . Personality is also shaped through such traits of physique as stature, pigmentation, strength, conformity of features to the culturally fashionable type, etc. Such characteristics influence a man's needs and expectations.' C. Kluckhohn and H. A. Murray, *Personality in Nature, Society and Culture*, New York, Alfred Knopf, 1948, p. 39.

'The personality is a configuration or *gestalt* made up of a great number of elements which have been organized and mutually adjusted to form a more or less coherent, functional whole. At the foundation of this configuration lie the innate, inherited qualities of the individual; such things as his capacity for receiving and responding to stimuli, for muscular coordination, for habit formation and for those complex processes of association which are subsumed under the term intelligence. All these qualities are, presumably, functions of the individual's organic structure and, as such, are influenced by heredity and biological mutation. Since we know that the organic structure is never identical for any two persons, the qualities in question might be expected to present a corresponding range of individual variation. Experimentally this can be shown to be the case, but unfortunately for those who believe in a genetic solution for all psychological and social ills, experiments also show the presence of a complicating factor of extreme importance. The qualities in question are not determined exclusively by heredity but are modified through their exercise. It seems that any one of them can be improved by training. There is good reason to believe that there are physiologically determined limits to what training can do for the individual. Thus no amount of it can transform a moron into an Einstein. However, the limits seem to be wide enough to permit of the same degree of innate ability showing markedly different results in interaction with environments of different sorts. Although psychologists are busily at work on the problem, they are still unable to distinguish between innate and acquired ability and until they can do this no conclusions as to the inheritance of psychological qualities can be really valid.' R. Linton, 'Some Functional, Social, and Biological Aspects of Offenses and Offenders,' *Federal Probation*, Vol. V, No. 2, p. 19.

Both heredity and environment are always involved in the process of establishing the complex traits analyzed in this research. We believe, however, that at least as a basis for fruitful hypotheses concerning the relationship to delinquency of biologically grounded traits, it was possible in *Physique and Delinquency* to distinguish from among traits shown to be associated with delinquency those which probably have an *essentially constitutional orientation* as defined above.

Physique and Delinquency yielded important clues regarding the relationship of the traits to the physique types and the role of these traits in creating a varied delinquency potential among boys of different body builds. However, there remains the other aspect of the problem to which the present volume is devoted: namely, the extent of participation of factors of family environment in developing not only the traits already established in *Physique and Delinquency* as varying among body types and therefore probably oriented in constitution, but also the traits *not* found to differ in incidence among the body types. There remains also an exploration of the *combined influence* of social factors and traits on delinquency.

II

SCOPE OF INQUIRY

INTRODUCTION

IT is well to re-emphasize that the current study of family environment and delinquency was initially designed as part of a two-pronged work, of which *Physique and Delinquency* was the first. There we were concerned with ascertaining: (*a*) which among 67 traits could be regarded as essentially 'constitutional' by reason of statistically significant variation in their incidence among nondelinquent boys of the four dominant body types—mesomorphic, endomorphic, ectomorphic and balanced; and (*b*) the differences in the delinquency potential of the four physique types.[1]

[1] The traits referred to are those which might be expected, in common experience, to facilitate or hamper the kinds of behavior subsumed under the legal term, delinquency. Of course, not all boys with a high delinquency *potential* in this sense ever become delinquent. To change a potentiality into an actuality, the influence of various other forces, usually sociocultural factors, must come into play. For example, mesomorphs comprise 60·1% of our delinquent sample. Examining the traits of the mesomorphic nondelinquents, it becomes evident that mesomorphs are more vigorous than the other body types. They are also less sensitive and have a lesser tendency to phantasy than boys of one or another of the remaining body types. In addition, they are less unstable emotionally, less burdened by emotional conflicts, less inhibited in motor responses to stimuli. They are relatively free, as a group, of such inhibitions to antisocial adventures as feelings of inadequacy or marked submissiveness to authority. Such traits are not in themselves necessarily criminogenic; but, unless they are channeled toward socially acceptable goals, they are just the kind of traits that might furnish the strength, daring, enterprise and dynamic tendency to unrestrained action that spell out a high delinquency potential, and such traits are in fact frequently found among delinquents. Apart from this, some of the traits found to have a special impact on the delinquency of mesomorphs are *not* usually typical of that physique; they are alien to the constitutional host. But they also contribute, through the internal disharmony they create, to selecting, from among all mesomorphs, those who do in fact become delinquent.

Ectomorphs, by contrast, comprise only 14·4% of our randomly selected sample of true delinquents. Ectomorphs are distinguished by the predominance of fragility and linearity and, relative to mass, by the largest brain and central nervous system and sensory exposure. Such a comparatively fragile morphologic type would not be likely to have many of the traits generally associated with the robust, energetic mesomorphic type; and this was indeed found to be true when the traits were related to each of the four physique types. Ectomorphs are less sturdy physically, more sensitive, more unstable emotionally. In general, they give the impression of a less smooth functioning and less well-integrated organism, finding its major outlets to frustration not in action but in internal emotional strain with resultant neurotic symptoms. Thus,

14

It will be recalled that the study of the origin of traits was limited in *Physique and Delinquency* to constitutional (*i.e.*, essentially genetic) influences in trait formation. Having already isolated 23 of the 67 traits as primarily constitutional in emphasis, our next step is to examine more closely those traits *not* found to vary among the body types and therefore not yet deemed to be fundamentally constitutional. The aim is to ascertain, within the limitations of our data, whether such traits are conditioned by family environment; or, if not related to any of the social factors encompassed in this study, whether they may be considered essentially 'inherent.' Finally, we propose to inquire into how traits and environmental factors *in combination* contribute to delinquency.

It was originally intended to encompass the entire analysis— constitutional and environmental aspects—within one volume. But this proved too massive and complex a task. This comprehensive inquiry was initially projected in 1949 just prior to the actual publication of *Unraveling Juvenile Delinquency*, the basic data of which continue to provide invaluable source materials not only for the present study but for several others. The first part of the projected over-all work, emphasizing the role of constitution in trait formation and criminogenesis, was, as already indicated, published in 1956, under the title *Physique and Delinquency*.[1] Meanwhile, the tabulation of data for the second part of the inquiry, dealing with sociocultural influences, had been proceeding.

DATA OF THE RESEARCH

The present study deals with certain physiologic, neurologic, psychologic and psychiatric *traits*, and with certain environmental *factors*. Appendix Exhibit B-2 presents a list of 66 of the original 67 traits with the percentage incidence among delinquents and nondelinquents of the particular subcategory (or combination of subcategories)

they have a far lower delinquency potential than mesomorphs. Why, then, are some ectomorphs delinquent when their potential for acting out aggressive behavior is so much lower than in the typical mesomorph? The reason is the over-reaction of ectomorphs to the pressures and tensions of family life which tend to transform a low delinquency potential into a delinquency actuality in a small proportion of instances. But the percentage of ectomorphs who in fact become delinquent remains low because of the unfitness of their traits to energetic, daring adventuresomeness. Those who do become delinquent are more likely to do so than mesomorphs if they are the sons of emotionally disturbed fathers, of working mothers, of mothers who give them little affection and supervision, or if they come from families not united in deed and spirit, or from broken homes.

[1] New York, Harper & Brothers.

15

used in *Physique and Delinquency*.[1] The traits are assigned the same identifying *numbers* as were given them in *Physique and Delinquency* and the numbers are consistently retained throughout this volume to facilitate cross-reference not only to *Physique and Delinquency* but to the textual discussions and Appendices of the present work.

Appendix Exhibit C-2 lists the 44 environmental factors encompassed in the present study (42 of which had been included in *Physique and Delinquency*),[2] the subcategories or combination of subcategories used, and the percentage incidence (for both delinquents and nondelinquents) of the respective subcategory (or combination of subcategories). The social factors, although assigned numbers in *Physique and Delinquency*, are now identified by *letters* which are retained throughout the text and Appendices.

In determining which of the numerous factors of family environment initially included in *Unraveling Juvenile Delinquency* should be used in *Physique and Delinquency* and in the present study, we decided to eliminate any concerning the grandparents of the boys, on the assumption that they are too remote from the personality and character traits of our subjects.

In order that the reader may more readily comprehend the scope of the present work, we have included in Appendix Exhibit B-1 the definitions of the 66 traits and in Appendix Exhibit C-1 the definitions of the 44 social factors.

OBJECTIVES OF THE ANALYSIS

The major questions we pose in this inquiry are: (*a*) Which traits are largely environmentally conditioned and by what social factors? (*b*) How do factors (reflecting family environment) and traits, in combination, bear on delinquency? As a preliminary to answering these questions it was necessary to relate each of the 66 traits to each of the 44 social factors. This resulted in a grand total of 2,904 correlation tables for the sample of 500 delinquents, and a like number for their matched nondelinquents. This proved a formidable task. It was followed by applying the same test for statistical significance used in the analysis of the data of *Physique and Delinquency*, to which reference is made below. After placing all reasonable safeguards (statistical and otherwise) around the materials, we can only suggest that the qualified and careful reader add his own interpretations of

---

[1] *Susceptibility to Contagion* has been omitted in this volume because the data were not in proper form for machine processing.

[2] The two additional factors are (O) *Usual Work Habits of Father* and (FF) *Age of Boy at First Breach in Family Life*.

16

the data to ours. If he does not always agree with us, he has available in the Appendices the necessary materials on the basis of which to arrive at judgments of his own.

TEST FOR SIGNIFICANCE

A word is necessary in regard to the test of statistical significance used in this inquiry, and previously applied in *Physique and Delinquency*. An explanation of the method was prepared by Professor Jane Worcester of the Harvard School of Public Health (whom we consult from time to time on statistical problems) and comprises Appendix A of *Physique and Delinquency*.[1] Dr. Worcester included a table comparing significances as determined by χ^2 (Chi-square) based on three 'degrees' of freedom with those (the least in each set of six comparisons) determined by the less familiar method of 'multiple comparisons':[2]

> The table shows, not unexpectedly, the close relationship between the two methods. If $P = <\cdot10$ had been used as the dividing line, χ^2 would have picked out 27 traits as showing significant variability over the physique types, whereas the method of multiple comparisons picks out 25. However, 24 traits are common to both groups. The advantage of the method of multiple comparisons is that it has allowed more definite statements as to how the physique types differ from one another.

The method of multiple comparisons, developed by Professor John W. Tukey of Princeton University and recommended for our use by Professor Frederick Mosteller of Harvard University, makes possible specific conclusions from the data, assuming of course a careful gathering and verification of the raw materials. In this connection, it is well to illustrate the care with which the social histories of the 500 delinquents and 500 matched nondelinquents of *Unraveling Juvenile Delinquency* had been gathered and which in turn provided us with the social data from which the materials for *Physique and Delinquency* and the present study have been derived. Space limitations made it impossible to include the 'Case of Henry W' in *Unraveling Juvenile Delinquency*, but we are incorporating it as Appendix A of the present work to show the steps taken to gather, collate and verify the social histories of the thousand boys involved.

[1] *Physique and Delinquency*, Appendix A, 'Explanation of Statistical Method,' by Professor Jane Worcester, Harvard School of Public Health, pp. 276 *et seq.*, with special reference to p. 281.
[2] *Physique and Delinquency*, Appendix A, p. 283.

Introduction

In the first three of five chapters to follow which deal with the origin of traits (Chapters III, IV and V), attention is focused on those traits (43 in all) which had *not* been found, in *Physique and Delinquency*, to vary significantly in incidence among the body types and which may therefore possibly be closer to the environmental than to the biologic end of the posited biosocial continuum. In Chapters VI and VII the focus is on the 23 traits which *had* been found, in *Physique and Delinquency*, to vary in incidence among the four body types, and therefore had been established as closer to the biologic than to the sociocultural zone of the biosocial spectrum. The question at issue is whether some of these latter may, on more intensive examination, be found to be the product of a relatively equal admixture of biologic and environmental influences.

To avoid repetition of qualifying phrases, we refer to traits as *constitutional* if they are identified as closer to the genetic than to the sociocultural end of the postulated biosocial continuum. Those which are more largely the product of environmental stimuli are referred to as 'conditioned' or 'environmental' or 'social' or 'sociocultural.' It is, of course, obvious that both genetic and external influences are involved in the formation of traits; the question is one of *emphasis* and of degree of association.

Only when the origin of the traits (within the scope of our data) has been determined is it possible to examine the major subject of our interest—how a child's family environment and his traits operate jointly or individually in contributing to his delinquency. Thereafter we can begin to consider the implications of the findings for the prevention and management of juvenile delinquency.

As in *Physique and Delinquency*, so in this volume, determination of the orientation of traits is derived from an inspection of the 500 *nondelinquents* who were the subjects of *Unraveling Juvenile Delinquency*; for it is necessary in the disentangling of factor-trait relationships to avoid the involvement of the presence of antisocial behavior with all its complexities.

ASSOCIATION BETWEEN FACTORS AND TRAITS

It will help to clarify our subsequent analyses concerning the origin of traits if we bear in mind the various types of relationships which are possible between social or cultural factors and physiologic or psychologic traits; for the discovery of statistically significant associations between factors and traits does not throw light on the *nature* of the relationships. Whether the linkage is *directly* sequential, or *indirectly* so *via* another trait or factor, or whether the linked trait-factor is in turn the *product* of a prior factor-trait combination, is often very difficult to say. All we can be reasonably sure of is that the relationship has occurred at an acceptable level of statistical reliability (*i.e.*, its occurrence by chance is extremely unlikely); and, not infrequently, that the linkage in question is one noted in clinical investigation, or one which common experience shows to exist. Proceeding upon these assumptions, we make analyses which we believe to be reasonable.

One possible explanation of an association between factor and trait is that it reflects the more or less *direct influence of the factor upon the trait*; or, to put it differently, it is probable that such a trait would not exist (or would exist in a different form or degree of intensity) in the absence of the factor found associated with it. We refer to such a factor-trait association as reflecting a *contribution* of the factor to the development of the trait.

A second possible explanation of an association between factor and trait is a reversal of the above sequence; that is, *the pre-existent trait in a boy serves as a stimulus to a more or less specific response of the human (father, mother, siblings) environment*.[1] Here the social (environmental) factor is not necessary to the existence of the trait but is nevertheless associated with it because of the frequency with which the trait attracts the factor. We refer to such an association as 'reactive' (*i.e.*, reflecting a *reaction* of the environment to a boy having the trait).

A third possible explanation of a significant association between factor and trait is that *the two are dynamically reciprocal in their influence*: given the trait, the factor is likely to follow; and given the factor, as a response to the trait, the trait is likely to be enhanced, crystallized, or deepened.

As to the relationship between factors, traits and *delinquency* (to be discussed in Chapters IX–XIII) still another dynamism may be involved: each element, standing alone, may not be sufficiently weighty to be reflected as an influence in the etiologic complex; but *together* they may be, either because the impact of the two (or more) combined is sufficient to make a telling difference in stimulating antisocial behavior; or because the influence of one, say the trait, does

---

[1] Compare the following: 'It is not the stimulus that is the crucial determinant in behavior that expresses personality; it is the trait itself that is decisive. Once formed, a trait seems to have the capacity of directing responses to stimuli into characteristic channels. This emphasis upon the dynamic response is variously recognized by many writers.' G. W. Allport, 'The Personality Trait,' *Psychological Theory*, M. H. Marx (ed.), New York, The Macmillan Co., 1952, pp. 503–7.

not become *criminogenic* except in the presence of the other, the factor, as a sort of catalytic agent. Similarly, it is conceivable that the presence of a criminogenic trait can be counteracted by an anticatalytic factor. In other words, an antisocial reaction can be either accelerated or retarded through the *simultaneous presence* of certain traits and factors.

All this is intended to remind the reader that association is not necessarily causation, and that much creative thought must *follow* the discovery of a statistically significant relationship between trait and factor. Readers with special professional competence in various relevant fields may not always agree with our interpretation of the meaning of one or another of the statistical patterns which are about to be analyzed. Our aim is not only to answer but also to raise significant questions; we do not hesitate to 'go out on a limb' when it seems, on the basis of a 'feel' for and much reflection upon the raw materials, that the limb will probably bear the weight of our reasoning.

Although the 44 sociocultural factors of family environment included in the present analysis obviously serve only as an index of many environmental circumstances, the absence of any significant association between factor and trait or even the presence of one association (since the probabilities are considerable that such an association could have occurred by chance) should lend support to our conclusion that such traits are essentially *genetic* in origin. On the other hand, instances in which at least two or more of the factors appear associated with traits found in *Physique and Delinquency* to be constitutionally oriented should lend weight to the inference that there are strong influences of *both* Nature and Nurture involved in the formation of a trait. No trait can be said to be absolutely 'pure' in the sense of being exclusively genetic without any environmental influence, intra- or extra-uterine. It is plasticity at birth and during the early formative years that makes possible the development of human personality under the impact of sociocultural influences. But traits apparently vary in degree of plasticity; and the question before us therefore is not which traits are exclusively genetic and which exclusively conditioned by environment, but, rather, which are more probably referable to the biologic end of a hypothetical biosocial continuum and which to the environmental.

We are of course aware that the analyses that follow deal with individual traits and individual factors. This particularistic approach has the major disadvantage of dissection of patterns or *Gestalten* instead of their treatment as dynamic wholes. But just as in the study of anatomy dissection is a first and indispensable step, so is it in the analysis of a social disease, namely *Juvenile Delinquency*. Before we can (in a planned later monograph) arrive at *Gestalten*, we must first try to pinpoint the nexus of influence as reflected in *individual* factor-trait foci.

PART I
ORIGIN OF TRAITS

III

TRAITS WHICH DO NOT VARY AMONG BODY TYPES: RELATED TO LESS THAN TWO SOCIAL FACTORS

INTRODUCTION

WE turn in this and the succeeding two chapters to the influence of certain aspects of the family environment on the development of those traits (43 in all) that were *not* found in *Physique and Delinquency* to vary in incidence among the body types and are therefore not as yet presumed to have a largely constitutional orientation. In Chapters VI and VII we shall consider further the 23 traits already found in the previous work to vary in incidence among the four body types and therefore presumed to be closer to the constitutional than to the sociocultural end of the postulated biosocial continuum.

The 43 physiologic and psychologic traits, the latter derived largely from the Rorschach and psychiatric studies carried on in connection with the gathering of data for the basic work, *Unraveling Juvenile Delinquency*, from which *Physique and Delinquency* and the present volume originate, are the following:

Developmental Health History
  1. Poor Health in Infancy
  3. Extreme Restlessness in Early Childhood
  4. Enuresis in Early Childhood

Neurologic Findings
  5. Irregular Reflexes
  7. Dermographia

Some Aspects of Intelligence
  11. Low Verbal Intelligence
  12. High Performance Intelligence
  13. Originality
  14. Banality
  15. Marked Power of Observation

25

16. Intuition
18. Common Sense
19. Unmethodical Approach to Problems
20. Potential Capacity for Objective Interests

Basic Attitudes to Authority and Society
22. Defiance
24. Ambivalence to Authority

Feelings of Resentment, Anxiety, Inferiority and Frustration
25. Enhanced Feeling of Insecurity
26. Marked Feeling of Not Being Wanted or Loved
27. Feeling of Not Being Taken Care Of
28. Marked Feeling of Not Being Taken Seriously
29. Feeling of Helplessness
30. Feeling of Not Being Appreciated
32. Feeling of Resentment

Feelings of Kindliness and Hostility
33. Poor Surface Contact with Others
34. Hostility
35. Marked Suspiciousness
37. Feeling of Isolation
38. Defensive Attitude

Dependence and Independence
40. Feeling of Being Able to Manage Own Life

Goals of Strivings
41. Narcissistic Trends
42. Receptive Trends

Some General Qualities of Personality
45. Emotional Lability
46. Lack of Self-Control
48. Compulsory Trends
49. Preponderance of Extroversive Trends
50. Preponderance of Introversive Trends

Deep-Rooted Emotional Dynamics
52. Suggestibility
54. Stubbornness
55. Adventurousness

Personality Orientation
62. Lack of Self-Criticism
63. Conscientiousness

Some Aspects of Mental Pathology
66. Neuroticism
67. Psychopathy

For definitions the reader is referred to Appendix Exhibit B-1 where the traits are presented by the same numbers assigned them in the above listing; and for the incidence of the traits among the delinquents and nondelinquents of *Unraveling* (and to which frequent reference is made in the text of the present work), the reader is referred to Appendix Exhibit B-2 (also by trait numbers).

A word of explanation is necessary concerning the method of analysis of the findings that follow in this and in the succeeding four chapters. It will be recalled from Chapter II that in order to determine the extent and the manner in which social factors (mainly pertaining to the family environment) contribute to the formation of a trait, it was necessary to correlate the trait with each one of 44 social factors encompassed in the inquiry. (These factors are listed and defined in Appendix Exhibit C-1.)

The statistically meaningful results of these correlations are presented trait by trait in Appendix D (also arranged in chronological order by trait number). An explanation has been given in Chapter II of the statistical method of multiple comparisons which has been applied to determine the significance of the variation in the incidence of the same trait among boys of differing social background. As an illustration (see Appendix Table D-43), the incidence of *masochistic trends* is found to differ significantly in boys from crowded homes as compared to those from uncrowded homes; in boys from families lacking ambition as compared to those reared in families who showed some evidences of wanting to improve their status; in homes in which there were meager recreational facilities as compared to those in which some opportunities for home play were provided; and so on.

Examination of the findings concerning one other trait might be helpful before proceeding with the analysis in this and succeeding chapters. See, for example, Appendix Table D-37, where the results are presented of the significant relationships found between the *feeling of isolation* and six (out of the 44) social factors.

With these preliminaries, the reader should be able to follow the analyses in the succeeding pages. Although not necessarily always agreeing with them, he will at least know by what method we have arrived at our judgments.

TRAITS NOT ASSOCIATED WITH ANY SOCIAL FACTORS

In *Physique and Delinquency* we suggested that there may well be, among the traits not found to be associated with any physique types, some that are constitutional in their orientation. However, since they were not found to vary significantly in incidence among the four body types, we could not, by that particular test of genetic involvement, determine whether they are closer to the constitutional than to the sociocultural zone of the biosocial continuum.

Now, however, we think it may be suggested that the traits not shown in *Physique and Delinquency* to vary in incidence among the body types, and also not found in the current inquiry to be related to any of the 44 social factors (or related to only one) may (like eye color, which is not linked to physique type) nevertheless still be largely of genetic determination. Only further and more intensive research on other samples of cases would determine the correctness of this assumption.

There are five such traits (among the 43 now under consideration) to which *not even one* of the 44 social factors embraced in this study is found to be significantly related.

   5. Irregular Reflexes
   16. Intuition
   33. Poor Surface Contact with Others
   45. Emotional Lability
   46. Lack of Self-Control

It must be borne in mind that although the factors included in this inquiry are indices of many important environmental influences, they are not exhaustive; no sample of factors can be.

TRAITS TO WHICH ONE SOCIAL FACTOR IS RELATED

We come now to a group of traits, also not shown in *Physique and Delinquency* to vary in incidence among the body types and therefore not deemed, by that criterion, to be constitutionally oriented, which are now found to be significantly associated with *only one* of the 44 social factors.

   1. Poor Health in Infancy
   4. Enuresis in Early Childhood
   19. Unmethodical Approach to Problems
   20. Potential Capacity for Objective Interests
   22. Defiance

28

24. Ambivalence to Authority
55. Adventurousness
67. Psychopathy

Whether or not the single association has occurred by chance it is impossible to say with assurance; however, it seems reasonable to suggest that if the trait were essentially the product of environmental conditioning, a statistically significant association would probably exist with more than a single social factor. Hence, although it appears reasonable to assume that such traits are closer to the biologic than to the sociocultural pole of the biosocial continuum, we are not completely secure in this conclusion and await further evidence. There may well be traits in which the relationship between factor and trait suggests an association not due to chance (*unmethodical approach to problems*, for example). The reader must judge for himself.

Poor health in infancy (Appendix Table D-1) refers to frequent and severe illnesses and low resistance to infection. Information on health was derived from the mothers, from hospital and social agency records, and from family doctors. Although less than 10% of the nondelinquents were in poor health as infants, a significantly higher proportion of them had fathers who themselves suffered from serious physical ailments. It is, however, not clear whether this relationship reflects a genetic or an environmental influence on a child's poor health in infancy.

Enuresis (Appendix Table D-4) refers to bedwetting beyond the years of its normal expectancy. A relationship is found between enuresis and the attitude of brothers and sisters to the child, for there is an excessive proportion of enuretics among youngsters who are not well accepted by their brothers and sisters in contrast to those who are well accepted. Whether this contributes to a child's enuresis or the unfriendly attitude of his brothers and sisters results because they find it difficult to tolerate the persistently enuretic sibling is an open question. At all events, the *single* relationship between trait and factor may well have occurred by chance. More important is the finding that no one of the other 43 social factors shows any statistically significant relationship to *enuresis*.

Unmethodical approach to problems (Appendix Table D-19) pertains to the way in which an intellectual problem or some task is typically attacked and how the individual attempts to master it. The presence of an association between this trait in a child and his rearing in a home that is generally unclean and disorderly shows that poor household management by parents may well contribute to the development in a child of a habit of planlessness in approaching

29

problems. Here is an instance in which the single relationship may be meaningful. Intensive clinical observation might clarify this.

Potential capacity for objective interests (*i.e.*, interests for their own sake as opposed to interests merely or predominantly for the sake of gaining prestige, earning money, having success, gaining attention, affection, protection, and the like) is still another trait found to be significantly related to only a single social factor (Appendix Table D-20). It appears to be more prevalent among boys brought up in homes in which the parents make some constructive provision for their child's use of leisure at home, since more youngsters so reared than those otherwise brought up are found to possess the competence under discussion. It is not unreasonable to assume that a boy's *potential capacity for objective interests* may be stimulated by constructive outlets for the use of his leisure, since this makes it less necessary for him to seek selfishly motivated interests.

Defiance (Appendix Table D-22), unlike social assertiveness, which is a rather superficial quality, pertains to aggressive self-assertion, born out of deep insecurity or weakness and therefore often indiscriminate in its aims and means and usually directed against somebody or some thing rather than toward a positive goal. The environmental factor of parental indifference to a son's interests, as reflected in their attitude toward entertaining the boy's playmates in the home, would appear to contribute to the development of this trait; for a significantly higher proportion of defiant youngsters are found among the group whose parents were indifferent to their son's friends than among those whose parents were actively friendly.

But while it is reasonable to assume that lack of parental concern for the son's interests has some bearing on the development of an attitude of *defiance*, it may at present be suggested that this trait is probably closer to the constitutional than to the sociocultural end of the somatosocial continuum, since only this single factor is related to *defiance*, and its chance association can not be ruled out.

Ambivalence to authority (Appendix Table D-24) is the result of contradictory or conflicting feelings, such as coexistence of defiant and submissive strivings or of assertive and dependent attitudes, all of which are basic attitudes toward authority and society.

Here, too, only one social factor has been found to be associated with a trait; but before discussing *ambivalence*, it should be borne in mind that a related trait, *defiance*, although also not found to vary among the body types, is nevertheless perhaps closer to the constitutional segment of the biosocial spectrum than to the sociocultural, and that two other related traits, *submissiveness* and *social assertiveness*, were classified in *Physique and Delinquency* as having essentially a constitutional orientation, an inference based on the finding that they vary significantly in incidence among the body types.

All this is relevant to an assessment of the trait of *ambivalence*. For in view of the findings regarding *defiance, social assertiveness* and *submissiveness*, it seems justifiable to suggest that *ambivalence to authority*, a trait involving an inconsistency of attitude and impulse as between these various psychologic tendencies, may in fact also be closer to the constitutional than to the sociocultural zone of the biosocial continuum.

This conclusion is reinforced by the present finding that only one of the numerous social factors included in this study, affection of mother for boy, is related to *ambivalence to authority*. Whether one may reason that deprivation of mother love largely contributes to a boy's ambivalence, or that an inherent tendency to ambivalence arouses a feeling of maternal indifference or even hostility toward a child, depends of course on whether one accepts as conclusive the inference so far made that the traits expressive of basic attitudes to authority and society are essentially of constitutional orientation.

Adventurousness (Appendix Table D-55), which has to do with an exceptional need for change, excitement and risk, would appear from our findings to be in some measure spurred by rearing in a home atmosphere reflecting a lack of parental aspirations; for a greater proportion of adventurous boys are found in homes in which the parents were devoid of ambition to improve the family status (through higher education for the children, sincere intent to move to a better neighborhood, provision of a more adequate home, plans to improve the family economic status, and such) than in households in which the parents showed some (even if not necessarily marked) desire for progress.

Be this as it may, the single existing relationship to an environmental factor would seem to justify the tentative placement of this trait, like the previous ones, among those that are probably more inherent than acquired.

Turning now to *psychopathy* (Appendix Table D-67), the final trait in the group of those found to be significantly related to only one of the 44 social factors, this is not a uniform and definite concept. As employed in *Unraveling Juvenile Delinquency*, *psychopathy* refers (following Bleuler and others) to all marked mental and emotional deviations that do not clearly belong in any other diagnostic group. 'Often a difference in degree of a disorder rather than of kind places a person in this category. This may be illustrated by saying that the psychopath is less ill than the psychotic and more ill than the neurotic. He is distinguished from the neurotic also by the fact that he is much more often openly destructive and antisocial or asocial. He is also usually less amenable than the neurotic to therapeutic or educative efforts. The most important trait of the psychopath is the fleeting, non-integrative, superficial quality of his personal relations.' [1]

It would appear that *psychopathy* is closer to the biologic than to the social end of the biosocial continuum; for it occurs despite the less traumatic aspect of exposure to a first break in the family life when the child is ten years of age or over rather than when he is under five (the most impressionable and pliable years for the formation of personality and character).

SUMMARY

We have thus far isolated 13 of the 43 traits which had not been found (in *Physique and Delinquency*) to vary in incidence among the body types of nondelinquents and about which it is now evident that correlation with each of the 44 social factors reveals either no statistically valid association, or, at most, not more than a single linkage (which may well have occurred by chance). Thus we venture the opinion that, despite their failure to meet the test of variation in incidence among physique types, these traits are, with two possible exceptions, more reasonably referable to the biologic than to the sociocultural zone of the biosocial continuum.

1. Poor Health in Infancy
4. Enuresis in Early Childhood
5. Irregular Reflexes
16. Intuition
19. Unmethodical Approach to Problems
20. Potential Capacity for Objective Interests
22. Defiance
24. Ambivalence to Authority
33. Poor Surface Contact with Others
45. Emotional Lability
46. Lack of Self-Control
55. Adventurousness
67. Psychopathy

As regards two of the traits—*enuresis* and *ambivalence to authority* —it is uncertain whether the relationship between trait and factor reflects a contributory influence of the factor to the trait formation or a reaction of the environment to a child characterized by the trait.

[1] Dr. Ernest G. Schachtel, in *Unraveling Juvenile Delinquency*, New York, The Commonwealth Fund, 1950, p. 240.

Traits Which Do Not Vary among Body Types

Our conclusion about the essentially biologic orientation of the traits discussed in this chapter can not, of course, be absolutely definite. Nor does it involve a denial of some tangible sociocultural influences; but the issue is whether constitution or conditioning *predominates*. The most that can be ventured in the light of the evidence in the present inquiry is that such traits are closer to the innate than to the environmental zone of the biosocial continuum.

IV

TRAITS WHICH DO NOT VARY AMONG BODY TYPES: RELATED TO TWO OR MORE SOCIAL FACTORS

INTRODUCTION

IN this and the following chapter, we consider 30 traits which had not been shown in *Physique and Delinquency*[1] to vary in frequency among the body types and are in the present analysis seen to be associated with two or more of the 44 social factors. This relationship is not always of a kind to suggest that the social factors have necessarily *contributed* to the development of a trait; in some instances, the relationship more reasonably suggests a *reaction* of the human environment to the person already possessing the trait, and in some it would appear that trait and factor are involved in a reciprocal dynamic interplay.

The relationships that reflect a social conditioning of the traits will emerge in the analysis, at the completion of which we shall be able to group: (*a*) the traits that are conditioned by social factors in a way suggesting that such influences do indeed contribute to their development; and (*b*) the traits which appear to be closer to the constitutional than to the social pole of the biosocial continuum, either because only one contributory relationship of factor to trait has emerged or because the existing relationships between factor and trait suggest the primacy of hereditary influences.

It should be recalled that the analysis of the relationships between traits and social factors is at this stage being made regardless of whether and how these characteristics may be involved in delinquency. Our interest at this point is to derive clues as to the major *orientation* of the traits, the better to understand their roles in delinquency. Beyond this stage we shall turn our attention to the involvement of traits and factors in the correction and prevention of delinquency.

[1] S. and E. T. Glueck, *Physique and Delinquency*, New York, Harper & Brothers, 1956.

34

Traits Which Do Not Vary among Body Types

The traits (involving some aspects of child health and development, some features of intelligence, and some characteristics that reflect feelings of resentment, anxiety, inferiority and frustration) found to be related to two or more social factors are:

3. Extreme Restlessness in Early Childhood
7. Dermographia
11. Low Verbal Intelligence
12. High Performance Intelligence
13. Originality
14. Banality
15. Marked Power of Observation
18. Common Sense
25. Enhanced Feeling of Insecurity
26. Marked Feeling of Not Being Wanted or Loved
27. Feeling of Not Being Taken Care Of
28. Marked Feeling of Not Being Taken Seriously
29. Feeling of Helplessness
30. Feeling of Not Being Appreciated
32. Feeling of Resentment
34. Hostility
35. Marked Suspiciousness
37. Feeling of Isolation
38. Defensive Attitude
40. Feeling of Being Able to Manage Own Life
41. Narcissistic Trends
42. Receptive Trends
48. Compulsory Trends
49. Preponderance of Extroversive Trends
50. Preponderance of Introversive Trends
52. Suggestibility
54. Stubbornness
62. Lack of Self-Criticism
63. Conscientiousness
66. Neuroticism

DEVELOPMENTAL HEALTH HISTORY

Our concern in relation to health history focuses on the characteristic, *extreme restlessness in early childhood,* and on *dermographia.*

Extreme restlessness in early childhood (Appendix Table D-3) refers to the chronic inability to 'sit still,' always wanting to be 'on the go,' as observed by parents, teachers and family physicians. Unlike any of the traits thus far analyzed, this one is found to be

35

related to *no fewer than eight social factors.* From the evidence, it would appear that excessive restlessness is, in part at least, the result of the home atmosphere in which a child is reared. It can be no accident that a far higher proportion of very restless youngsters were found in homes in which the child was witness to the parents' overt incompatibility than in homes in which he was reared by one parent, usually the mother, who had long since separated from her mate, thereby sparing the child exposure to the parents' obvious disharmony. Since it is not likely that parents are incompatible *because* of their child's restlessness, overt parental friction may indeed be regarded as contributory to the development of *extreme restlessness* in a child.

There is evidence, also, that rearing by an emotionally disturbed mother contributes to a child's restlessness; for a higher proportion of agitated youngsters were found to be the sons of such mothers than of mothers who were not emotionally disturbed.

The remaining six factors found to be related to *extreme restlessness in early childhood,* instead of indicating a contribution of the human environment to the formation of the trait, may reflect the *response* of parents and brothers and sisters to a child already emotionally restless—such a factor, for example, is the parents' provision of at least some recreational facilities for the youngster.

As to some of these environmental influences, however, the influence *may* be of factor on trait; such as, for example, the possibility that an unfavorable attitude of family members toward a child contributes to the development of his restlessness. The same is true of the fact that a greater proportion of fathers and/or mothers of restless boys resorted to threats of severe chastisement or actually used corporal punishment on them; and of the indifference or hostility of siblings toward an extremely restless brother. These attitudes and practices may be interpreted as contributory to the development of extreme restlessness in a child rather than as a reaction of family members to it; or it may be that what is involved is a vicious circle of reciprocal influence.

Dermographia (Appendix Table D-7) is another aspect of a child's developmental health history with which we are concerned. This is a condition indicated by reddish tracings on the skin made in response to a light stroking with a fingernail; it would seem to reflect some physiologic sensitivity. Relationships are found between *dermographia* and seven social factors, but their linkage to this physiologic sign is not clear. For example, a disproportionately high percentage of boys one or both of whose parents did not themselves have any history of delinquency were found to show this evidence of skin sensitivity. One may speculate from this that delinquent parents are less likely to rear children who are physiologically sensitive.[1] But whether one is dealing here with a linkage that is essentially genetic or represents largely a sociocultural connection, it is difficult to say.

There are two additional associations that may throw light on the question of whether *dermographia* is closer to the constitutional than to the social end of the biosocial progression. One of these has to do with self-respect of the parents. (This refers to their attitude toward protecting the family name, as reflected in embarrassment about any irregularity in the behavior or status of any member of the family and to their preference for self-help as opposed to outside financial relief or other aid.) A higher proportion of physiologically sensitive boys were found in self-respecting families than in those lacking in self-regard.

We seem to be dealing here, as in the case of the trait of *aestheticism* (Chapter VII), with a characteristic that is somehow related to the quality of the *background* of a boy; for the more 'refined' family milieu contributes a higher proportion of physiologically sensitive children. This inference is supported by two other factors significantly associated with *dermographia* which also reflect the better family background of 'thin-skinned' boys: such boys were more frequently found to have parents who were warmly hospitable to entertaining their son's friends at home and who made at least some provision for the boy's 'under-the-roof' recreational needs.

Further indices of the more wholesome family background of boys who are perhaps more delicately organized than other boys (as judged by *dermographia*) are found in the significantly high proportion of such youths whose mothers never resorted to physical punishment and who gave them proper supervision.

Nevertheless, it appears to us that since the more favorable home conditions noted above may be themselves due to a greater physiologic sensitivity of the parents, *dermographia* may possibly have genetic determinants.

SOME ASPECTS OF INTELLIGENCE

We turn now to several intellectual traits, beginning with *verbal intelligence* and then *performance intelligence, originality, banality, power of observation* and *common sense.*

[1] Lombroso's claim that the 'born criminal' is characterized by excessive tatooing has frequently been misinterpreted as 'inheritance' although it is clearly a cultural practice. Lombroso really referred to this practice as indicating a physiologic sensitivity, which might very well be a genetic characteristic. He also spoke of the absence of remorse, *i.e.*, moral insensitivity, among his group of born criminals.

Verbal intelligence (Appendix Table D-11) consists essentially of the capacity to do intellectual tasks requiring the use of abstract reasoning and memory, in which the approach to meaning tends to be through intermediate symbols rather than through concrete physical things. There is some suggestion in the findings that a psychologically and physically uncomfortable home atmosphere interferes with the capacity for intellectual tasks requiring the use of abstract reasoning and memory.[1]

Boys reared in homes in which the parents were overtly unhappy in their relationship to one another and constantly on the verge of an open breach are more likely to manifest *low verbal intelligence* (I.Q. below 80) than are youngsters whose parents separated when they were little (not older than three years), the children remaining with one parent, usually the mother. Here is some evidence that intelligence tests are not independent of cultural opportunities. In further support of the finding that lack of harmony under the home roof contributes in some way to *low verbal intelligence* is the higher proportion of such boys who were treated with indifference by their brothers and sisters. And one more piece of evidence of the possible role of the home atmosphere in conditioning verbal ability rests in the higher proportion of boys reared in overcrowded homes who were found to have verbal intelligence of less than 80. This latter finding suggests that the multiplicity of circumstances (social, psychological, economic) which result in overcrowded homes have some bearing on impeding the capacity to carry out intellectual tasks that call for the use of abstract reasoning and memory, in which the approach to meaning tends to be via a structure of intervening symbols rather than through tangible things.

While not denying the probably dominant role of natural endowment in determining the scope and nature of intelligence,[2] and bearing in mind that in the pilot research (*Unraveling Juvenile Delinquency*) the delinquents and nondelinquents had been essentially matched in respect to general or global intelligence, the foregoing

[1] Attention is called to the fact that in the original study from which the materials are derived (*Unraveling Juvenile Delinquency*) 'global intelligence' (I.Q. according to standard intelligence tests) was *controlled*, the 500 delinquents and the matched 500 nondelinquents having essentially similar intelligence distributions. This fact renders more meaningful the differences in the *constituents* of intelligence which emerge from comparison of the two groups.

[2] In *Physique and Delinquency* (pp. 63–4) it was found that while *low verbal intelligence* did vary significantly among the body types of the delinquents (despite the matching of delinquents with nondelinquents in global intelligence) there was no significant variation among the nondelinquents. This led us to say that 'it cannot be concluded that *verbal intelligence* is of constitutional orientation, although other evidence may establish it to be hereditary.'

evidence impels to the view that, within certain margins, the expression of *verbal intelligence* is affected by environmental opportunity or handicap. It must be concluded that parental incompatibility, unsympathetic attitudes on the part of siblings and crowding in the home are influences contributory to low verbal ability.

Performance intelligence (Appendix Table D-12) relates to the 'hand-minded' aspects of intelligence in which the approach to meaning tends to be by way of direct physical relationships, with a minimum of dependence on intermediary symbols and abstractions. How is this trait affected by the environmental factors in this study?

There is evidence in the findings that a permissive home atmosphere (as reflected in lax discipline by the mother in contrast to erratic discipline) somehow contributes to the performance ability of a youngster. Perhaps he has more freedom to develop manipulative skills in a home climate free of restriction. This is, however, but the barest of clues and needs intensive exploration through clinical analysis of other samples of cases.

There are two other factors in regard to which a significant relationship to performance ability occurs: cleanliness and neatness of the home and rearing in a household in which the routines of daily living are systematized (specific mealtimes, study hours, playtime, bedtime, and the like). A higher proportion of boys of good performance ability (I.Q. over 100) were brought up in such homes than were reared in households where there was sporadic or constant disorder and uncleanliness.

We consider, next, the psychologic trait of *originality* (Appendix Table D-13), which is reflected in an unconventional way of perception, experience or thought. It is important to note that *originality* can be either rewarding or destructive. In its positive aspects, this trait is a genuine, often productive expression of the personality; in its negative form, it may lead to estrangement from the community, to a 'lack of common sense,' to 'queerness' and the like.

Four of the 44 sociocultural factors bear a significant relationship to the trait of *originality*. First, it would appear that a higher proportion of boys characterized by this trait had mothers who were erratic workers (going from job to job, largely to escape their home responsibilities), rather than mothers who were full-time homemakers. Also, the failure of a mother to give competent supervision to a youngster, leaving him mainly to his own devices or in the hands of an irresponsible person, appears to contribute to the formation of an unconventional way of perception, experience or thought involved in the trait of *originality*. This is supported by the finding that the unconcern of parents for their son (as reflected in inhospitality to his playmates and lack of provision for his use of leisure in the home) is also associated with the development of *originality*, which, as has been pointed out, may lead to a lack of common sense, to queerness and the like. In other words, *'originality,'* at least in its more undesirable aspects, is seemingly fostered by absence of a warm and understanding relationship between mother and child, leaving the son without adequate moorings in the family and without guidance from his parents; his unconventional perceptive inclinations may thus develop as a reactive defensive expression of his ego.

Banality (Appendix Table D-14) is defined as the complete or comparative inability to think in other than the most commonplace terms and concepts. A linkage is found between this trait and rearing in a home which lacks cultural refinement, or in a careless and irresponsible household climate, reflected in a family's inability or unwillingness to manage its income to cover essential needs. Both of these home influences apparently derive from a mediocrity of family life which appears to have something to do with stunting a boy's capacity to think in other than the most unimaginative and humdrum terms.

Whether two additional associations with *banality*—use of physical punishment by the father and threatening or scolding by the mother —result from a boy's banality, or, contrariwise, the trait derives from his parents' unsympathetic disciplinary practices, is an open question. Despite the fact that the emphasis probably varies in different families, the trait and the conduct of father and mother are probably bound in a reciprocal dynamism.

Still another aspect of intelligence is *marked power of observation* (Appendix Table D-15), which includes the ability both to observe accurately and to maintain such accuracy of observation at a fairly constant level. If there is any relationship at all between this trait and any of the environmental circumstances involved in our series of 44 social factors, it rests in the matter of concern of parents for a child. For in contrast to inadequately supervised youths, an excessive proportion of boys with *marked power of observation* are found among those whose mothers keep close watch on their leisure-time activities, providing the son with safe and constructive outlets in clubs or playgrounds, or, if personally unable to do so, delegating this task to a responsible adult. This is supported by two additional findings which also reflect parental concern and interest in a youngster, *i.e.*, in the higher proportion of markedly observant boys whose parents welcomed their playmates into the home or whose parents make some provision for leisure-time pursuits at home.

Evidently, boys about whom parents are constructively concerned, over whom they watch and for whose leisure time they make whole-some provision are more likely to develop or sharpen their powers of observation than are children whose activities are of little concern to parents.

Turning now to *common sense* (Appendix Table D-18), defined as the capacity to think and act in the ways of the community, it has been found that an only child is less likely to possess this useful faculty. Evidently, youngsters deprived of the opportunity to learn to adapt themselves to peers within the confines of the family circle are not so likely to learn how to think and act in the ways of the community as are children who have siblings. Youngsters who are closely supervised by the mother, and those who are provided with play facilities at home, are somewhat more likely to develop the faculty of *common sense* than are those who are deprived of this protected, but normalizing, outlet for their energies.

FEELINGS OF RESENTMENT, ANXIETY, INFERIORITY AND FRUSTRATION

Next we are concerned with the traits: *enhanced insecurity or anxiety, marked feeling of not being wanted or loved, feeling of not being taken care of, marked feeling of not being taken seriously, feelings of helplessness and powerlessness, of not being appreciated, of resentment.* In learning how these evidences of anxiety and frustration develop, we may derive some hints as to how to prevent or minimize their formation.

While insecurity and anxiety are emotional involvements not only in pathological individuals but also in so-called 'normal' persons, the *enhanced feeling of insecurity* (Appendix Table D-25) designates a state in which this feeling exerts a decidedly stronger influence within the personality dynamics—either quantitatively or qualitatively—than is usual in the average person. This feeling, however, may remain largely unconscious.

Lack of wholesome parental interest in a child, especially on the part of the mother, appears to contribute to the development of excessive *feelings of insecurity or anxiety.* This is evidenced in the significantly higher proportion of youngsters having this trait among those whose mothers were lax in their discipline (allowing the children to do as they please, even to running about the streets without any supervision) in contrast to boys who were controlled with firmness and kindness. The maternal influence in question is further evidenced by the finding that an excessive proportion of insecure and anxious boys are the sons of delinquent mothers or are among those who

41

were left by the mother to their own devices without guidance, or are found among children whose parents do not provide them with home recreational outlets beyond an occasional book or toy.

The role of lack of parental interest in a child in the development of *enhanced feelings of insecurity* is further evident in the excessive proportion of markedly insecure boys among those whose parents were not ambitious to improve the family's socioeconomic status, or who belonged to families in which the interpersonal ties were not very close.

The many dangers to a child's emotional development inherent in his feeling of not being wanted or loved is our next concern.

A *marked feeling of not being wanted or loved* (Appendix Table D-26) is the conviction, often repressed and unconscious, that one is not accepted, not included, even rejected by others; the early childhood sense of lack of positive human relationships to a particular group or persons, especially to parents and other members of the family. It may lead, by way of compensation, to an exaggerated need for affection, recognition or success.

This feeling is currently found associated with three of the social factors included in this inquiry: rearing in an overcrowded home, lack of positive acceptance by brothers and sisters, and overstrict (contrasted with lax) discipline of the boy by his father.

This suggests a basic problem in child-rearing—the need for discipline as a method of teaching a child the rules of life and thereby minimizing occasions for frustration, pain and disappointment, and, simultaneously, the need to provide a climate of kindliness to counteract the child's conception that parental strictness is a sign of lack of love.

Turning next to the *feeling of not being taken care of* (Appendix Table D-27), the conception that there is no active interest on the part of others (especially the parents) or help from them in situations in which the child deems himself entitled to such interest and aid, once crystallized, may outlast the particular situation which produced it. Strikingly, there is a statistical relationship between this feeling and 17 social factors—by far the greatest number of associations revealed in our analysis and, in fact, more than with any other trait encompassed in this inquiry.

Among the social conditions related to the *feeling of not being taken care of,* and which probably contribute to the crystallization of the trait, are: overcrowding of the home, which suggests that a child's occasional need for privacy is not respected; rearing in an ambitionless atmosphere; a home in which life is haphazard and uncertain, as reflected in a lack of planfulness in the use of the family's income and the absence of established routines. Such an atmosphere must indeed engender the feeling in a child that he is not being taken care of. Also contributing to this sense of abandonment is the father who is an employment liability (as reflected in his loafing, laziness, dishonesty, waywardness, vagabondage); such a parent obviously cannot inspire confidence and a sense of security in a child.

Low standards of conduct on the part of one or another family member are also contributory to the development of the *feeling of not being taken care of*; inadequate supervision by the mother, as well as other evidences of parental failure to show interest and real concern for the child—indifference or open hostility of the parents toward entertaining the boy's friends at home; meager provision by the parents for his play outlets, as well as a complete lack of recreation by the family as a group; permissiveness on the part of a mother who, if not always lax, swings erratically between laxity and overstrictness so that a child never learns what to expect from parental authority; resort to physical punishment by a father, rather than to less drastic means of control. It also emerges that an excessive proportion of youngsters who are not loved by the father develop the *feeling of not being taken care of*. Evidently, a child reacts to such deprivation by lack of confidence in his parents; for a significantly disproportionate segment of boys who were emotionally unattached to one or both parents developed the *feeling of not being taken care of*. It is reasonable to assume, therefore, that emotional attachment of a child to his parents depends in large measure on the child's feeling that he is being protected and well looked after by them. Evidently, also, a boy who feels that he is not well taken care of reacts by not accepting his father as a pattern for emulation.

Marked feeling of not being taken seriously (Appendix Table D-28) is the impression that one's person, interests, ideas and wishes are not acknowledged and not treated as deserving of respect and consideration for their own sake. This is frequently produced in childhood (often inadvertently) by making a child feel that whatever he does is mere 'child's play,' especially if his wishes and interests are not consulted and do not coincide with those of his parents.

Six factors in this study appear to develop this feeling. Some of them were found to contribute to other evidences of insecurity and anxiety: overcrowding in the household, lack of adequate provision for home recreation, indifference or inhospitality to a child's friends, overstrictness by a mother whose rigidity may well give a child the feeling that she has no respect for him. In addition, there is evidence that rearing by an emotionally disturbed mother, or by one whose absence from the home in gainful employment is unpredictable in

43

that she works erratically and mainly to escape from household obligations, also contributes to a youngster's *feeling of not being taken seriously*.

The feeling of not being taken seriously often leads in turn to a *feeling of helplessness* (Appendix Table D-29), a frequent, important, and often unconscious kind of insecurity, in which the individual feels incompetent, especially as regards changing or influencing anything, and most particularly the course of his own life.

This serious emotional attitude is engendered by the unhappy circumstance of being brought up by a delinquent mother, living in crowded quarters, rearing in a home in which the family income is not systematically assigned to provide for the basic necessities (thereby creating an atmosphere of uncertainty about whether such needs will be met), subjection to physical punishment or careless supervision of a child by his mother. It is developed also by an over-strict (compared to lax) disciplinary attitude on the part of the father, or by his resort to physical punishment (rather than to less drastic disciplinary measures) in order to 'tame' an unmanageable child.

Discipline by the mother which is lax or erratic rather than firm and kindly also contributes to the development of a *feeling of helplessness and powerlessness* in a youngster. The same is true of a lack of cordiality of parents to the son's friends and neglect to provide proper outlets for his recreational activities under the home roof.

We next consider the *feeling of not being appreciated* (Appendix Table D-30), which refers especially to the impression that one's qualities, gifts, intentions and achievements are not sufficiently thought of or valued. It often occurs in association with grandiose ideas and opinions about oneself—conscious as well as unconscious.

Parental unconcern for a child (reflected in indifference or outright inhospitality of parents to the friends of a youngster and their failure to provide adequate recreational facilities for him in the home) appears to play a telling role in developing the feeling on the part of a child that he is not recognized or appreciated.

Finally, we consider the *feeling of resentment* (Appendix Table D-32), which is the sense of frustration, envy or dissatisfaction, with particular emphasis on the negative wish that others be denied satisfactions or enjoyments one has himself lacked rather than on the positive hope or attempt to better one's own situation.

As is true of *ambivalence to authority*, so of *resentment*, there is an association between the trait and mother-love. Although it may be that resentment would naturally arise from deprivation of maternal affection, a reciprocal mechanism, suggested by the possibility that the mother finds it difficult to give warm affection to a youngster

44

who is resentful, must also be considered. However, supportive evidence for the first view is strong, since it is also found that a disproportionately high percentage of resentful boys had mothers who were erratic in their behavior as evidenced by their unpredictable absence from home in gainful employment, often to escape from household responsibilities. It is also found that children of mothers who are permissive in discipline suffer in greater measure from *feelings of resentment* than do youngsters who are treated with firmness and kindness by the mother.

In the next chapter we continue our discussion of the relationships between social factors and those traits which had not been shown in *Physique and Delinquency* to vary in incidence among the body types, and which are now found to be significantly related to two or more of the 44 social factors encompassed in this inquiry.

V

ADDITIONAL TRAITS WHICH DO NOT VARY AMONG BODY TYPES: RELATED TO TWO OR MORE SOCIAL FACTORS

INTRODUCTION

IN this chapter we continue the discussion concerning the relationships between social factors and those traits not found in *Physique and Delinquency* to vary in incidence among the body types (and therefore not referable by that test to the constitutional zone of the biosocial continuum). The presumption is that, if such relationships reflect a contribution by the environmental factor to the development of the trait, the trait may be regarded as closer to the sociocultural area of the biosocial continuum than to the constitutional or innate.

Our concern in this chapter is with the traits reflecting feelings of hostility, suspicion, isolation; dependence and independence; goals of drives; some general qualities of personality; deep-rooted emotional dynamics; personality orientation; and, finally, some aspects of mental pathology.

FEELINGS OF HOSTILITY, SUSPICIOUSNESS AND ISOLATION

At the outset we consider the development of feelings of *hostility*, *suspiciousness*, and *isolation*—traits which are interrelated and all of which were shown, in *Unraveling Juvenile Delinquency*, to be significantly more characteristic of youthful transgressors than of non-delinquents.

Hostility (Appendix Table D-34) refers to conscious or unconscious unfriendly impulses against others without good reason. There is in this kind of dynamism an accompanying fear that those against whom the impulse is directed are themselves hostile.

It is quite generally accepted by psychiatrists that a child's hostility to others is, among other things, the product of parental hostility to the child (unconscious as well as conscious). The present findings would appear to give statistical confirmation to this clinical experi-

46

ence: for a significantly greater proportion of youngsters whose fathers and/or mothers were either carelessly indifferent or downright hostile to them, than of boys not typically subjected to such parental neglect, were found to have deep-seated feelings of *hostility*.[1] Erratic discipline by the father (sometimes very harsh, sometimes lax) or overstrictness on the part of the mother also appear to be associated with feelings of *hostility* in children.

There are further bits of evidence regarding the circumstances that contribute to a youngster's feelings of *hostility*: one of these is the unpredictable absences of a mother from the home in erratic outside employment; for sons of mothers who flit from job to job (largely to escape household responsibilities) are, in significantly greater measure, found to be hostile youngsters than are children of women who are full-time homemakers. It was found, also, that sons of alcoholic fathers or of fathers with serious physical ailments (to the point of affecting their employment) are hostile in greater measure than are sons of sober or of physically healthy fathers. This is likewise the case in regard to boys reared in households of low conduct standards (as evidenced by drunkenness, delinquency or immorality in one or more members of the immediate family group).

Marked suspiciousness (Appendix Table D-35) has to do with indiscriminate or exaggerated mistrust of others, unwarranted by the actual situation. The person is usually not aware that he is unduly suspicious; he thinks rather that he is being merely cautious, or 'realistic,' or that he is in fact being persecuted.

Suspiciousness evidently develops more readily in youngsters one or both of whose parents are foreign-born than among boys of all-native parentage. Perhaps it grows out of cultural tension between the Old-World standards of the parents and the values which the native-born child acquires from his school or playtime peers.

Rearing by parents who are ambitionless (meaning in effect that they have no sense of purpose and direction) seems also to act as a stimulus to the conditioning of this trait; for a significantly greater proportion of boys brought up by such parents are characterized by an exaggerated mistrust of others than are youngsters whose parents showed some inclination to improve the family's status (as

---

[1] The reader is reminded that a very important feature of *Unraveling Juvenile Delinquency* is the fact that the investigators in one line of inquiry were not permitted to consult the findings on any boy under examination by them made by investigators in other aspects of the study; thus contamination of raw materials was prevented. It is this feature which makes the subsequent statistical comparisons of the delinquents with the nondelinquents and the intercorrelations of the data from the various areas of *Unraveling* particularly impressive. See *Unraveling Juvenile Delinquency*, New York The Commonwealth Fund, 1950, p. 17.

reflected in seeking more rewarding occupations, moving to more wholesome neighborhoods or to more adequate living quarters, planning for higher education or vocational training for their children, and the like).

Lack of intelligent concern of parents for a child, reflected in failure to provide for his recreations, appears also to be involved in developing *suspiciousness* in the youngster, since a significantly higher ratio of boys whose parents did not provide more than the most meager recreational outlets (*e.g.*, only an occasional toy) than of other boys are found to be unduly mistrustful of others.

Another clue to the environmental influences that contribute to the development in a child of mistrust of others is found in the age of a youngster at the first breach in the family group (by death, desertion, separation, divorce of parents, or prolonged absence of one or both parents resulting from illness or imprisonment). A significantly greater proportion of boys who experienced such a break in the normal family relationships when under five years of age developed mistrust of others than of those who were five to ten years of age when so great an emotional revolution in their lives occurred.

Next to be considered is the *feeling of isolation* (Appendix Table D-37), that is, the sense of being alone, often combined with a feeling of helplessness and of not being sufficiently capable of either giving or receiving love and affection. It may be accompanied by an appearance and even a subjective conviction of being very 'sociable,' illustrated, for instance, by the person who is constantly 'on the go' and always 'making friends,' but acting essentially to escape awareness of his own extreme emotional isolation.

It would appear from our findings that a mother's shortcomings in relation to her child (as reflected in her erratic absences from the home in hit-or-miss jobs, in lax discipline, and in failure to give suitable supervision) all contribute materially to the development within the youngster's personality dynamics of a *feeling of isolation* from people and from the world.

Also contributory to this crippling emotional state is a lack of intelligent parental concern for the child's wholesome development (reflected in inadequate provision for recreational opportunities under the home roof and in lack of interest in his playmates) as well as rearing in an overcrowded home. We can only speculate on the reasons why this latter circumstance bears a relationship to the *feeling of isolation*. Perhaps it is the lack of a sense of privacy, the necessity for outward conformity to the needs of others in such an uncomfortable situation, which causes some children to turn inward in order to escape from what is to them an unpleasant or threatening reality.

We next consider the characteristic described as a *defensive attitude* (Appendix Table D-38). This pertains to unwarranted defensiveness, either exaggerated in proportion to the attack or directed against an imaginary aggressor. It appears to result in part from rearing by a mother who is herself a delinquent, or from growing up in a family in which the ties are not close and warm. About this, too, one can only speculate in the absence of more specific clinical information. The tenuous atmosphere of a home in which such conditions prevail may well cause a child to become self-conscious about his unfortunate circumstances and result in compensatory behavior such as exaggerated defensiveness.

DEPENDENCE AND INDEPENDENCE; GOALS OF DRIVES

The *feeling of being able to manage one's life* (Appendix Table D-40) is a deep-seated confidence that one can handle one's problems and tasks without leaning unduly on others.

One source of this feeling of competence would appear to be the fortunate circumstance of rearing in a closely knit family. Another lies in the affection and interest of the parents in their children, as suggested by the preponderance of boys with a sense of competence whose mothers were firm and kindly in their discipline.

Another root influence of the feeling of being able to manage the affairs of life is rearing by parents who are very much concerned about the welfare of their children as reflected in friendliness toward a son's playmates and in at least some provision for his leisure hours at home.

It is clear enough from our findings that it is the warmth and concern of parents which contributes to a youngster's confidence that he can meet life's problems.

A striking contrast is shown in the relationship of parental behavior to the evolution of *narcissistic trends* (Appendix Table D-41), that is, self-love, leading to an increased need for power, superiority, prestige, status and admiration. As is the case regarding the preceding trait, two social factors, both however reflecting *lack* of parental concern for the welfare of their children, appear to contribute to the development of the trait of *narcissism*: a higher proportion of narcissistic youngsters are the offspring of parents so uninterested in the welfare of their children as to be inhospitable to their playmates; and/or of parents who make no effort to provide at least some family group recreations in which they and their children can happily participate together.

49

It seems reasonable to assume that deprivation of family group activities (such as picnics, visits to relatives, auto rides, movie attendance and the like) tend to develop excessive self-love in children as one type of compensatory mechanism.

Receptive (oral) trends (Appendix Table D-42) constitute a typical way in which some persons satisfy their emotional needs through an unconscious expectation that they will somehow be taken care of by others without feeling obliged to make any effort to assume any responsibility of their own. This tendency may take a passive form (waiting for someone else to provide what one desires); or it may express itself in more affirmative channels (leading to outwardly expressed greed or to attempts to secure the desired object without effort, as by theft or without assuming any obligations).

As might be anticipated, it is found that rearing in a home in which there is evidence of incompetence and inadequacy or lack of concern of the parents for the child contributes to the development in some boys of a need to make up for these unwholesome aspects of home life by a largely unconscious 'devil-may-care' attitude.

In relating *receptive trends* to the 44 factors of social background, it is found that a significantly greater proportion of boys reared in homes in which there is parental carelessness in the management of household affairs, especially in the handling of finances, have such feelings in their personality-character structure. Further evidence of the part played by parental lack of concern for a child in engendering in him the kind of irresponsible self-centeredness that is reflected in *receptive trends* is seen in the excessive proportion of youngsters reared by mothers so uninterested in them as to fail to provide close supervision, leaving the children to their own devices without guidance or in the care of irresponsible persons. It is evident also in the greater proportion of such boys from families in which group recreations were not engaged in, as contrasted with the lower proportion of boys with *receptive trends* in families in which group recreations were common.

Finally, parental indifference as a contributory factor in the development of *receptive trends* is further shown by the excessive proportion of such boys among those whose parents were not friendly to the child's playmates and who made no provision for his leisure hours at home.

SOME GENERAL QUALITIES OF PERSONALITY

We turn now to certain more permeative personality dynamisms. The first of these, *compulsory trends* (Appendix Table D-48), includes not only typical neurotic compulsions, but the less evident cases of rigidity—that is, traits not permitting of flexible adaptation to changing situations. *Compulsory trends* reflect rather mechanical attempts to defend the self against conscious or, more often, unconscious anxiety.

Of the 44 social factors with which this trait was systematically intercorrelated, eight were found which appear to be significant in contributing to the persistent anxiety against which *compulsory trends* are a defense. All of these factors obviously reflect unconcern on the part of the parents for the welfare of the child and appear to be the result of his growing up in an unclean and disorderly household, a home in which life is confused and in which the income is not systematically managed; rearing by parents devoid of self-respect or of ambition to improve their status; growing up in a household in which there are only the most meager provisions for the child's recreational needs; bringing up by a mother who does not carefully supervise her child. Apart from all these undesirable under-the-roof conditions, there is evidence that, as regards discipline, complete permissiveness (laxity) on the part of a mother, or an erratic swinging from extremes of overstrictness to extreme permissiveness, are also influential in crystallizing *compulsory trends* in a youngster in his attempt to defend himself against the malaise of largely unconscious but very disturbing anxiety.

A *preponderance of extroversive trends* (Appendix Table D-49) in the personality dynamism reflects a ready tendency to discharge tensions in emotional outlets or in motoric action.

The interpretation of one of the relationships uncovered between such trends and social factors must be considered in connection with the analysis that follows regarding *introversive* trends. This has to do with emotional disturbance in the mother. The association revealed between affective maternal disturbance (psychoses, psychoneuroses, psychopathies, epilepsies, sex perversions, delirium tremens, marked emotional instabilities, and other extreme liabilities of personality such as marked impulsiveness) and extroversiveness in the child suggests that a *preponderance of extroversive trends* is more likely to be found among boys who were reared by emotionally healthy mothers, while, as will be seen below, an excessive proportion of sons of emotionally (and/or physically) ill mothers are found to be *introversive*.

Two other statistically significant correlations have to do (one directly, one indirectly) with the father–son relationship. It would appear that the tendency toward extroversion is enhanced by affection of the father for his son and by rearing in a home in which the father, rather than the mother, takes the leadership in family affairs.

A *preponderance of introversive trends* (Appendix Table D-50) reflects the tendency to pile up tensions by an emphasis on the creative mental processes, a living more 'within oneself,' and by difficulty in relating emotionally to others. This appears by definition to represent a response that is essentially opposite to extroversion; for a disproportionately high percentage of sons of physically ill and/or emotionally ill fathers are found to be *introversive*. The same is true, also, in regard to boys who are constantly exposed to overstrict (as contrasted with lax) discipline by the father.

One additional factor appears to play a role in the evolution of *introversive trends*. This has to do with the attitude of parents regarding the entertainment of a child's friends in the home, an inhospitable manner being associated with introversiveness among a greater proportion of such youngsters than among those from homes where parents welcome the child's playmates. This indication of lack of concern for the son's needs evidently contributes to his tendency to withdraw into himself.

DEEP-ROOTED EMOTIONAL DYNAMICS; PERSONALITY ORIENTATION

Suggestibility (Appendix Table D-52) describes a tendency to be easily swayed by an appeal to one's feelings despite one's better judgment.

Correlating this trait with the 44 social factors reveals that influences stemming from an early break-up in normal family relationships contribute to the development of *suggestibility* in a youngster, since an excessively higher proportion of boys who suffered a breach in home ties before they were five years old are found to be suggestible than of boys who were older when such disruption in family life first occurred.

Another influence contributing to the development of *suggestibility* in a youngster is erratic discipline by the father, in contrast with firm but kindly restraint. Such fluctuation between extremes of harshness and complete permissiveness must be very unsettling and confusing to a child.

There is evidence also that suggestible boys are more likely to find the father unacceptable as a role-figure for emulation. Whether this strained relation between father and son is largely the *result* of the boy's suggestibility, or is initially and essentially the product of the son's lack of attachment to his father, is hard to say. Perhaps intensive clinical observations would clarify the issue.

Additional Traits Which Do Not Vary among Body Types

Stubbornness (Appendix Table D-54) is perhaps largely the result of thwarted dynamic qualities. That this frustration should be somehow related to a child's weak affective ties to his parents comes as no surprise, whatever the dynamic sequence may be. Of all the 44 factors included in this inquiry, a clear relationship to *stubbornness* is found with only two: lack of attachment of a son to his father and to his mother. Stubborn boys, as a group, are not fond of their parents. It is doubtful whether lack of affection of a boy for his parents accounts for his *stubbornness*. The sequence is probably the reverse. Intensive clinical tracing of relationships would throw further light on this question.

Because of the lack of any clearly contributory relationship of any of the 44 factors to the development of *stubbornness*, we must for the present consider this trait to be closer to the biologic than to the social pole of the bipolar continuum.

Lack of self-criticism (Appendix Table D-62) is the incapacity and unwillingness to assay one's own faults and virtues, abilities and liabilities. This appears to be associated with being reared in an unwholesome atmosphere, a likelihood reflected in the excessive proportion of youngsters with this characteristic who were brought up by delinquent mothers or by parents who lacked family pride and self-respect; or in a household in which the children were denied the stability of remaining in one or two places of residence, being instead frequently uprooted during their early years.

Conscientiousness (Appendix Table D-63) has to do with scrupulousness about achieving one's aims. This trait appears to flourish more easily among youngsters reared in a healthy and wholesome atmosphere than among other boys—a fact reflected in the greater proportion of conscientious youngsters in families in which the mother gives or provides adequate supervision, is firm and kindly in her discipline; in which both parents show genuine interest in a child's friends, and provide him with suitable play facilities under the home roof. Also contributory to the desirable trait of *conscientiousness* is rearing in a home in which the father is not burdened with physical ailments, so that he can fulfill his role as a parent without the handicap of a debilitating illness.

The effect of rearing in a planful and dynamic home on the development of *conscientiousness* in a child is further reflected in the greater proportion of boys with this trait found in homes in which the parents carefully budget the family income and in which they show concern to improve the family's socioeconomic status.

It should also be noted that proportionately high percentages of conscientious youngsters are found to be warmly attached to the father and to regard him as an acceptable model for emulation. These factors of emotional attachment to the father and his acceptability as a role-symbol may, however, represent rather the response of a conscientious child to parental attitudes and actions than influences that contribute to the *development* of *conscientiousness* in the first place; or there may well be a reciprocal involvement.

SOME ASPECTS OF MENTAL PATHOLOGY

Turning now to more fixed syndromes of mental malaise, the first diagnostic pattern to be considered is *neuroticism* (Appendix Table D-66). If this interfered with efficient adaptation, a boy was classified as a *marked* neurotic; otherwise, as a mild neurotic. Marked neuroticism was defined by the experienced psychiatrist who interviewed the boys in connection with *Unraveling Juvenile Delinquency* as a condition in which the individual suffers from more than average insecurity and anxiety (conscious or unconscious) against which he develops protective devices differing quantitatively or qualitatively from the culturally accepted ones and leading to conflicts which are, as a rule, not solvable by him for the time being. Mild neuroticism, on the other hand, was defined as a condition that does not prevent the individual from relatively efficient adaptation. In addition to the boys who, on the basis of psychiatric interview, were diagnosed as marked or mild neurotics, there are those who could not clearly be placed in one or the other diagnostic category but who nevertheless evidenced recognizable neurotic personality trends.

Within the limits of the factors in the present research, how did these various aspects of neuroticism develop? [1]

According to our findings, *neuroticism* (marked, mild or trends) would appear to be the product of a faulty relationship with the mother and also of weak family ties. A higher proportion of youngsters whose mothers were found to be overstrict, harsh, or especially demanding, were also found to be markedly neurotic or to show neurotic trends than youngsters whose mothers were not overly restrictive in the management of the child.

It is clear also that an excessive proportion of boys reared in families in which there was an absence of strong affective bonds among the members developed into neurotics. This is the case also in regard to youngsters reared by delinquent mothers or mothers

---

[1] We are of course aware of the existence of the 'neurotic constitution.' The analysis in the text is concerned with the influence of certain intimate family relationships in contributing to the syndrome of *neuroticism*.

unpredictably absent from the home in sporadic outside employment.

We have now completed the analysis of the orientation of the 43 (of 66) traits which had not been found in *Physique and Delinquency* to vary in incidence among the body types. These traits, it will be remembered, were therefore not classified as essentially constitutional. There were, however, 23 traits in *Physique and Delinquency* which had been classed as fundamentally constitutional. Before presenting a summary of the findings, we must next focus attention on a further examination of the orientation of these 23 traits. In the light of the data in the present work, can it still be said that these traits are all essentially constitutional? Or must some of them now be placed toward the center of our postulated biosocial continuum?

VI

CONTRIBUTION OF ENVIRONMENTAL FACTORS TO CONSTITUTIONAL TRAITS

INTRODUCTION

THE 23 traits shown in *Physique and Delinquency*[1] to vary significantly in incidence among the body types (and therefore assumed to have an essentially constitutional orientation) are as follows:

6. Cyanosis
8. Tremors
9. Genital Underdevelopment
10. Strength of Hand Grip
17. Tendency to Phantasy
21. Social Assertiveness
23. Marked Submissiveness to Authority
31. Fear of Failure and Defeat
36. Destructiveness
39. Marked Dependence on Others
43. Masochistic Trends
44. Destructive-Sadistic Trends
47. Vivacity
51. Sensitivity
53. Feeling of Inadequacy
56. Uninhibited Motor Responses to Stimuli
57. Emotional Instability
58. Aestheticism
59. Sensuousness
60. Acquisitiveness
61. Unconventionality
64. Impracticality
65. Emotional Conflicts

[1] S. and E. T. Glueck, New York, Harper & Brothers, 1956.

CONSTITUTIONALLY-ORIENTED TRAITS PROBABLY NOT
LARGELY DEPENDENT ON ENVIRONMENTAL FACTORS

First, we can dispose of five of the above traits in which no relationship has been found to any of the factors or the relationship of one and sometimes two factors to the trait does not reflect a contribution of the factor to the development of the trait, but, rather, expresses the reaction of a person in the immediate environment (father, mother) to the boy with a given trait, or explains the attitude of a boy to such a person.

6. Cyanosis
8. Tremors
9. Genital Underdevelopment
47. Vivacity
59. Sensuousness

In the case of *tremors* and *sensuousness*, significant relationships were not found to exist between these and any one of the 44 social factors.

As regards *cyanosis* (Appendix Tables D-6 and E-6), a higher proportion of cyanotic boys were found to have been physically punished by the father and a higher proportion, emotionally unattached to the mother. The meaning of these associations is obscure and may be accidental. However, it is well to note that in *Physique and Delinquency* ectomorphs were found to be more cyanotic than endomorphs and this is true also of cyanotic boys who were given physical punishment by the father.

As regards *genital underdevelopment* (Appendix Tables D-9 and E-9), a reflection of physical immaturity, a disproportionately high percentage of such boys were found to be attached to the father. Perhaps they have a greater need than more mature youngsters for a father's love and protection. Here, also, it is well to note that a higher proportion of genitally underdeveloped boys were found in *Physique and Delinquency* to be endomorphic and ectomorphic rather than mesomorphic, and this is now found to be the case among genitally underdeveloped boys having a strong father attachment.

As regards *vivacity* (Appendix Tables D-47 and E-47), defined as 'liveliness' of behavior, the findings suggest that vivacious youngsters are more likely than others to be threatened or scolded by the mother. As this probably represents the response of the mother to the exuberant conduct of a son (behavior she evidently finds difficult to manage), this relationship is classifiable as 'reactive' of factor to trait rather than as a contribution of the factor to the formation of the trait. In

Physique and Delinquency we learned that endomorphic boys (round, fat) are as a group less vivacious than boys of other body builds. However, we do not now find that there is any difference in the extent to which vivacious boys of one or another body build are threatened or scolded by the mother.

Two traits among the 23 which vary in incidence among the body types—*social assertiveness* and *fear of failure and defeat*—are found to be significantly related to no more than one social factor in a way to suggest a contribution of the factor to the development of the trait. *Social assertiveness* (Appendix Tables D-21 and E-21), unlike self-assertion which usually implies a genuine spontaneity, refers to the more superficial trait of asserting one's will and ambitions. This tendency appears to be enhanced in situations in which a father's discipline is lax (instead of overstrict or firm but kindly), leading to the implication that the essentially latent tendency to *social assertiveness* is fostered in a highly permissive atmosphere.

Analyzing this trait in terms of physique type, it is found that *social assertiveness* is in general far less characteristic of endomorphs than of boys of other body builds; however, there is no evidence that a father's disciplinary laxity bears any significantly greater relationship to the social assertiveness of boys of one body build than of another.

As to *fear of failure and defeat* (Appendix Tables D-31 and E-31), which is a frequent consequence of anxiety, this appears to be considerably influenced by permissiveness (laxity) in discipline on the part of the mother; for those boys whose mothers allowed them to do as they pleased are found to be more generally characterized by such fear than are boys whose mothers were firm and kind in discipline and even than those whose mothers vacillated between permissiveness and overstrictness.

It is to be noted, however, that, although ectomorphs (the thin, linear, fragile type) were not in general found to be more highly characterized by *fear of failure and defeat* than mesomorphs (the sturdy, muscular body build), it now appears that a significantly greater proportion of ectomorphic than of mesomorphic boys had not been restricted by the mother in their activities.

Thus far, seven of the traits found in *Physique and Delinquency* to vary in incidence among the body types are not shown to be associated with any, or at most with only one, of the 44 social factors in a way suggestive of a contribution of the factor to the development of the trait. It would seem reasonable, therefore, to infer that these traits are indeed closer to the biological than to the environmental end of the biosocial continuum. As previously stated, caution would dictate that evidence of at least two significant factor-trait relationships should exist before it can be said that a trait is possibly nearer to the cultural than the constitutional area of the biosocial continuum.

We turn now to 16 traits found in *Physique and Delinquency* to vary in incidence among the body types (thus permitting an inference of an essentially biologic orientation) but which in the present inquiry are also found to be significantly associated with at least two of the 44 social factors.

A few of these relationships clearly reflect the predominance of hereditary influences in the formation of the traits (*sensitivity* and *aestheticism*). As for the other traits, it will become evident in the analysis that the influence of both heredity and environment are markedly involved in their formation.

Strength of hand grip (Appendix Tables D-10 and E-10), which we look upon as evidence of good vitality, was measured by a standard hand dynamometer. Although a grip averaging 75 kilograms or more for both hands had previously been shown to vary significantly in incidence among the body types (permitting an inference of an essentially biologic orientation), relationships were nevertheless also found between five of the 44 social factors and vigorous hand grip. Three of these relationships suggest a reaction of parents to marked vigor in a son, rather than conditions precedent to a child's vitality: provision of recreational facilities in the home, suitable supervision of boy by mother, and firm but kindly discipline of boy by mother. Some readers may not agree with this interpretation, but the nature of the factors involved tends to support it.

Another finding would seem to indicate that the latent energy of a youngster is *blocked* by the traumatic effect on him of frequent bickering between the parents (reflecting, as it often does, their lack of love for each other), or by an early break in the family life (separation, desertion, divorce, or death of one or both parents, or the prolonged absence of a parent from the home due to illness or imprisonment); for an excessive proportion of youngsters exposed to parental friction or subjected to a breach in the family life when under five years of age were boys with *low dynamometric strength*.

Considering now the various body types, a markedly excessive proportion of mesomorphs were found in *Physique and Delinquency* to have a vigorous hand grip. We know from other aspects of our study of boys of this body type that mesomorphs are also more extroversive (*i.e.*, tend more than other body types to discharge their energies in

59

action). It comes as no surprise, therefore, to find that a far higher proportion of mesomorphic boys than boys of other body builds had been provided by their parents with adequate home recreational facilities. This would appear to support the prior inference that some environmental factors operate as a *response* to a pre-existing trait in a boy rather than that the trait is conditioned by any particular sociocultural influence.

As in the case of home recreation, a far higher proportion of mesomorphs than of boys of other body builds had been firmly but kindly disciplined by the mother and were closely supervised by her. Evidently youngsters of this body build (characterized as they are by greater energy, more extroversiveness, and less conventionality) invite attention from their parents; and this is reflected in firm handling and close watching, as well as in the provision of home recreational facilities.

Be this as it may, it would seem that a child's vitality as reflected in a strong hand grip is clearly not the result of the adequacy or inadequacy of recreational outlets in the home or of a mother's disciplinary or supervisory practices, but rather the reverse—that a boy's bursting energy, demanding outlets of some kind in the home, conditions in some measure the behavior of parents toward him.

Tendency to phantasy (Appendix Tables D-17 and E-17) refers to the inclination to invent something not taken from reality or a combination of elements taken from reality but spun together in a way which does not conform to reality. *Phantasy* may be productive or receptive; actually, there are many intermediate states and combinations of these two extremes. In either case, a tendency to rumination may lead merely to an arbitrary neglect of certain elements in reality or to a consistent elaboration of well perceived elements into a product of phantasy.

Adding to the constitutional impulsion of certain youngsters to escape into phantasy are certain deleterious circumstances in the home, such as rearing by an emotionally disturbed father or a seriously ill mother; growing up in a home in which family group recreations are unknown; having parents who do not welcome their child's playmates into the home; being deprived of one or both parents before the age of five. Children exposed to such circumstances and who are already inclined to phantasy life would appear to be further propelled by such social influences into an escape from reality. Certainly, in the early years, before the child finds companions in the school and on the streets (our youngsters grew up before the era of widespread television), a resort to phantasy life would appear to be almost inevitable.

Although boys of balanced physique and ectomorphs were in general found to have a greater *tendency to phantasy* (as contrasted with mesomorphs), those of balanced physique (*i.e.*, with approximately equal components of endomorphy, mesomorphy and ectomorphy in the body structure) even more than the mesomorphic boys retreated into phantasy as a result of rearing in an inimical home atmosphere (rearing by an emotionally ill father, in homes where a breach occurred in normal family ties due to the separation, divorce, desertion, or death of a parent before the boy was five years old; rearing in a home where family group recreations were uncommon; or in one which discouraged a boy from inviting his friends to the home). The difficulty which boys of balanced physique have in harmonizing the three largely contradictory major biologic tendencies that characterize this physique (mesomorphy, endomorphy, ectomorphy) makes it more likely that they, in contrast to boys of the other physiques, would seek escape into phantasy in the face of such inimical home conditions; while mesomorphs appear to be the least likely to resort to such unrealistic adjustment to the stresses of life.

Marked submissiveness (Appendix Tables D-23 and E-23) is the abandonment of self-assertion in an attempt to gain security by submitting to those who are believed stronger (originally, one or both of the parents; later, also, the more anonymous power of institutions, public opinion, conventional usage and the like). This constitutionally-oriented trait is in general found to occur most frequently among sons of emotionally disturbed fathers. Indifference or hostility of father to son also appears to contribute to the development of this characteristic in a boy.

As to specific body types, it is to be especially noted that endomorphs are more submissive to authority than either mesomorphs or ectomorphs, and that the role of an emotionally disturbed father in stimulating marked submissiveness in a son is greater in the case of endomorphs than of ectomorphs.

Destructiveness (Appendix Tables D-36 and E-36), the tendency to destroy, to hurt or to be negativistic, may be directed against others or against one's self. Usually both trends run parallel, one often being more manifest, the other more suppressed. *Destructiveness* derives essentially from a difficulty in sublimating hostile feelings. It is not to be confused with *destructive-sadistic trends*, which pertain to *goals* of drives.

Rearing by unhappy parents (*i.e.*, those who quarrel continuously) is in the present analysis found to contribute more significantly to the development of *destructiveness* than rearing by parents whose

61

hostility to one another, if it exists, is not corrosive because the father or mother abandoned the family home. One loving parent evidently provides a more wholesome atmosphere for a child than rearing by two who are overtly incompatible. Another factor that appears to add to a child's *destructiveness* is rearing by a mother whose absence from the home in gainful employment is unpredictable because of its irregularity. Still other factors contributing to the development of *destructiveness* are rearing in crowded homes or by parents who are careless or unconcerned about their children (as reflected in neglect to plan the use of the family income to cover such absolute necessities as food, rent, clothing and insurance).

With reference to the influence of such factors in stimulating the trait of *destructiveness* among the various body types, it is clear that the effect of a crowded home and an erratically employed mother on the sensitive ectomorph is greater than on boys of other body builds, especially endomorphs, in enhancing a latent tendency to destroy, to hurt, or to be negativistic.

Not only incompatible parents, but those who do not welcome their children's friends, who provide only the most meager of recreational outlets at home, and who are careless about observing even rudimentary household routines, stimulate the latent *destructiveness* of children. But there is no definitive evidence that these circumstances have a greater bearing on the essentially innate trait of *destructiveness* among youngsters of one body structure than of another.

Finally, indifference or out-and-out hostility of brothers and sisters to a boy may contribute to bringing out his latent destructive tendencies; but the possibility should not be neglected that the unfriendliness of siblings may itself be their reaction to the hurtful, negativistic brother in their midst. There is no statistically significant evidence that siblings are more indifferent or actually hostile to a destructive brother of one body build than of another.

Marked dependence on others (Appendix Tables D-39 and E-39) is defined as the tendency to cling to others rather than to stand on one's own feet.

Relating the trait of *dependence* to our series of social factors, this predisposition appears to be significantly enhanced by an early break in the family life (before the boy was five), and also results from rearing by an inadequate father; for a significantly greater proportion of markedly dependent youngsters were the sons of emotionally disturbed fathers and/or of fathers who were liabilities to their employers; and a significantly higher proportion had been subjected to corporal punishment by the father.

There is evidence, too, that laxity in discipline by the mother (as contrasted with kindly but consistently firm handling) enhances a boy's need to be dependent, to cling to anyone who appears strong and who may be a potential protector. (This is evidence of a child's need for consistent limits to be set to his behavior.)

In *Physique and Delinquency* it was noted that endomorphs have a greater predisposition to *marked dependence on others* than do youngsters of balanced type. Now it is found that none of the social factors which have a bearing on the formation of this trait acts selectively on the body types.

Masochistic trends (Appendix Tables D-43 and E-43) reflect a tendency to suffer and to be dependent on others. In relating social factors to *masochistic trends*, it is found that rearing in overcrowded homes and/or by parents lacking in ambition to improve the family circumstances, as well as deprivation of recreational and companionship outlets, all contribute significantly to the development of *masochism*. In addition, a greater percentage of youngsters brought up in homes lacking in unity (as reflected in the total absence of family group recreations) were found to be masochistic.

Lax discipline and careless supervision by a mother appear also to contribute disproportionately to a child's masochism. Something of this unwholesome maternal influence has already been reflected in its contribution to the trait of *marked dependence on others*.

Except for a lesser influence on the development of *masochistic trends* in boys of balanced physique of parents who were indifferent to their playmates, none of the other social influences contributing to the development of a masochistic tendency to suffer and to be dependent on others is found to have a greater influence on children of one body structure than on those of another.

Destructive-sadistic trends (Appendix Tables D-44 and E-44), as previously indicated, are not to be confused with *destructiveness* (which arises from an inability to sublimate feelings of hostility); for *destructive-sadistic trends* pertain to the *goals* of hostile drives. These deal with typical ways in which the individual tries to satisfy his needs—in this case, with a tendency to hurt or destroy others.

Eight out of nine factors of the home background clearly contribute to the development of such trends in the personality (and seven of these have already been found to be related to the development of *destructiveness*): unwillingness of parents to entertain a child's friends; lack of recreational facilities in the home; rearing in disorderly or in overcrowded homes; rearing by parents who are so careless in the management of the family's economic resources that essential needs were not regularly provided for; rearing in a home in which the child was exposed to a generally stormy emotional relationship between the parents (in contrast to one in which children were spared direct contact with parental discord because the parents had long since separated, the boy usually remaining with his mother); rearing by an erratically employed mother (the kind who flits from one job to another, working only sporadically and with the prime purpose of satisfying a strong need to get away from her home responsibilities) as contrasted with upbringing by a mother who was employed steadily and who in accordance with our findings in 'Working Mothers and Delinquency' [1] was generally more planful about providing for the supervision of her children and the conduct of the household in her absence; rearing in households in which the daily routines were relatively unplanned; and, finally, growing up in disorderly homes.

As regards the relationship between *destructive-sadistic trends* and the acceptability of a boy by his brothers and sisters, it is not clear whether the failure to accept him contributes to the development of such antisocial trends in a boy's personality or whether, on the contrary, his brothers and sisters did not accept him *because* he was sadistic. Perhaps, here, as in other trait-factor linkages, there is a reciprocal influence.

Like *destructiveness*, *destructive-sadistic personality trends* have been found in *Physique and Delinquency* to be more characteristic of ectomorphs than of other body types. By and large, deleterious home and family influences appear more likely to contribute to the development of *destructive-sadistic trends* among ectomorphs than among endomorphs. This is certainly true of the influence of rearing in crowded and in disorderly homes; in homes in which the income was poorly managed and the household routine careless; by mothers who were not too concerned about their household responsibilities (as reflected in flitting from job to job).

These findings are supportive of the ones in *Physique and Delinquency* (Exhibit 13, p. 240), in which it was discovered that ectomorphic boys reared in a deleterious home environment are more likely to become delinquent than are boys of other body builds reared in a similar environment.

In the next chapter, the analysis of the contribution of environmental factors to constitutional traits is continued.

---

[1] See S. and E. T. Glueck, 'Working Mothers and Delinquency,' 41, *Mental Hygiene* No. 3, July 1957.

VII

CONTRIBUTION OF ENVIRONMENTAL FACTORS TO ADDITIONAL CONSTITUTIONAL TRAITS

INTRODUCTION

WE proceed with our discussion of the traits found in *Physique and Delinquency* to be essentially constitutional in orientation but which in the present inquiry are also found to be related to two or more social factors. The question before us is whether any of these traits may now be considered as closer to the center of our postulated biosocial continuum or may still be looked upon as essentially genetic in their orientation.

FURTHER ANALYSIS OF CONSTITUTIONAL TRAITS

Sensitivity (Appendix Tables D-51 and E-51) is an acute awareness of conflicting situations and stimuli and of their implications, resulting in some inhibition of action. Relationships were established between this trait and two of the 44 social factors, an excessive proportion of sensitive children being found among those whose parents were self-respecting, as well as among boys whose mothers had emotional disturbances. These findings certainly do not suggest that such circumstances contribute to a boy's *sensitivity*; they may rather reflect the presence of '*sensitivity*' in the parents. The limited study of the genetic transmission of specific psychologic traits makes it difficult to do more than speculate on the meaning of these findings. The trait of *sensitivity*, however, belongs, in our judgment, among those in which a direct and marked contribution of factors of the social environment is not found.

It should be noted that ectomorphs and boys of balanced physique are more characterized by *sensitivity* than are boys of other body types.

Inadequacy (Appendix Tables D-53 and E-53), which is an inability to express or conduct oneself with a fair degree of efficiency, appears to be more prevalent among sons of mothers who are themselves delinquent than among sons of nondelinquent mothers; among boys reared in families lacking in ambition; and among those who were the youngest of the family group.

The feeling of *inadequacy*, which was found in *Physique and Delinquency* to be in general more characteristic of ectomorphs and boys of balanced type than of mesomorphs, is still seen, in children reared in ambitionless families, to be more clearly characteristic of ectomorphs than of mesomorphs. Similarly, the feeling of *inadequacy* is more characteristic of boys of balanced physique than of mesomorphs among boys who happened to be the youngest in the family.

Uninhibited motor responses to stimuli (Appendix Tables D-56 and E-56), which is the direct behavioral resolution of tension, is among the constitutionally-oriented traits found to be associated with two or more of the social factors included in this study.

We note that a higher proportion of youngsters who are in the middle birth rank among brothers and sisters tend to *uninhibited motor responses to stimuli* than of children of other birth rank. It may be that, being in the least 'favored' position in the family constellation (*i.e.*, not the *only*, or *oldest*, or *youngest* child), they more freely develop a latent tendency to motoric action in order to gain some of the attention usually bestowed on the oldest and the youngest child in a family.

It also appears that exposure to a breach in the normal home ties, to unpleasant home surroundings (as reflected in uncleanliness and disorderliness), and to haphazard living from day to day (shown in lack of planning for use of the family income) somehow contribute to a tendency to *uninhibited motor responses to stimuli*; for a significantly higher proportion of boys reared in such a confused environment than of other boys are found to possess this characteristic.

It has previously been established (in *Physique and Delinquency*) that the tendency to *uninhibited motor responses to stimuli* is more characteristic of mesomorphs than of boys representative of other body builds, and it is now found that the deleterious influence of an unpleasant home and that of being a middle child also play more of a role in fostering extroversion of action among mesomorphs than they do among endomorphs and ectomorphs.

Emotional instability (Appendix Tables D-57 and E-57) is reflected in a lack of harmonious, integrated and appropriate feelings and reactions. It was shown in *Physique and Delinquency* that ectomorphs as a group are more unstable emotionally than are boys of other body builds, the ectomorphic habitus, with its greater surface area in proportion to its mass and its consequently excessive sensory exposure

66

to the outside world, reacting more intensely to emotion-arousing influences than do other physique types.

In the current study it is found that this constitutionally-oriented trait is present to a significantly greater extent among firstborn children than among those in the middle position. We do not know the meaning of this. If it has any significance, it is not clear; but we do not find that a higher proportion of firstborn ectomorphic children are unstable emotionally than of those of other body builds.

The findings indicate also that affectional ties of emotionally unstable children to the father and to the mother are more tenuous and that such children less readily accept the father as a pattern for emulation. Some readers, especially those trained in Freudian psychology, may conclude that a child's *emotional instability* is the *result* of affect-starvation rather than a selective reaction engendered by the child's innate emotional make-up which contributes to his lack of attachment to his parents and his inability to accept his father as a pattern for emulation. The latter interpretation is strengthened by the finding that it is indeed the ectomorphs, as a group the least emotionally stable of all the body types, who are more generally not attached to the father and find him not acceptable, compared to emotionally unstable boys of other physiques.

As for lack of attachment to the mother, definitive statistical findings have not emerged; although, percentagewise, the same pattern is suggested by the higher incidence of emotionally unstable ectomorphs than of boys of other body builds who are unattached to the mother.

Aestheticism (Appendix Tables D-58 and E-58) is the impulse for the more refined, discriminating and artistic. A significantly greater proportion of ectomorphs than of youngsters of other body builds have this tendency. Although this trait was classified in *Physique and Delinquency* as essentially constitutional, a significant relationship has been established in the present inquiry between *aestheticism* in children and 11 of the 44 social factors encompassed here. Whether aesthetically-inclined children are the offspring of parents who are themselves 'refined,' or their being surrounded by more favorable conditions in the home largely contributes to the cultivation of refined tastes, is the question to be determined. Probably both sets of influences are reciprocally involved. The facts, as revealed within the confines of the present inquiry, are that boys of more cultivated tastes are more often found in what may be termed homes of better 'quality' despite economic marginality, *i.e.*, homes that are clean and neat, in which the financial conditions are more stable, in which there is a well planned routine, and in which the family income is carefully budgeted. So, also, a greater proportion of aesthetic children are found in homes in which the parents are self-respecting; such children are more often the sons of mothers who give them suitable supervision and of fathers who are firm and kindly (rather than erratic) in their discipline. Boys of refinement appear also to stem largely from homes in which some recreational facilities are provided or in which family group recreations are not unusual; and in which the parents are typically hospitable to their child's play-mates. There is evidence, also, that a higher proportion of youngsters with an impulse for the refined, discriminating and artistic than of other boys are warmly attached to the father.

Here, as in the case of *sensitivity*, we find relationships that do not necessarily reflect a direct contribution of environmental factors to the trait (which is constitutional in its orientation) but in which there is rather a suggestion that aesthetically-inclined parents (inferred from the way in which the parents conduct their home affairs) are more likely to have *aesthetic* children.

Examination of Appendix Table E-58 clearly indicates not only that a greater proportion of ectomorphs (than of mesomorphs or endomorphs) were shown in *Physique and Delinquency* to be aesthetic, but also that all the conditions which are now found to be related to *aestheticism* are likewise more prevalent in the home environment of the ectomorphs (than of mesomorphs or endomorphs). This finding bears out the suggestion that although some reciprocal influence may exist between *aestheticism* and sociocultural factors, it would appear more likely, in the light of the evidence, that this is an essentially inherited tendency.

Acquisitiveness (Appendix Tables D-60 and E-60) refers to the inclination to accumulate money or other material things over and above any desire for their immediate use. There is some evidence in the present findings that this constitutionally-oriented trait, which is more characteristic of ectomorphs than of endomorphs or boys of balanced type, may be linked to the response of some youngsters to environmental stresses; for there is an excessive proportion of markedly acquisitive youngsters among those reared in overcrowded homes and in homes providing meager recreational facilities, and among boys who, with the arrival of a new baby, are dethroned from their favored status of youngest child in the family.

Regarding the various somatotypes, it is found that *acquisitiveness* is more characteristic of mesomorphs and ectomorphs who were brought up in overcrowded homes or who occupied the middle rank in the family. There is, however, no reliable statistical evidence that deprivation of recreational outlets at home plays a differential role in contributing to the *acquisitiveness* of one or another of the body types, although, percentagewise, it would appear that ectomorphs and mesomorphs deprived of adequate recreational facilities are more inclined to be acquisitive than are endomorphic boys or boys of balanced type.

Conventionality (Appendix Tables D-61 and E-61) may be defined as a preference for the safe and familiar. According to the findings in *Physique and Delinquency* a significantly higher proportion of endomorphs than of other body types have this characteristic. In contradistinction to this, a lower proportion of ectomorphs and mesomorphs than of endomorphs tend to be conventional.

Looking now at the association between *unconventionality* and various sociocultural factors of the home, we find that unconventional youngsters are in excessive measure the sons of mothers and/or fathers with alcoholic habits. They are also to an excessive degree boys whom the father, mother or siblings did not love and accept; they are youngsters who were not warmly attached to the father; more of them are found in families in which the ties between members were not close and warm.

Since it was found, in *Physique and Delinquency*, that a tendency to conventional behavior has an essentially constitutional orientation, the possibility must not be overlooked that parents or brothers and sisters find it more difficult to love unconventional children, who probably keep them constantly in a state of tension by their behavior. However, this may involve reciprocal dynamisms; and although evidence was adduced in *Physique and Delinquency* that *conventionality* is essentially focused in constitution, the possibility should not be ignored that lack of attachment of parents to a son is in some measure the result of his deep-rooted inclination to unconventional attitudes or conduct.

It is of particular significance that, although in general a greater proportion of ectomorphs than of mesomorphs and endomorphs are characterized by *unconventionality*, rearing in a noncohesive family is now found to have more of an influence on the development of *unconventionality* among endomorphs than among mesomorphs or ectomorphs. But rearing by an alcoholic father or by a father who is hostile to his son contributes more to developing *unconventionality* in an ectomorph than in an endomorph. This diverse effect of a similar set of several influences on boys of different body types lends support to the conclusion that constitutional make-up, in its interaction with the most intimate mechanisms of culture (that is, those that operate in the home) can not be ignored. It would seem unnecessary to emphasize this, were it not for a tendency to ignore or greatly to minimize constitutional predisposition in the etiologic complex of delinquency.[1]

Impracticality (Appendix Tables D-64 and E-64) is the inclination not to consider the feasibility of any contemplated course. The findings arising from the current study show that an excessive proportion of boys who lack good practical sense are the sons of emotionally disturbed mothers and of mothers who do not give them some fair degree of supervision. They show also that an excessive proportion of only children are impractical. This somatically-oriented proclivity is evidently heightened in a youngster who has the psychological difficulty inherent in being an only child, one who is so often the subject of oversolicitousness on the part of the parents.

It has also emerged that a significantly excessive proportion of fathers and mothers of impractical youngsters were erratic in the discipline of their sons during the formative years. So, also, a greater proportion of impractical boys are found not to be warmly attached to their parents and not to accept the father as an ego-ideal or pattern for emulation. Such boys were also, to a greater extent than youngsters with a practical sense, reared in families lacking in self-respect, and in families devoid of a feeling of 'all for one, one for all.'

This evidence suggests that a trait so useful for realistic adaptation as *practicality*, although having some roots in the soma, is greatly influenced by familial structure and by intimate under-the-roof relationships.

Generally, *impracticality* has been found to be more characteristic of ectomorphs than of mesomorphs, and it now appears that rearing by emotionally disturbed mothers conditions the development of *impracticality* among ectomorphs as contrasted to mesomorphs.

Emotional conflicts (Appendix Tables D-65 and E-65) reflect an inability to reconcile opposite feelings or attitudes or contradictory goals, not only in respect to persons most intimately related to a youngster (mother, father, siblings, companions), but also as regards more generalized emotion-arousing objects or institutions (religion, the community) and their standards. In *Physique and Delinquency* it was learned that ectomorphic youngsters as a group are to a greater extent conflict-ridden than are mesomorphic boys or those of balanced type. Because of this difference in the incidence of the trait the conclusion was reasonable that the *tendency to emotional conflict* is probably constitutional in orientation.

[1] See S. Glueck, 'Theory and Fact in Criminology,' 7, *British Journal of Delinquency*, October 1956, pp. 92–109; and 'Ten Years of Unraveling Juvenile Delinquency,' Vol. 51, No. 3, *Criminal Law, Criminology and Police Science*, September–October 1960, pp. 283–308.

Now it is found that a greater proportion of conflict-ridden boys were reared in families lacking cohesiveness; that a significantly excessive proportion were not attached to the father and/or the mother; that significantly more of them regarded the father as unacceptable as a pattern for emulation; and/or that more boys with *emotional conflicts* were not accepted warmly by their siblings.

It would seem that only one of the relationships found between emotionally-conflicted boys and exposure to environmental stresses reflects a contribution of the stress (family incohesiveness) to the trait. All the other relationships are apparently reflective of the behavior of already conflict-ridden children toward their parents or siblings.

Referring to specific physique types, it is of interest to note that a greater proportion of ectomorphs from stressful homes were in emotional conflict as contrasted with mesomorphs and boys of balanced type. Thus, rearing in an atmosphere of family disharmony, as well as lack of attachment to parents, evidently strengthens an already latent tendency in ectomorphs and also appears to increase *emotional conflicts* in boys of balanced type.

SUMMARY

A prime objective of the present and several prior chapters has been to see how the findings of *Physique and Delinquency*, in respect to the essentially constitutional orientation of certain traits, stand up in the light of the correlation of these traits with 44 factors of family life. If, on the whole, these traits, which were previously considered essentially constitutional because of significant variations in their incidence among diverse body types, are not now found to be significantly associated with any of the social factors embraced in this study, it may reasonably be assumed that they do indeed belong at the constitutional end of the postulated biosocial continuum. On the other hand, those traits in which there is a heavy involvement of social influence must be placed somewhere toward the center of the heredity–environment continuum; for the clear relationship of both constitutional and sociocultural influences denotes the presence of both genetic roots and great plasticity, that is, an essentially strong and uniform participation of both Nature and Nurture in their development. It has also been found that certain sociocultural factors are associated with certain psychologic–physiologic traits, not as contributory to their formation but rather as *reactive* responses of persons in the boy's home environment to the existence of such traits in the organism.

It is, of course, recognized that there may be other sociocultural influences than the 44 encompassed in this study; but we believe the most important ones, because they are the earliest and most intimate as far as the conditioning of traits is concerned, are those reflecting parent–child relationships in the home during the first few years of life.

The findings brought to light in the present chapter may be thus summarized.

(*a*) There are seven traits (found in *Physique and Delinquency* to vary significantly in incidence among the body types and therefore deemed to be oriented toward the constitutional end of the biocultural continuum) which in the present analysis are *not* found to be related to any of the 44 social factors in a way that reflects a *contributory* influence of the factor to the development of the trait. On the contrary, the association between trait and factor, where it exists, seems rather to express the *reaction* of the human environment (parents, siblings) to a boy with the pre-existent trait or, at most, to indicate that the factor somewhat reinforces an essentially inherent trait.

6. Cyanosis
8. Tremors
9. Genital Underdevelopment
47. Vivacity
51. Sensitivity
58. Aestheticism
59. Sensuousness

(*b*) To these seven traits may be added the four following traits, also shown in *Physique and Delinquency* to vary in incidence among the body types and therefore to be essentially constitutional in orientation and now found to be related to only one social factor in a way to reflect a *contributory* influence of the factor on the trait.

21. Social Assertiveness
31. Fear of Failure and Defeat
57. Emotional Instability
65. Emotional Conflicts

(*c*) There are two traits shown in *Physique and Delinquency* to vary among the body types but found in the present analysis to be related to two social factors in a way which suggests a *contributory* influence of the factor to the development of the trait.

10. Strength of Hand Grip
23. Marked Submissiveness to Authority

Contribution of Factors to Additional Constitutional Traits

(*d*) Three traits previously judged to be constitutional in orientation are now found to be related to three of the 44 social factors in a way indicating that the sociocultural factors of the home played a *contributory* role in the development of the trait.

53. Feeling of Inadequacy
60. Acquisitiveness
61. Unconventionality

(*e*) The remaining seven traits which had been found in *Physique and Delinquency* to vary significantly in incidence among the four body types are far less rigid in their constitutional structure than supposed, because they are now seen to be related to *four or more* social factors in a way which suggests that these home influences contributed to the development of the trait, often however acting selectively on one or another of the body types.

17. Tendency to Phantasy
36. Destructiveness
39. Marked Dependence on Others
43. Masochistic Trends
44. Destructive-Sadistic Trends
56. Uninhibited Motor Responses to Stimuli
64. Impracticality

Before closing this chapter, it should again be pointed out that in the formation of most traits there is very probably some constitutional involvement. The aim of the analysis has been to discover the traits which are more clearly influenced by constitutional derivation than by sociocultural conditioning, *i.e.*, far more rigid than the traits noted in (*e*) above, in which there is a considerable involvement of environmental influence. A sharp and fast heredity–environment cleavage can, of course, not be made; but it seems reasonable to conclude that the traits listed in (*a*) above, in which no contributory influence of any of the 44 social factors could be found, are indeed probably referable to the constitutional zone of the biosocial continuum; and the traits in (*b*), although less clearly referable to the biologic end-zone of the biosocial progression, should probably be placed 'left of center' toward the genetic end of the continuum; while the traits in (*c*) and (*d*) should probably be more definitely placed in the socially conditioned area of the postulated biosocial continuum.

VIII

SUMMARY OF TRAIT FORMATION

INTRODUCTION

THE analysis of the derivation of the traits initially studied in *Physique and Delinquency*[1] is now completed. Since our initial postulation of a biosocial continuum appears to gain support from the current findings, it will be helpful to clarify the meaning of this concept. As already stated, not one of the traits included in this study is exclusively, of course, either of genetic or of sociocultural origin. It is obviously impossible, by the very nature of our materials, to arrive at any final judgment regarding the *specific role* of heredity in the origin of traits. It is therefore more correct to speak of the *formation* of the traits rather than of their origins, because they all originate genetically (whether from a single gene or combination of genes); but they also all reflect some environmental influence. The question is one of *probable* constitutional or sociocultural *emphasis* in the evolution of the developed trait as it was found to exist among the boys examined. If it be concluded that some traits are nearer to the constitutional than to the sociocultural border of the biosocial continuum, there is also an implication that the traits in question are more *fixed* in their innate form or tendency than are traits demonstrably influenced in their development by several sociocultural factors. The degree of this rigidity of a trait can, of course, not be determined by our method of analysis; all that can be said is that certain traits are evidently close to the *center* of a biosocial axis because they bear significant statistical relationships *both to the type of physique involved and to a considerable number of environmental factors*, while other traits are referable by such analysis to points at a greater distance from the center, either toward the constitutional or toward the sociocultural pole of the postulated continuum.

It is generally accepted, however, that whatever genetic basis may exist for physiologic or psychologic traits, there is an obscure intrauterine environmental influence at play, as well as an observable extrauterine one. In suggesting that evidence exists which makes it

[1] S. and E. T. Glueck, New York, Harper & Brothers, 1956.

74

reasonable to refer a particular trait, in relative emphasis of influence, either to the constitutional or to the sociocultural pole of a postulated biosocial gradation, we drew on findings presented in *Physique and Delinquency* that certain traits, by reason of their significant variation in incidence among the different physique types, are probably anchored largely in soma (constitution). This, as we have indicated, does of course not imply that there has been no conditioning influence of one or more social factors on the evolution of such traits. However, the statistically significant variations in the incidence of certain of the traits (23 in all) among the body types justifies the assignment of these traits, in the absence of persuasive evidence to the contrary, to the biologic area of the biosocial continuum.

It is probable that many traits are largely governed not by single genes but by combinations of genes. However, such complex traits are also the product of an interplay of genetic and sociocultural influences, and the issue as to these is, likewise, not as between one or the other influence but rather a matter of emphasis of one over the other.

We have also noted that certain traits are heavily influenced by sociocultural factors in the home; and without ignoring the participating influence of constitution, it has seemed to us legitimate to place them toward the environmental end of the biosocial continuum. Only further research, involving traits and factors similar to those included in the present study, can confirm, contradict or modify the results of our analysis. Meanwhile, there appears to be reasonable ground for ordering the traits in the present inquiry along the postulated biosocial continuum. In this connection, it should be obvious that researches such as this give promise of throwing light on a very important area of psychology, quite apart from any relevancy to the dynamics of delinquency.

TRAIT FORMATION: BY TRAIT

A summary of the findings in the prior five chapters regarding trait orientations, as determined in *Physique and Delinquency* and in the current work, can now be made. Anyone wishing to examine the trait-factor relationships should consult Appendix D, where each trait is presented by the number assigned in *Physique and Delinquency* and used throughout this work.

Constitutional Traits. The following traits appear to be closer to the constitutional than to the sociocultural pole of the biosocial continuum; for (*a*) they were found in *Physique and Delinquency* to vary in incidence among the body types and (*b*), correlatively, they have either *not* been found in the current study to be related to any social factors or shown to be related to only one and, in a very few instances, two environmental influences.

6. Cyanosis
8. Tremors
9. Genital Underdevelopment
10. Strength of Hand Grip
21. Social Assertiveness
23. Marked Submissiveness to Authority
31. Fear of Failure and Defeat
47. Vivacity
51. Sensitivity
57. Emotional Instability
58. Aestheticism
59. Sensuousness
65. Emotional Conflicts

In the light of the clearly significant variation in incidence of these traits among divergent body types, we feel justified in assigning them to the constitutional end of our posited biosocial continuum.

Probably Constitutional Traits. The following traits we consider to be of probable constitutional orientation because, although *not* shown in *Physique and Delinquency* to vary in incidence among the body types, they are, in the present analysis, either not found to be related to any of the 44 social factors or related to only one—an association which might well have occurred by chance—or the relationships are such that they can not be classified as contributing to the development of the trait.

1. Poor Health in Infancy
4. Enuresis in Early Childhood
5. Irregular Reflexes
7. Dermographia
16. Intuition
19. Unmethodical Approach to Problems
20. Potential Capacity for Objective Interests
22. Defiance
24. Ambivalence to Authority
33. Poor Surface Contact with Others
45. Emotional Lability
46. Lack of Self-Control
54. Stubbornness
55. Adventurousness
67. Psychopathy

The rationale for the inference that these traits are probably of constitutional derivation, despite the absence of any significant variation in their incidence among the body types, is that there are traits (such as eye color) which are clearly constitutional though not known to be linked to any specific body structure. We reason, further, that if the traits in question were moulded essentially by environmental influences, more than one social factor among the 44 we studied should have been found to be associated with them.

Constitutional and Socially Conditioned Traits. We come next to a group of traits which, although varying in incidence among the body types and by that test probably constitutional in derivation, have in the present study been found to be related to three or more social factors in a way suggesting that these factors have contributed to their development. This would appear to mean that such traits although probably genetic in orientation are referable to an area part way between the constitutional and the sociocultural poles of the biosocial continuum.

17. Tendency to Phantasy
36. Destructiveness
39. Marked Dependence on Others
43. Masochistic Trends
44. Destructive-Sadistic Trends
53. Feeling of Inadequacy
56. Uninhibited Motor Responses to Stimuli
60. Acquisitiveness
61. Unconventionality
64. Impracticality

Socially Conditioned Traits. We turn now to those traits *not* previously found to vary in incidence among the body types—and by such test therefore not essentially constitutional—and now found to be related to three or more social factors in a manner suggesting that the factors have indeed contributed to the formation of the trait.

11. Low Verbal Intelligence
12. High Performance Intelligence
13. Originality
15. Poor Power of Observation
18. Common Sense
25. Enhanced Feeling of Insecurity
26. Marked Feeling of Not Being Wanted or Loved
27. Feeling of Not Being Taken Care Of
28. Marked Feeling of Not Being Taken Seriously

29. Feeling of Helplessness
32. Feeling of Resentment
34. Hostility
35. Marked Suspiciousness
37. Feeling of Isolation
40. Feeling of Being Able to Manage Own Life
42. Receptive Trends
48. Compulsory Trends
49. Preponderance of Extroversive Trends
50. Preponderance of Introversive Trends
62. Lack of Self-Criticism
63. Conscientiousness
66. Neuroticism

These comprise the traits which may be regarded as the most plastic among all the 66 we have studied. *Sociocultural conditioning* has evidently had a considerable influence in their formation.

Traits Not Clearly Constitutional or Conditioned. In addition to these groups of traits is one which, although not found to vary in incidence among the body types, is now seen to be related to only two social factors in a way suggesting that the factors may have contributed to formation of the traits. It is not clear whether such traits are closer to the constitutional or to the sociocultural end of the biosocial continuum. Further research is necessary in order more clearly to disentangle the relative emphasis of Nature and Nurture in their development.

3. Extreme Restlessness in Early Childhood
14. Banality
30. Feeling of Not Being Appreciated
38. Defensive Attitude
41. Narcissistic Trends
52. Suggestibility

TRAIT FORMATION: BY TYPES OF TRAITS

As we now have before us the findings on the relative roles of heredity and environment in the formation of the 66 traits, we are in a position to make a somewhat more meaningful summary of the traits by types. The bearing of these findings on the etiology of delinquency, its prevention and its management, will emerge later.

Physical Conditions. First, as regards physical conditions (which encompass *poor health in infancy, restlessness in early childhood, enuresis in early childhood, irregular reflexes, cyanosis, dermographia,*

78

tremors, genital underdevelopment, strength of hand grip), it would appear that most of these are primarily of constitutional orientation, either because they were found in *Physique and Delinquency* to vary in incidence among the body types, or, though not found to vary among physique types, they are not now found to be related to any of the 44 social factors or to only one.

It should be pointed out, however, that although *extreme restlessness* (which does not vary in incidence among the body types) is now found to be associated with two social factors of a kind which would appear to aggravate an already pre-existent condition in a child (rearing by an emotionally disturbed mother and/or by incompatible parents), it may in its emphasis be closer to constitutional than to environmental influences. Only intensive studies of very restless children from the time of the earliest evidence of this characteristic would provide a definitive answer.

EXHIBIT VIII–1. CERTAIN PHYSICAL CONDITIONS AND THE
SOCIAL FACTORS CONTRIBUTING TO THEIR
DEVELOPMENT

1. Poor Health in Infancy (PC)
3. Extreme Restlessness in Early Childhood (?)
    K. Emotional Disturbance of Mother
    V. Parents Incompatible But Not Separated
4. Enuresis in Early Childhood (PC)
5. Irregular Reflexes (PC)
6. Cyanosis (C)
7. Dermographia (PC)
8. Tremors (C)
9. Genital Underdevelopment (C)
10. Strength of Hand Grip (C)
    V. Parents Compatible
    FF. Boy Ten Years of Age or Older at First Breach in Family Life

Legend:
    C = Constitutional.
    PC = Probably Constitutional.
    ? = Not Clearly Constitutional or Socially Conditional

Aspects of Intelligence. Concerning certain intellectual characteristics, it has been found that *verbal intelligence, performance intelligence, originality, power of observation,* and *common sense* (none of which varies in incidence among the body types) appear to be closer to the sociocultural than to the constitutional border of the biosocial axis; for three or more social factors have been found to contribute to the development of each of these traits. One trait, the *tendency to phantasy*, although varying in incidence among the body types, is to some extent influenced in its formation by certain environmental circumstances so that it clearly results from a combination of innate and environmental influences.

On the other hand, three aspects of intelligence—*intuition, unmethodical approach to problems, potential capacity for objective interests*—not found in *Physique and Delinquency* to vary in incidence among the body types, and also not now found to be related to any (or to only one) of the 44 social factors, must, for the present, be regarded as of probable constitutional orientation. *Banality*, also not found in *Physique and Delinquency* to vary in incidence among the body types and now found to be related to two social factors in a way suggesting their contribution to its development, can not be definitively classified as largely of sociocultural orientation.

EXHIBIT VIII–2. CERTAIN ASPECTS OF INTELLIGENCE AND THE SOCIAL FACTORS CONTRIBUTING TO THEIR DEVELOPMENT

11. Low Verbal Intelligence (S)
    B.   Crowded Home
    V.   Parents Incompatible But Not Separated
    JJ.   Indifference or Hostility of Siblings to Boy
12. High Performance Intelligence (S)
    C.   Clean and Orderly Home
    Q.   Well Planned Household Routine
    LL.   Lax Discipline of Boy by Mother
13. Originality (S)
    X.   Mother Occasionally Employed Outside Home
    Y.   Unsuitable Supervision of Boy by Mother
    AA. Parents Inhospitable to Boy's Companions
    BB. Meager Recreational Facilities for Boy in Home
14. Banality (?)
    P.   Poor Management of Family Income
    R.   Lack of Cultural Refinement in Home
15. Marked Power of Observation (S)
    Y.   Suitable Supervision of Boy by Mother
    AA. Parents Interested in Boy's Companions
    BB. Adequate Recreational Facilities for Boy in Home
16. Intuition (PC)
17. Tendency to Phantasy (C/S)
    J.   Emotional Disturbance of Father
    M.   Serious Physical Ailment of Mother
    Z.   Lack of Family Group Recreations
    AA. Parents Inhospitable to Boy's Companions
    FF. Boy less than Five Years of Age at First Breach in Family Life

18. Common Sense (S)
    Y.   Suitable Supervision of Boy by Mother
    BB. Adequate Recreational Facilities for Boy in Home
    DD. Middle or Youngest Child in Family
19. Unmethodical Approach to Problems (PC)
    C.   Unclean and Disorderly Home
20. Potential Capacity for Objective Interests (PC)
    BB. Adequate Recreational Facilities for Boy in Home

Legend:
   PC = Probably Constitutional.
   C/S = Constitutional and Socially Conditioned (probably close to center of biosocial continuum).
   S = Socially Conditioned.
   ? = Not Clearly Constitutional or Socially Conditional

Basic Attitudes to Authority and Society. Basic attitudes to authority and society are those which are important for the genesis and establishment of the individual's psychological situation in the community. Attitudes toward authority are of special importance since, in our culture, most individuals experience society as authority, at first through the medium of the family (the parents), later through society's agencies (school, church, and like social institutions). These attitudes concern basic ways in which the individual attempts to establish his place, his security, and his share in society and in life. These may be identified as *social assertiveness, defiance, submissiveness* and *ambivalence to authority.*

All four traits are found to be closer to the constitutional than to the sociocultural area of our postulated biosocial continuum. However, the trait of *submissiveness,* which was shown in *Physique and Delinquency* to vary in incidence among the body types and was therefore classified as essentially constitutional in orientation, is apparently stimulated by the presence in the home of an emotionally disturbed father and by one who is indifferent or hostile to his son.

EXHIBIT VIII–3. SOME BASIC ATTITUDES TO AUTHORITY AND SOCIETY AND THE SOCIAL FACTORS CONTRIBUTING TO THEIR DEVELOPMENT

21. Social Assertiveness (C)
    KK. Lax Discipline of Boy by Father
22. Defiance (PC)
    AA. Parents Indifferent to Boy's Companions
23. Marked Submissiveness to Authority (C)
    J.   Emotional Disturbance of Father
    HH. Indifference or Hostility of Father to Boy
24. Ambivalence to Authority (PC)

Legend:
  C = Constitutional.
  PC = Probably Constitutional.

Feelings of Resentment, Anxiety, Inferiority and Frustration. An analysis of the formation of eight traits reflecting attitudes or moods of resentment, anxiety, inferiority and frustration has been made: *enhanced feeling of insecurity, marked feeling of not being wanted or loved, feeling of not being taken care of, marked feeling of not being taken seriously, feeling of helplessness, feeling of not being appreciated, fear of failure and defeat, feeling of resentment.* With one clear exception—the *fear of failure and defeat*—and possibly the *feeling of not being appreciated,* all the traits in this series appear to be appreciably conditioned by certain aspects of the home environment. It is to be noted that many more such elements contribute to the *feeling of not being taken care of* and the *feeling of helplessness* than is true of the other traits in the group.

EXHIBIT VIII–4. FEELINGS OF RESENTMENT, ANXIETY, INFERIORITY AND FRUSTRATION AND THE SOCIAL FACTORS CONTRIBUTING TO THEIR DEVELOPMENT

25. Enhanced Feeling of Insecurity (S)
    G. Delinquency of Mother
    T. Lack of Family Ambition
    Y. Unsuitable Supervision of Boy by Mother
    BB. Meager Recreational Facilities for Boy in Home
    CC. Lack of Family Cohesiveness
    LL. Lax Discipline of Boy by Mother
26. Marked Feeling of Not Being Wanted or Loved (S)
    B. Crowded Home
    JJ. Indifference or Hostility of Siblings to Boy
    KK. Overstrict Discipline of Boy by Father
27. Feeling of Not Being Taken Care Of (S)
    B. Crowded Home
    O. Poor Work Habits of Father
    P. Poor Management of Family Income
    Q. Careless Household Routine
    T. Lack of Family Ambition
    U. Poor Conduct Standards of Family
    Y. Fair or Unsuitable Supervision of Boy by Mother
    Z. Lack of Family Group Recreations
    AA. Parents Indifferent or Inhospitable to Boy's Companions
    BB. Meager Recreational Facilities for Boy in Home
    HH. Indifference or Hostility of Father to Boy

    KK. Overstrict Discipline of Boy by Father
    LL. Lax/Erratic Discipline of Boy by Mother
    MM. Physical Punishment of Boy by Father
28. Marked Feeling of Not Being Taken Seriously (S)
    B.   Crowded Home
    K.   Emotional Disturbance of Mother
    X.   Mother Occasionally Employed Outside Home
    AA. Parents Indifferent or Inhospitable to Boy's Companions
    BB. Meager Recreational Facilities for Boy in Home
    LL. Overstrict/Lax Discipline of Boy by Mother
29. Feeling of Helplessness (S)
    B.   Crowded Home
    G.   Delinquency of Mother
    P.   Poor Management of Family Income
    Y.   Unsuitable Supervision of Boy by Mother
    AA. Parents Indifferent to Boy's Companions
    BB. Meager Recreational Facilities for Boy in Home
    KK. Overstrict Discipline of Boy by Father
    LL. Lax/Erratic Discipline of Boy by Mother
    MM. Physical Punishment of Boy by Father
    OO. Physical Punishment of Boy by Mother
30. Feeling of Not Being Appreciated (?)
    AA. Parents Indifferent or Inhospitable to Boy's Companions
    BB. Meager Recreational Facilities for Boy in Home
31. Fear of Failure and Defeat (C)
    LL. Lax Discipline of Boy by Mother
32. Feeling of Resentment (S)
    X.   Mother Occasionally Employed Outside Home
    II.   Indifference or Hostility of Mother to Boy
    LL. Lax Discipline of Boy by Mother

Legend:
    C = Constitutional.
    S = Socially Conditioned.
    ? = Not Clearly Constitutional or Socially Conditional.

Feelings of Hostility. These encompass six traits—*poor surface contact with others, hostility, marked suspiciousness, destructiveness, feeling of isolation,* and *defensive attitude.* Although *destructiveness* had been found in *Physique and Delinquency* to vary in incidence among the body types, it is now apparent that seven of the social factors have an impact on its development, thus moving this constitutional trait closer to the center of the biosocial continuum. By contrast, *poor surface contact with others,* although not varying in incidence among the body types, is probably of constitutional orientation since not even one relationship between the social factors and this trait has been found. As to a *defensive attitude,* we prefer to err on the side of caution and say that it is not clear whether conditioning influences or constitutional predisposition play the dominant role in its formation.

The remaining traits in this group, *hostility*, *marked suspiciousness* and *feeling of isolation*, are all found to be conditioned by various factors in the family life.

EXHIBIT VIII–5. FEELINGS OF KINDLINESS AND HOSTILITY AND THE SOCIAL FACTORS CONTRIBUTING TO THEIR DEVELOPMENT

33. Poor Surface Contact with Others (PC)
34. Hostility (S)
    H.   Alcoholism of Father
    L.   Serious Physical Ailment of Father
    U.   Poor Conduct Standards of Family
    X.   Mother Occasionally Employed Outside Home
    HH. Indifference or Hostility of Father to Boy
    II. Indifference or Hostility of Mother to Boy
    KK. Erratic Discipline of Boy by Father
    LL. Overstrict Discipline of Boy by Mother
35. Marked Suspiciousness (S)
    B.   Crowded Home
    E.   One or Both Parents Foreign Born
    T.   Lack of Family Ambition
    BB. Meager Recreational Facilities for Boy in Home
    FF. Boy less than Five Years of Age at First Breach in Family Life
36. Destructiveness (C/S)
    B.   Crowded Home
    P.   Poor Management of Family Income
    Q.   Careless Household Routine
    V.   Parents Incompatible But Not Separated
    X.   Mother Occasionally Employed Outside Home
    AA. Parents Indifferent or Inhospitable to Boy's Companions
    BB. Meager Recreational Facilities for Boy in Home
37. Feeling of Isolation (S)
    B.   Crowded Home
    X.   Mother Occasionally Employed Outside Home
    Y.   Fair Supervision of Boy by Mother
    AA. Parents Indifferent or Inhospitable to Boy's Companions
    BB. Meager Recreational Facilities for Boy in Home
    LL. Lax Discipline of Boy by Mother
38. Defensive Attitude (?)
    G.   Delinquency of Mother
    CC. Lack of Family Cohesiveness

84

Legend:
    PC = Probably Constitutional.
    C/S = Constitutional and Socially Conditioned (probably close to center of biosocial continuum).
     S = Socially Conditioned.
     ? = Not Clearly Constitutional or Socially Conditioned.

Dependence and Independence. As regards *marked dependence* (tendency to cling to others rather than stand on one's own feet), it appears that five social factors are related to its development: father's emotional disturbance, his use of physical punishment, and his poor work habits, mother's lax discipline of boy, and early break in home ties (when boy less than five). Thus, *marked dependence*, found in *Physique and Delinquency* to vary in incidence among the body types, is nevertheless seen to be considerably influenced by sociocultural factors and therefore must now be placed closer to the center of the postulated biosocial gradation.

Independence of others, reflected in the *feeling of being able to manage one's own life*, a trait *not* found in *Physique and Delinquency* to vary in incidence among the body types, is now revealed to be conditioned by four aspects of the family environment. It must, therefore, be looked upon as closer to the sociocultural than to the biologic pole of the biosocial continuum.

EXHIBIT VIII-6. FEELINGS OF DEPENDENCE AND INDEPENDENCE AND THE SOCIAL FACTORS CONTRIBUTING TO THEIR DEVELOPMENT

39. Marked Dependence on Others (C/S)
    J.   Emotional Disturbance of Father
    O.   Poor Work Habits of Father
    FF.   Boy less than Five Years of Age at First Breach in Family Life
    LL.   Lax Discipline of Boy by Mother
    MM. Physical Punishment of Boy by Father
40. Feeling of Being Able to Manage Own Life (S)
    AA.   Parents Interested in Boy's Companions
    BB.   Adequate Recreational Facilities for Boy in Home
    CC.   Marked Cohesiveness of Family
    LL.   Firm Discipline of Boy by Mother

Legend:
    C/S = Constitutional and Socially Conditioned (probably close to center of biosocial continuum).
     S = Socially Conditioned.

Goals of Strivings. As regards goals of strivings, which refer to typical ways in which the individual tries to satisfy his needs by *narcissistic, masochistic, receptive (oral),* or *destructive-sadistic trends,* two of the traits in the group (*masochistic trends* and *destructive-sadistic trends*) were found in *Physique and Delinquency* to vary in incidence among the body types. However, as they are now shown also to be influenced by a number of sociocultural factors, it would appear appropriate to place them in the central area of the postulated biosocial continuum.

As to *receptive (oral) trends,* which had *not* been found to vary in incidence among the body types, it is now evident that they tend to the sociocultural rather than to the constitutional edge of the postulated spectrum, for at least five social factors have been found to have a bearing on the development of this characteristic.

As regards *narcissistic trends,* since only two relationships between social factors and the trait have been found, a judgment as to its position in the biosocial progression has to be reserved.

EXHIBIT VIII–7. CERTAIN GOALS OF STRIVINGS AND THE SOCIAL FACTORS CONTRIBUTING TO THEIR DEVELOPMENT

41. Narcissistic Trends (?)
   Z.   Lack of Family Group Recreations
   AA. Parents Indifferent or Inhospitable to Boy's Companions
42. Receptive Trends (S)
   P.   Poor Management of Family Income
   Y.   Unsuitable Supervision of Boy by Mother
   Z.   Lack of Family Group Recreations
   AA. Parents Indifferent or Inhospitable to Boy's Companions
   BB. Meager Recreational Facilities for Boy in Home
43. Masochistic Trends (C/S)
   B.   Crowded Home
   T.   Lack of Family Ambition
   Y.   Fair Supervision of Boy by Mother
   Z.   Lack of Family Group Recreations
   AA. Parents Indifferent to Boy's Companions
   BB. Meager Recreational Facilities for Boy in Home
   LL. Lax Discipline of Boy by Mother
44. Destructive-Sadistic Trends (C/S)
   B.   Crowded Home
   C.   Unclean and Disorderly Home
   P.   Poor Management of Family Income
   Q.   Careless Household Routine
   V.   Parents Incompatible But Not Separated
   X.   Mother Occasionally Employed Outside Home
   AA. Parents Inhospitable to Boy's Companions
   BB. Meager Recreational Facilities for Boy in Home

Summary of Trait Formation

Legend:
   C/S = Constitutional and Socially Conditioned (probably closer to center of biosocial continuum).
   S = Socially Conditioned.
   ? = Not Clearly Constitutional or Socially Conditioned.

Some General Qualities of Personality. There are six traits encompassed in general qualities of personality. Of these, *emotional lability, lack of self-control* and *vivacity* have been found to be essentially constitutional in orientation; while *compulsory trends, preponderance of extroversive trends* and *preponderance of introversive trends* appear to be essentially environmental in development.

EXHIBIT VIII–8. SOME GENERAL QUALITIES OF PERSONALITY
AND THE SOCIAL FACTORS CONTRIBUTING TO THEIR DEVELOPMENT

45. Emotional Lability (PC)
46. Lack of Self-Control (PC)
47. Vivacity (C)
48. Compulsory Trends (S)
   C.   Unclean and Disorderly Home
   P.   Poor Management of Family Income
   Q.   Careless Household Routine
   S.   Lack of Family Self-Respect
   T.   Lack of Family Ambition
   Y.   Fair Supervision of Boy by Mother
   BB. Meager Recreational Facilities for Boy in Home
   LL.   Lax/Erratic Discipline of Boy by Mother
49. Preponderance of Extroversive Trends (S)
   K.   No Emotional Disturbance of Mother
   W.   Dominance of Father in Family Affairs
   HH. Affection of Father for Boy
50. Preponderance of Introversive Trends (S)
   J.   Emotional Disturbance of Father
   K.   Emotional Disturbance of Mother
   M.   Serious Physical Ailment of Mother
   AA. Parents Inhospitable to Boy's Companions
   KK. Overstrict Discipline of Boy by Father

Legend:
   C = Constitutional.
   PC = Probably Constitutional.
   S = Socially Conditioned.

Deep-Rooted Emotional Dynamics. The seven traits included here are: *sensitivity, suggestibility, inadequacy, stubbornness, adventurousness, uninhibited motor responses to stimuli,* and *emotional instability.*

It is of special import that with the exception of *suggestibility* all have been established, either in *Physique and Delinquency* or in the present inquiry, as of constitutional orientation. As regards *suggestibility*, to which only two factors are related, judgment as to its position on the biosocial continuum must be reserved. It is to be noted that *inadequacy* and *uninhibited motor responses to stimuli*, both found in *Physique and Delinquency* to be essentially constitutional in orientation, are now shown to be related to at least three social factors in a way that suggests a contribution of the factor to the development of these two characteristics. They should therefore probably be included among the more plastic traits and placed around the central area of the biosocial continuum. They certainly appear to be in rather substantial measure the product of both genetic and environmental forces.

EXHIBIT VIII–9. DEEP-ROOTED EMOTIONAL DYNAMICS AND THE
SOCIAL FACTORS CONTRIBUTING TO THEIR DEVELOPMENT

51. Sensitivity (C)
52. Suggestibility (?)
    FF.   Boy Less than Five Years of Age at First Breach in Family Life
    KK. Erratic Discipline of Boy by Father
53. Feeling of Inadequacy (C/S)
    G.   Delinquency of Mother
    T.   Lack of Family Ambition
    DD. Youngest Child in Family
54. Stubbornness (PC)
55. Adventurousness (PC)
    T.   Lack of Family Ambition
56. Uninhibited Motor Responses to Stimuli (C/S)
    C.   Unclean and Disorderly Home
    P.   Poor Management of Family Income
    DD. Middle Child in Family
    EE. Broken Home
57. Emotional Instability (C)
    DD. Firstborn Child in Family

Legend:
    C = Constitutional.
    PC = Probably Constitutional.
    C/S = Constitutional and Socially Conditioned (probably close to center of biosocial continuum).
    ? = Not Clearly Constitutional or Socially Conditioned.

Appetitive-Aesthetic Tendencies. All three traits reflective of appetitive-aesthetic tendencies—*aestheticism, sensuousness, acquisitiveness*

Summary of Trait Formation

—were found in *Physique and Delinquency* to vary among the body types. As regards the first two of these traits, not one of the 44 social factors in the present work has been shown to have contributed to their development, but three social factors are found to be involved in the formation of *acquisitiveness*. This latter trait must therefore now be placed toward the center of our biosocial continuum.

EXHIBIT VIII–10. APPETITIVE-AESTHETIC TENDENCIES AND THE
SOCIAL FACTORS CONTRIBUTING TO THEIR DEVELOPMENT

58. Aestheticism (C)
59. Sensuousness (C)
60. Acquisitiveness (C/S)
    B.   Crowded Home
    BB.   Meager Recreational Facilities for Boy in Home
    DD.   Middle Child in Family

Legend:
    C = Constitutional.
    C/S = Constitutional and Socially Conditioned (probably close to center of biosocial continuum).

Personality Orientation. Our discussion of basic personality orientation has centered upon four traits—*unconventionality, lack of self-criticism, conscientiousness, impracticality*. Two of these traits (*unconventionality* and *impracticality*) were found in *Physique and Delinquency* to vary in incidence among the body types and therefore considered to be essentially constitutional in orientation, but they must now be moved closer to the center of the postulated biosocial continuum. The other two traits (*lack of self-criticism* and *conscientiousness*) can now be classified as closer to the sociocultural than to the constitutional zone of the continuum.

EXHIBIT VIII–11. PERSONALITY TRAITS AND THE SOCIAL
FACTORS CONTRIBUTING TO THEIR DEVELOPMENT

61. Unconventionality (C/S)
    H.   Alcoholism of Father
    I.   Alcoholism of Mother
    CC. Lack of Family Cohesiveness
62. Lack of Self-Criticism (S)
    G.   Delinquency of Mother
    S.   Lack of Family Self-Respect
    QQ. Frequent Moving
63. Conscientiousness (S)
    L.   No Serious Physical Ailment of Father

P. Good Management of Family Income
T. Family Ambitious
Y. Suitable Supervision of Boy by Mother
AA. Parents Interested in Boy's Companions
BB. Adequate Recreational Facilities for Boy in Home
LL. Firm Discipline of Boy by Mother
64. Impracticality (C/S)
K. Emotional Disturbance of Mother
S. Lack of Family Self-Respect
Y. Unsuitable Supervision of Boy by Mother
CC. Lack of Family Cohesiveness
DD. Only Child in Family

Legend:
C/S = Constitutional and Socially Conditioned (probably close to center of biosocial continuum).
S = Socially Conditioned.

Some Aspects of Mental Pathology. Finally, we treat three aspects of mental pathology—*emotional conflicts*, *neuroticism* and *psychopathy*. On the basis of findings in *Physique and Delinquency* and in the present inquiry, *emotional conflicts* and *psychopathy* are found to be of constitutional and probable constitutional orientation, respectively. As regards *neuroticism*, since four social factors were shown to have contributed to its development, it must be considered as closer to the conditioned than to the genetic pole of the biosocial continuum.

EXHIBIT VIII–12. SOME ASPECTS OF MENTAL PATHOLOGY AND
THE SOCIAL FACTORS CONTRIBUTING TO THEIR DEVELOPMENT

65. Emotional Conflicts (C)
CC. Lack of Family Cohesiveness
66. Neuroticism (S)
G. Delinquency of Mother
X. Mother Occasionally Employed Outside Home
CC. Lack of Family Cohesiveness
LL. Overstrict/Lax Discipline of Boy by Mother
67. Psychopathy (PC)

Legend:
C = Constitutional.
PC = Probably Constitutional.
S = Socially Conditioned.

COMMENTS

Among the foregoing analyses of factor-trait relationships are a few that may raise questions in the minds of readers, since the results appear to run counter to expectation. But in calling attention to puzzling findings, we must not overlook the fact that *most of the traits emerge in accordance with expectancy and clinical experience.*

It should also be remembered that, as is true of all research, this study deals with *samples* of factors and of traits and not of all possible ones. While many of the traits are of high importance to behavior and misbehavior, and the sociocultural factors have great significance both in predictive power and causal involvement, neither the catalogue of traits nor the list of factors is, of course, complete. Certain more subtle traits of physiologic-endocrinologic essence and certain psychologic indices of importance to the motivation of conduct are not included in this study; and, likewise, certain familial and extrafamilial sociocultural forces which play an important role in the conditioning of behavior are not encompassed in this inquiry.

We recognize that such unavoidable facts make it hard to arrive at definitive conclusions. But we have assumed that the greater the number of associations of factors with a trait, the more probably is the developed trait attributable to environmental impacts following birth than to innate constitutional (genetic) influences. However, by the very nature of our materials and the inherent complexity of genetic study, it can not be concluded with certainty that even *many* correlations between various sociocultural factors and a particular trait rule out completely the possibility of some hereditary predisposition. *Per contra*, as to traits inferred by the analysis in *Physique and Delinquency* to be oriented essentially toward the constitutional edge of the biosocial continuum (because of significant variations in their incidence among widely differing physique types), and now not found to be related to any (or at most to be associated with only one or two) sociocultural factors, we have found confirmation of the original conclusion in *Physique and Delinquency* that such traits are essentially genetic and therefore less plastic than others.

As regards traits in the formation of which our analyses in *Physique and Delinquency* did *not* disclose evidence of constitutional involvement, and with which more than two sociocultural associations have emerged in the present inquiry, we conclude that such traits are probably quite plastic and environmentally oriented.

Finally, as to traits in which there is evidence of biologic orientation but also of relationship to several sociocultural factors, we have concluded that they fall near the center of the hypothetical biosocial continuum; or, to put it differently, that Nature and Nurture have contributed about equally to their formation.

These are, perforce, crude quantitative distinctions. We recognize that there is also a qualitative difference in the influence of various sociocultural factors. It may well be, for example, that a factor such as *affection of mother for boy* is so powerful and permeative in its influence that the impact of this single environmental circumstance is equivalent to, or even surpasses, the influence of several other factors. But we know of no way to measure this with any exactness, and we are therefore forced to the not unreasonable assumption that, ordinarily and generally, a valid distinction can be made that is based on the *number* of environmental factors found to influence a trait.

In all this, the fact that we are dealing with samples and that there may be other influences involved must be borne in mind; but this does not necessarily militate against the type of analysis—partial though it may be—made in the foregoing pages, nor against the significant findings that have emerged. At the very least, these findings are clues suggestive of rewarding hypotheses which can be tested on other samples of cases by other investigators.

The reader may feel baffled, as we have sometimes been, by our inability to reach firm conclusions regarding the *primacy* of a trait or of a sociocultural influence with which that trait is found to be statistically associated, as well as about the possibility that factor and trait are tied together in a reciprocal dynamic circle. It seems to us that careful, intensive clinical study might throw further light on these factor-trait involvements. We have done the best we can, both in determining temporal sequences when building up the case histories on which our researches are based, and in putting forward the device of employing statistical variation in incidence among widely differing somatotypes as a basis for a rational inference about the essentially constitutional orientation of some of the traits analyzed. However, as already pointed out, while the presence of such variation permits of a reasonable inference of essentially genetic involvement in the formation of a trait, its absence does not necessarily permit a firm conclusion that the trait is essentially grounded in environmental conditioning; for, as in the case of eye color, for example, there are undoubtedly genetic traits which are not linked to somatotype.

The reader will recall another difficulty encountered in this type of pioneering analysis of the orientation of physiologic and psychologic traits; namely, the determination as to whether a sociocultural factor is a *reactive* phenomenon in response to the pre-existence of a given trait or is itself a strong contributing influence in the formation of the trait.

In interpreting the data, we have resorted to experience, reason and judgment. As indicated at various points in the discussion, there may well be differences of opinion as to whether a trait is fundamentally genetic or essentially environmental. We welcome efforts by other investigators, with richer and more varied experience, to add to the clarification of the generating forces of these traits.

Finally, there is another important point to which we have already made brief reference: in order to analyze the data intensively, we have perforce had to relate each one of the 66 traits to each one of the 44 factors. We are fully aware that by such fragmentation something vital in the total organized pattern may be lost; but we are also aware that correlations and analyses of broad and poorly defined 'patterns' or 'groups' or 'subcultures' entail perhaps a greater risk. It is relatively simple to speak in broad generalizations about patterns and cultures; but such discussions hardly meet the basic scientific test of at least reasonable precision of concept and fact. This does not, of course, mean that we do not recognize the value of efforts to find common denominators and a patterning or *Gestalt* in the multiple single traits and factors embraced in a study such as this. But patterning must begin with the building stones, inductively arrived at, and only then proceed to a structure of interrelated elements.

In a study now in contemplation, we will lend ourselves to the task of integrating individual traits into inductively arrived-at patterns.

PART II

Family Environment, Traits
and Delinquency

IX

SOCIAL FACTORS, TRAITS AND DELINQUENCY

INTRODUCTION

SOME readers are perhaps wondering what may be the bearing on a study of *Family Environment and Delinquency* of the findings in the prior chapters which deal with analyses of the origins of 66 traits. It should be recalled that most of these traits were previously found (in *Unraveling Juvenile Delinquency*) to be significantly more characteristic of delinquents than of nondelinquents; and thereby they may be regarded as involved, at least indirectly, in criminogenesis. But a few of the traits analyzed in the foregoing chapters have *not* been found, in themselves, to be criminogenic. What is their meaning for delinquency? It will soon become evident that certain social factors assume a sort of catalytic significance in rendering such normally neutral traits criminogenic. It might be mentioned, at this point, by way of illustration, that the following traits, although not found in *Unraveling Juvenile Delinquency* to occur more frequently among delinquents than among nondelinquents, when existing in boys reared under specific inimical environmental circumstances, appear to be given criminogenic potency: *introversive trends, intuition, performance ability, feeling of not being taken care of*. They will be considered in their proper place in the ensuing chapters.

The important influence of family environmental factors in conditioning traits has already become evident. Even certain characteristics which may be legitimately regarded as essentially hereditary are moulded and enhanced in the human workshop and emotional arena of the home. Apart from *poor health in infancy*, which is essentially biologic in origin, even such traits as *extreme restlessness in early childhood* are seriously affected by environmental pressures involving family life, such as parental incompatibility or emotional illness of the mother—to review but a few. The environmental involvement is not always clear, and here and there we have suggested a circular or reciprocal influence of Nature and Nurture; but the dominant role of the home environment in the shaping of character

97

and personality cannot be gainsaid. The influence is apparent even in such traits as *verbal* and *performance intelligence* (often assumed to be purely genetic) in which such factors as parental incompatibility, lack of sympathy of siblings, crowding of home, cleanliness and orderliness of the household, and permissiveness in discipline are involved.

The influence of home and family are implicated even in such traits as *originality*, which tends to be conditioned by inadequate maternal oversight of the boy and lack of parental concern to welcome his playmates into the home. The under-the-roof environment is also operative in the development of such traits as *banality*, *marked power of observation* and *common sense*, in which there are conditioning linkages with such factors as rearing in a home without cultural refinement, or one with other signs of mediocrity of family life, improper disciplinary practices, inadequate provision for the child's leisure time—to note but a few.

So, also, such more complex psychologic traits as *feelings of resentment*, *anxiety*, *inferiority*, *frustration*—all tending to weaken and cripple personality and character—are related to early conditioning in the home. Lack of parental interest in the child, lax or erratic discipline, improper supervision, lack of family ambition, parental laziness or dishonesty leading to the child's rejection of the father as a symbol for emulation, lack of parental love for the child and many other unwholesome influences—all well known, yet too frequently unrecognized—must be taken into account in the assessment of the generative or formative influences on traits that can become anti-social in expression.

Thus, despite the genetic roots of many characteristics, a potent involvement of early childhood influences in the home is also operative in the development and moulding of traits of personality and character of a crippling kind which add to the child's incompetence to meet the demands of life that are made on him in the ever-widening world outside the borders of 'home.'

DELINQUENCY-RELATED TRAITS

But let us now consider the traits which have been previously shown to have a linkage with delinquency.

If we know what aspects of a child's rearing contribute to the formation of traits which are in general more significantly characteristic of delinquents than of nondelinquents, there arises some hope that specific targets in family life can be found and dealt with preventively both on an individual basis and in a broad prophylactic 'public health' program. In this connection it is important for those in the therapeutic professions to take note of the findings thus far made in this inquiry that certain delinquency-linked traits are less plastic than others; that they are probably attributable essentially to innate constitution and not as malleable or subject to specific environmental reconditioning or re-education as the less deep-rooted and less fixed traits. The rigid traits can be dealt with only by diversion into constructive, or at least harmless, channels.

The traits which are less likely to be responsive to social management through broad but specifically-targeted preventive efforts are those appearing in Chapter VIII under the headings, *Constitutional* and *Probably Constitutional*. Traits which are closer to the constitutional end of our postulated biosocial continuum than to the socio-cultural should be recognized as relatively 'fixed.' On the other hand, those which are largely socially conditioned are more likely to respond to efforts at constructive manipulation of that portion of the child's environment which contributes to the formation of the traits (these are listed in Chapter VIII under the title, *Socially Conditioned*); while those which because of relatively equal genetic and environmental influence are therefore placed somewhere toward the center of the biosocial continuum (see Chapter VIII) offer the greatest challenge to the therapeutic professions.

DELINQUENCY-RELATED SOCIAL FACTORS CONTRIBUTING TO FORMATION OF DELINQUENCY-RELATED TRAITS

As an introduction to considering how family environment operates on delinquency, we are now in a position to take the first step, which is to focus attention factor by factor on those delinquency-linked traits with which each delinquency-related social factor has been found to be associated in a way to suggest a contribution of the factor to the development of the trait.

In Exhibit IX–1 presentation is made of these factors and the traits to the formation of which the factor appears to have contributed.

EXHIBIT IX–1. SELECTIVE IMPACT OF DELINQUENCY-RELATED SOCIAL FACTORS ON DELINQUENCY-RELATED TRAITS

B.   Crowded Home
    11. Low Verbal Intelligence
    35. Marked Suspiciousness
    36. Destructiveness (*Meso./Ecto.* vs. Endo.)
    37. Feeling of Isolation
    44. Destructive-Sadistic Trends (*Meso./Ecto.* vs. Endo.)
    60. Acquisitiveness (*Meso./Ecto.* vs. Endo./Bal.)

C. Unclean and Disorderly Home
    19. Unmethodical Approach to Problems
    44. Destructive-Sadistic Trends (*Ecto.* vs. *Endo.*)
    56. Uninhibited Motor Responses to Stimuli (*Meso.* vs. Endo./Ecto.
F. Delinquency of Father
G. Delinquency of Mother
    38. Defensive Attitude
    53. Feeling of Inadequacy
    62. Lack of Self-Criticism
H. Alcoholism of Father
    34. Hostility
    61. Unconventionality (*Meso./Ecto.* vs. *Endo.*)
I. Alcoholism of Mother
    61. Unconventionality
J. Emotional Disturbance of Father
    17. Tendency to Phantasy (*Endo./Ecto./Bal.* vs. *Meso.*)
K. Emotional Disturbance of Mother
    3. Extreme Restlessness in Early Childhood
    64. Impracticality (*Ecto.* vs. *Meso.*)
L. Serious Physical Ailment of Father
    34. Hostility
    63. Lack of Conscientiousness
M. Serious Physical Ailment of Mother
    17. Tendency to Phantasy
N. Financial Dependence of Family
O. Poor Work Habits of Father
P. Poor Management of Family Income
    36. Destructiveness
    42. Receptive Trends
    44. Destructive-Sadistic Trends (*Ecto./Bal.* vs. *Endo.*)
    56. Uninhibited Motor Responses to Stimuli (*Meso.* vs. Endo./Ecto.)
    63. Lack of Conscientiousness
Q. Careless Household Routine
    36. Destructiveness
    44. Destructive-Sadistic Trends (*Ecto.* vs. *Endo.*)
R. Lack of Cultural Refinement in Home
S. Lack of Family Self-Respect
    62. Lack of Self-Criticism
    64. Impracticality (*Endo.* vs. *Meso.*)
T. Lack of Family Ambition
    35. Marked Suspiciousness
    53. Feeling of Inadequacy (*Ecto.* vs. *Meso.*)
    55. Adventurousness
    63. Lack of Conscientiousness
U. Poor Conduct Standards of Family
    34. Hostility

100

V.   Incompatibility of Parents
      3. Extreme Restlessness in Early Childhood
      11. Low Verbal Intelligence
      36. Destructiveness
      44. Destructive-Sadistic Trends
X.   Erratic Employment of Mother
      32. Feeling of Resentment
      34. Hostility
      36. Destructiveness (*Ecto.* vs. Endo.)
      37. Feeling of Isolation
      44. Destructive-Sadistic Trends (*Ecto.* vs. Endo.)
Y.   Unsuitable Supervision of Boy by Mother
      15. Poor Power of Observation
      18. Lack of Common Sense
      37. Feeling of Isolation
      42. Receptive Trends
      63. Lack of Conscientiousness
      64. Impracticality
Z.   Lack of Family Group Recreations
      17. Tendency to Phantasy (*Ecto./Bal.* vs. Meso.)
      41. Narcissistic Trends
      42. Receptive Trends
AA. Parents Indifferent or Inhospitable to Boy's Companions
      15. Poor Power of Observation
      17. Tendency to Phantasy (*Bal.* vs. Meso./Ecto.)
      22. Defiance
      30. Feeling of Not Being Appreciated
      36. Destructiveness
      37. Feeling of Isolation
      41. Narcissistic Trends
      42. Receptive Trends
      44. Destructive-Sadistic Trends
      63. Lack of Conscientiousness
BB.   Meager Recreational Facilities for Boy in Home
      15. Poor Power of Observation
      18. Lack of Common Sense
      20. Absence of Potential Capacity for Objective Interests
      30. Feeling of Not Being Appreciated
      35. Marked Suspiciousness
      36. Destructiveness
      37. Feeling of Isolation
      42. Receptive Trends
      44. Destructive-Sadistic Trends
      60. Acquisitiveness
      63. Lack of Conscientiousness
CC. Lack of Family Cohesiveness
      38. Defensive Attitude

61. Unconventionality (*Endo.* vs. **Meso./Ecto.**)
64. Impracticality
65. Emotional Conflicts (*Ecto./Bal.* vs. **Meso.**; *Ecto.* vs. **Endo.**)
DD. Middle Child in Family
    56. Uninhibited Motor Responses to Stimuli (*Meso.* vs. **Endo./Ecto.**)
    60. Acquisitiveness (*Meso./Ecto.* vs. **Bal.**)
EE. Rearing in Broken Home
    56. Uninhibited Motor Responses to Stimuli (*Meso.* vs. **Endo./Ecto.**)
FF. Boy less than Five Years of Age at First Breach in Family Life
    17. Tendency to Phantasy (*Bal.* vs. **Meso.**)
    35. Marked Suspiciousness
    52. Suggestibility
GG. Rearing by Parent Substitutes
HH. Indifference or Hostility of Father to Boy
    34. Hostility
II. Indifference or Hostility of Mother to Boy
    32. Feeling of Resentment
    34. Hostility
JJ. Indifference or Hostility of Siblings to Boy
    11. Low Verbal Intelligence
KK. Unsuitable Discipline of Boy by Father
    21. Social Assertiveness
    34. Hostility
    52. Suggestibility
LL. Unsuitable Discipline of Boy by Mother
    32. Feeling of Resentment
    34. Hostility
    37. Feeling of Isolation
    63. Lack of Conscientiousness
MM. Physical Punishment of Boy by Father
OO. Physical Punishment of Boy by Mother
PP. Threatening or Scolding of Boy by Mother
QQ. Frequent Moving
    62. Lack of Self-Criticism
RR. Indifference or Hostility of Boy to Father
SS. Unacceptability of Father to Boy for Emulation
TT. Indifference or Hostility of Boy to Mother

Note: The body type(s) on which the social factor is found to have the greatest impact is indicated in italics.

The criminogenic relationship of the social factors to these delinquency-linked traits derives from their role in stimulating or moulding such traits which have been shown, in *Unraveling Juvenile Delinquency*, significantly to differentiate delinquents from nondelinquents

However, it is to be noted that of the 41 delinquency-related factors, 11 (delinquency of father, financial dependence of family, poor work habits of father, lack of cultural refinement in the home, rearing by substitute parents, physical punishment of boy by father and/or mother, threatening or scolding of boy by mother, hostility of boy to father and/or mother, unacceptability of father for emulation) have *not* been clearly found in this research to contribute to the formation of any one of the 54 delinquency-related traits. Until further evidence comes from other researches we must tentatively assume that whatever bearing these factors in a child's home environment may have on the genesis of his acting out antisocial behavior, it is not through their contribution to the formation of traits that have been found in *Unraveling* to be related to delinquency. Since, however, these 11 factors of home life have *themselves* been found, in *Unraveling*, to distinguish delinquents from nondelinquents, our question now is (among others) whether these factors have a direct bearing on delinquency or operate only on boys already possessing certain characteristics.

Apart from this question, there is also the question whether the delinquency-linked factors influence antisocial behavior only indirectly, through their effect on the formation of delinquency-related traits, or whether they, in addition, *function in connection with certain traits* (regardless of whether these traits are themselves delinquency-linked or not), thereby adding to a child's delinquency impulsion. Finally, we hope to ascertain whether these combined influences of social factors and physiologic-psychologic traits act with relatively equal potency on boys of the various body types.

The reader is asked to bear in mind that there is a difference between the analysis of social factors associated with the development of traits (Chapters III–VIII) and the examination of the *criminogenic pattern of factors and traits* which is the subject of Chapters X–XIII.

METHOD OF ANALYSIS OF FAMILY INFLUENCES AND TRAITS OF BOY ON DELINQUENCY

In Appendix F is presented, trait by trait, the percentage incidence of each trait among delinquents from worse as opposed to better sociocultural backgrounds (for example, *crowded* versus *uncrowded* homes, *broken* versus *unbroken* homes) as well as the *differences* in the percentage incidence of each trait among delinquents and nondelinquents from worse as opposed to better sociocultural backgrounds.

Examination and analysis of Exhibit IX–2 will serve to illustrate the method of analysis in the ensuing chapters concerning the meaning of the above-mentioned differences. This exhibit deals with the differences in *emotional lability* among delinquents and non-delinquents from crowded as opposed to uncrowded homes; those reared in broken versus unbroken homes; those brought up by emotionally disturbed mothers as opposed to those reared by emotionally normal mothers; those whose mothers were employed sporadically outside the home versus those whose mothers were full-time housewives; boys who were deprived of paternal affection versus those who were loved by the father.[1]

EXHIBIT IX–2. EMOTIONAL LABILITY

Factors and Subcategories	Delinquents		Differences between Emotionally Labile Delinquents and Nondelinquents in Each Subcategory	
	Percentages of the Respective Subcategory Totals	Significance of Variations between Subcategories	Percentages of the Respective Subcategory Totals	Significance of Variations between Subcategories
B. *Crowding of Home*				
More than Two Occupants per Bedroom	49·3%	⎱·10	33·4%	⎱·10
One or Two Occupants per Bedroom	40·7		21·2	
K. *Emotional Disturbance of Mother*				
Present	53·1%	⎱·02	33·6%	⎱·05
Absent	37·1		18·7	
X. *Usual Occupation of Mother*				
Occasionally Employed Outside Home	51·7%	⎱·10	36·3%	⎱·10
Regularly Employed Outside Home	42·5		23·7	
Housewife	39·7		20·4	
EE. *Rearing in Broken Home*				
Yes	47·6%	⎱·05	32·1%	⎱·05
No	37·2		17·1	
HH. *Affection of Father for Boy*				
Indifferent or Hostile	49·0%	⎱·05	30·9%	⎱·05
Warm	34·8		15·5	

[1] Only those findings emerging from the correlations between the trait (*emotional lability*) and each one of the 44 sociocultural factors encompassed in this inquiry are presented in which a probability of 0·10 or better was found between delinquents and

If there is a greater significant variation (as tested by the method of multiple comparisons) in the *differences* between delinquents and nondelinquents possessing a certain trait *and* reared in an inimical environment, it can be concluded that the influence of the social factor on the delinquency impulsion of the boys was enhanced by their possession of the particular trait.

In the light of such findings, we reason throughout Chapters X–XIII that *a social factor acts selectively on the delinquency of boys possessing certain traits.* To put the matter differently, where there is more of a variation in the incidence of a trait as between delinquents and nondelinquents from an inimical environment than between delinquents and nondelinquents from a more favorable environment, it can be concluded that it is not the social factor alone, or the trait alone, which contributes to the operative distinction between delinquents and nondelinquents, but rather the *combined impact of factor and trait.*

Readers who wish to check our analyses of the data, point by point, should refer to the tables in Appendix F. Although we believe the statistical basis for our conclusions is sound, some readers may disagree with our interpretations in certain instances. Further research of a similar nature on other samples, aided by intensive clinical observations, can help to decide the issue where such differences of interpretation occur.

If progress is to be made in the prevention of delinquency and if the targets of prophylactic effort are to be more clearly defined, it is essential to discover these particularistic associations as a basis for later integration.

In the following four chapters, we proceed, factor by factor, with the analysis of the role of family environment and traits on delinquency, to see if we can delve more searchingly than has been possible in our prior researches into how a child's rearing affects his proneness to delinquency. This pattern of development of our research and thinking seems to us to be a reasonable way of orderly progression from general eclecticism to disciplined eclecticism.

nondelinquents from more, as opposed to less, inimical environmental backgrounds. The reader interested in reviewing the technical details of the method of multiple comparisons which we utilized in *Physique and Delinquency* and in the present research is referred to that work, Appendix A, 'Note on Statistical Method,' prepared by Professor Jane Worcester of the Harvard School of Public Health, and to page 17 of the present work.

X

PATHOLOGY OF PARENTS, TRAITS AND DELINQUENCY

INTRODUCTION

THE consideration of the *impact on delinquency of a child's family environment in association with certain traits he possesses* is divided into four segments: first, factors reflecting pathology in the parents, which is the subject of the present chapter; then, some aspects of the home atmosphere, in Chapter XI; family relationships, in Chapter XII; and, finally, evidences of parental unconcern for the boys, in Chapter XIII.

It is unfortunate that we could not have incorporated into our inquiry many more aspects of the family environment and also many more traits. But our task is already Herculean and we must make the first approach to it segmentally in the hope that such factors (44) and traits (66) as we could incorporate at least serve as indices of many other factors and traits. Even if our roster of factors and traits is partial, the findings are bound to shed at least *some* light on the dark places of crime causation. Despite the apparent limits of our data, they are nevertheless far more intensive and extensive than any as yet furnished by any researches into the causes of juvenile crime.

In the present chapter we are concerned with the impact on the delinquency of children of rearing by parents who are or have been delinquents; who are alcoholic; who are emotionally disturbed. We are concerned also with the contribution to the delinquency of children of rearing by parents who have physical ailments of so serious a nature as to interfere with their daily functioning; by parents who are inadequate in meeting the demands of life as judged by their poor employment history.

We shall consider first the effect of this kind of pathology in a father on the delinquency of his children; and then its effect when occurring in the mother.

106

PATHOLOGY OF FATHER

Delinquency of Father (Appendix Tables F-30, F-33, F-42). Turning now to the role of a father's delinquency on that of his son, we already know that paternal criminality does not contribute to the development of any of the delinquency-related traits encompassed in this research. But delinquents are to a greater extent than nondelinquents the sons of delinquent fathers, and this means that rearing by a father who is or has been a criminal does indeed have some bearing on the delinquency of his son. How? We gain some insight from an analysis of the traits which show significant variations in the differences between delinquents and nondelinquents whose fathers were delinquent as opposed to those whose fathers were not criminal.

From this analysis it appears that boys who have a *feeling of not being appreciated*, who *lack good surface contact with others*, or who have *receptive trends* in their personality structure (all traits previously found to be more characteristic of delinquents than of non-delinquents) are even more likely to develop into delinquents if reared by a father who is himself a criminal than if brought up by a noncriminal father.

Such findings may partially explain why *all* sons of criminalistic fathers do not become delinquent merely by 'differential association' with criminalistic fathers (and, we are tempted to reason, with delinquent peers).

Alcoholism of Father (Appendix Tables F-30, F-37, F-50). Unlike the role of delinquency of the father, which has not been found to contribute to the development of any delinquency-related traits, rearing by an alcoholic father has been shown to contribute to the development of the traits of *hostility* and *unconventionality*. In this indirect way, alcoholism of the father is involved in the delinquency of a son.

However, this gives us only part of the answer: obviously, not all children of chronic drinkers become delinquents. Rearing by an alcoholic father is but one of many environmental pressures on a child that propel him into an antisocial reaction to life. In the present inquiry it becomes clear that certain traits, if present in sons of alcoholic fathers, add to their delinquency potential—the *feeling of not being appreciated*, the *feeling of isolation*. In addition, one trait which is, however, no more characteristic of delinquents than of non-delinquents—*introversiveness*—also adds to the delinquency potential of sons of alcoholic fathers. These findings, limited as they are, already suggest that individual social factors, as deleterious as they may be, may not directly impel children to delinquency; they may

107

operate, rather, through the intermediary of certain traits to the formation of which they contribute and/or through the pre-existent presence in children of certain traits which may result in an antisocial reaction to the pressures of daily life. In other words, the factor (in this instance, a father's alcoholism) acts selectively on children having certain characteristics. Of course, this is only part of the story. There are obviously other social pressures and other traits in children which are cumulatively impelling to delinquency. What they are, how they work in combination, we hope to ascertain in our next volume. Clearly, before we can define patterns of interrelated factors and bio-social traits we must first isolate the individual strands that enter into the criminogenic patterns or complexes. We do not see how this can be avoided in any truly fundamental analysis of a complex organic whole.

Emotional Disturbance of a Father (Appendix Table F-53). We continue our factor–trait analysis by considering the impact on children of rearing by an emotionally disturbed father, which has been found in the present study to contribute to a youngster's *tendency to phantasy*. Since this tendency occurs more frequently among delinquents than nondelinquents, a father's emotional disturbance contributes to his son's delinquency potential in this indirect fashion. How his emotional aberration plays a more direct role in the delinquency of his children is suggested by our present finding that if a child has a *feeling of inadequacy* he is more likely to become delinquent than is a youngster with the same trait who is the son of an emotionally healthy father.

Serious Physical Ailment of Father (Appendix Table F-59). As regards the role of a father's severe illness in the delinquency of his children, it should first be reiterated that this has been found to contribute to the development of *hostility* in some children as well as to a *lack of conscientiousness* in others. A father who is handicapped by illness cannot always fulfill his proper role of guidance and example to a child; and this fact may account for the development of these antisocial traits in a son. In addition, it must be remembered that *hostility* and a *lack of conscientiousness* are in themselves delinquency-related traits; so it can be said that in this *indirect* way rearing by a physically ill father may contribute to the delinquency of his children.

As regards the more direct bearing of serious physical ailments of a father on the delinquency of his son, our findings reveal only one relationship of significance to delinquency, namely, through the trait of *sensuousness* (inclination to the free indulgence of appetites). Although a father's physical illness does not contribute to the development of *sensuousness* (a constitutional trait), we now find that, when

108

occurring in a boy who is the son of a seriously ill father, *sensuousness* is more likely to impel to delinquency than when it occurs in a youngster whose father is not seriously ill. This may reflect decreased opportunity by the father to discipline and control a sensuous boy; but since the significance of the relationship between a father's illness and his son's enhanced tendency to delinquency is not clear, perhaps the relationship is accidental.

Poor Work Habits of Father. Although more fathers of delinquents than of the control group were seen (in *Unraveling Juvenile Delinquency*) to have poor work habits, this factor has not been found in our current study to contribute to the development of any delinquency-related traits. Nor have any traits been found which enhance the delinquency potential of sons of industrially inadequate fathers.

PATHOLOGY OF MOTHER

It will soon become evident to the reader that pathology in the mother plays perhaps an even greater role in the delinquency of youngsters than does the father's pathology. A mother is generally closer, both emotionally and physically, to young children. It is generally considered by clinicians that the greatest psychologic damage done to children by the inimical aspects of their immediate home environment occurs during the first few years of life, and it is therefore to be expected that the mother's influence during these early years has a greater impact on children than that of the father.

Delinquency of Mother (Appendix Tables F-17, F-42). As is true of the impact of a father's criminalism on the delinquency of a boy, so of the criminalism of the mother: for, in *Unraveling Juvenile Delinquency*, a far higher proportion of the mothers of the delinquents than of the nondelinquents had a history of antisocial conduct. It now appears that the indirect influence on a child's delinquency of rearing by a criminalistic mother is partly independent of a boy's character and personality, for we have found that the only delinquency-related character traits to the formation of which the antisociality of the mother contributes are a *defensive attitude*, a *feeling of inadequacy*, a *lack of self-criticism*.

But the current inquiry into the characteristics of the sons of criminalistic mothers reveals that youngsters having a *tendency to phantasy* or having *receptive trends* are more likely to develop antisocially than are children whose mothers are not delinquent.

The implications of these findings are not clear to us. However, some readers may venture interpretations. To us it would seem that, at best, these findings can be regarded only as highly suggestive.

Alcoholism of Mother (Appendix Table F-16). Excessive indulgence in alcohol was in general found to be more prevalent among the mothers of the delinquents than of the nondelinquents. In the present inquiry, it has appeared that a mother's excessive drinking contributes to the development of only one of the delinquency-related traits encompassed in this research—*unconventionality*. In addition, we now find, however, that youngsters who are *intuitive* are more likely to be impelled toward delinquency if their mothers are alcoholics than if their mothers are not excessively addicted to alcohol. *Intuition* does not always lead to constructive results; if it is combined with a lack of mental control or with flightiness, it may lead to an entirely distorted mental picture of a situation and to quite an inadequate solution of a problem. It is to be noted that, of itself, *intuitiveness* was, however, not found in *Unraveling Juvenile Delinquency* to be more characteristic of delinquents than of nondelinquents.

Emotional Disturbance of Mother (Appendix Tables F-28, F-40, F-45, F-47, F-49). A higher proportion of delinquents than of non-delinquents were found in *Unraveling Juvenile Delinquency* to have been reared by emotionally disturbed mothers. In the current study, it appears that a mother's affective disturbance contributes to the formation of only two delinquency-related traits: *extreme restlessness* and *impracticality*. To the extent that these traits play a role in delinquency, a mother's emotional disturbance may thus be indirectly charged with the delinquency of her child.

However, we now find that the presence of certain traits in the sons of emotionally disturbed mothers has a significantly greater bearing on their delinquency than is true of youngsters reared by mothers who are not emotionally ill. This is the case in regard to *emotional lability* in children. Likewise, *vivacity* (an essentially constitutional trait) when occurring in sons of emotionally disturbed mothers is more likely to propel the boys into delinquency than if it characterizes the sons of emotionally normal mothers. And so, too, as regards a *preponderance of extroversive trends* in the personality, a *feeling of being able to manage one's life* without help from others, and also the *absence of a feeling of not being taken seriously*.

Serious Physical Ailment of Mother (Appendix Tables F-24, F-61). Serious physical diseases in the mother (as cancer, diabetes, Bright's disease, severe cardiovascular ailments, crippling arthritis or rheumatism, diseases of the nervous system) have been found to contribute to the development or enhancement of only one of the delinquency-related traits encompassed in our inquiry—namely, *tendency to phantasy*. If a mother can not share enough of herself with a child, the development of phantasy life on his part would appear to be a natural result in a youngster already so prone (for this is a constitutionally-oriented trait).

We now learn that a boy who is *ambivalent to authority* or *unconventional* in his attitudes is more likely to become delinquent if he is the son of a seriously ill mother than of a mother who is not severely ill. Her incapacitating illness must, in some measure at least, disrupt her functioning as a homemaker, so that she cannot give to an ambivalent or unconventional youngster the stabilizing supervision he requires.

Industrial Incompetence of the Mother (Appendix Tables F-12, F-45, F-65). In *Unraveling Juvenile Delinquency* it was shown that although almost equal proportions of mothers of delinquents and of nondelinquents were regularly engaged in gainful employment, a considerably higher percentage of mothers of delinquents were sporadic workers (now and then engaged in domestic service, cleaning and scrubbing, factory work, waiting on tables, entertaining in cafés and restaurants, and similar activity). We have already learned that the mother who works sporadically (and often largely to satisfy her own whims or to escape from household activities) contributes to the development of *hostility, destructive-sadistic trends,* and *destructiveness* in her children, and also to *feelings of isolation* and *resentment* in them. Perhaps they sense her lack of concern for their well-being as she satisfies her own urge for change and excitement in irregular out-of-the-home activity. Through the development of such delinquency-related traits in youngsters it can certainly be said that, *indirectly,* the mother's erratic absences from home contribute to the delinquency of her children.

We now find that children with *emotional conflicts,* with *labile temperaments,* with *low performance ability,* are more likely to become delinquents if their mothers are unpredictably absent from home than are such children of regularly employed mothers, or of mothers who do not work at all.[1]

It should be evident from the foregoing analysis that the significance of the findings in this chapter and also in the succeeding chapters derives from the observation that *certain inimical social factors in the family life become more criminogenic in the presence of certain traits in children; that, in other words, the evident enhancement of the criminogenic potency of such traits occurs when they are present in children reared in certain malignant sociocultural conditions.* We are also learning from this analysis that it is not only the greater incidence

[1] The interested reader is referred to a paper by the authors, 'Working Mothers and Delinquency,' *Mental Hygiene,* July 1957, Vol. 41, No. 3, pp. 327–52.

of certain inimical factors in the rearing of delinquents than of non-delinquents that is significant for the determination of etiologic mechanisms in delinquency (as determined in *Unraveling Juvenile Delinquency*), but also that *certain sociocultural circumstances operate as catalytic agents in the delinquency of children possessing certain character traits regardless of whether these traits are in themselves neutral as concerns criminogenesis or are, in general, found to be more characteristic of delinquents than of nondelinquents.*

The importance of this conception goes beyond the problem of delinquency. It is significant for psychology and sociology; for it begins to show the manner in which specific environmental pressures operate in exerting a *selective* influence on the behavior of children having certain characteristics, be these essentially constitutional or essentially conditioned in their orientation.

The analysis of the factor-trait dynamics is continued in the next chapter.

XI

SOME ASPECTS OF HOME CLIMATE, TRAITS AND DELINQUENCY

INTRODUCTION

IN the prior chapter, relating to the influence on delinquency of certain elements of parental pathology (criminalism, alcoholism, emotional and physical illness, industrial incompetence), we learned that such factors are implicated in the criminogenic process not only by contributing to the formation of delinquency-related traits in children but by their malignant catalytic influence on youngsters already possessing certain traits, regardless of whether these are in themselves related to delinquency. So far in the analysis, it appears that the activation to delinquency comes from the *combination* of inimical social factors and the presence in children of certain traits.

We begin now to understand why not all sons of criminalistic fathers become delinquent. If such an influence as 'differential association' were alone or predominantly the etiologic agent,[1] all, or at least the great majority, of boys who come into contact with anti-social parents, ideas or values would become delinquents. This is obviously not the case. But, apart from this affirmative evidence, the findings in *Unraveling Juvenile Delinquency* (Table IX–10) indicate that 32% of the 500 *nondelinquents* were also the sons of criminalistic fathers. It is obvious, then, that an oversimplified explanation such as differential association is not adequate, and that clusters of social pressures (a finding already brought out in *Unraveling Juvenile Delinquency*) and/or the combined influence of inimical social conditions and certain pre-existent traits in children influence their delinquency potential.

The presence in a boy, for example, of a *feeling of not being appreciated* (shown in *Unraveling Juvenile Delinquency* to be generally more characteristic of delinquents than of nondelinquents) results in

---

[1] See S. Glueck, 'Theory and Fact in Criminology,' *British Journal of Delinquency*, Vol. VII, No. 2, October 1956, pp. 92–109.

a significantly greater incidence of delinquency among sons of criminalistic fathers than among those of noncriminal fathers. (The data are set forth in the prior chapter.)

We shall now proceed to an examination of other inimical aspects of the home atmosphere (*i.e.*, those which, according to *Unraveling Juvenile Delinquency*, are more common to the background of delinquents than of nondelinquents), in an effort to determine why and how these factors participate in the genesis of delinquency, or, to put it differently, in the weakening of defenses against antisocial behavior. We shall be concerned with the evidence produced in this inquiry which, though not providing conclusive answers, at least opens up rewarding reflection on the criminogenic influences of various other conditions surrounding a boy, such as certain cultural factors, the economic circumstances of his rearing, certain physical aspects of the home, and some aspects of the atmosphere of the home.

CULTURAL FACTORS

Culture Conflict between Parents and Children. Culture conflict growing out of the differing standards and customs of parents of foreign birth and children of native birth has, like poverty, been generally looked upon as a major crime-inducing factor. However, a significant difference was not found in the proportion of foreign-born parents among the delinquents and nondelinquents of *Unraveling Juvenile Delinquency*, although the similarity between the delinquents and nondelinquents in this regard may be partly ascribable to the preliminary matching of the two sets of cases by ethnic origin.

Cultural Refinement of Home (Appendix Tables F-9, F-19, F-59). Another aspect of cultural influence on delinquency is provided by the absence of good taste in the home practices or furnishings; for the households of delinquents were shown in *Unraveling Juvenile Delinquency* to lack elements of cultural refinement to a significantly greater extent than the homes of nondelinquents. Evidence to this effect has been adduced from the existence of a lack of appreciation of the more aesthetic things of life, such as good music, art, literature, tasteful home decoration. Since the nondelinquents were originally selected for the research from a socioeconomic level very like that of the delinquents, the lower degree of cultivation in the homes of the delinquents must have some significance for delinquency. Nevertheless, the absence of cultural refinement has not been found to contribute to the development of any of the delinquency-related traits encompassed in this research. However, we can offer a few clues as o how the lack of cultural interests in the home may contribute to he delinquency of some children; for it now becomes clear that the presence of certain constitutional (or probably constitutional) traits among children reared in homes devoid of cultural interest—namely, *physical immaturity* (as reflected in *sexual underdevelopment*), *sensuousness*, an *unmethodical approach to problems*—is more likely to contribute to delinquency than is the presence of one or another of these same traits in boys reared in homes in which there is at least some cultural refinement. Such traits, with the exception of *genital underdevelopment*, may be classified as criminogenic because they were found in *Unraveling Juvenile Delinquency* to be significantly more characteristic of the delinquents than of the control group.

ECONOMIC CONDITIONS

Financial Dependence of Family (Appendix Tables F-11, F-30). By economic dependency we refer to those situations in which the income of a household is so small and so irregular that the family must resort to welfare agencies or relatives for almost continual assistance; in other words, the family is not self-sustaining, usually because of the prolonged illness or industrial incapacity of the breadwinner or of his desertion of wife and children. In considering this, it should be kept in mind that the 500 delinquents and their 500 matched nondelinquents were all reared in equally 'underprivileged neighborhoods' and that, almost without exception, they stemmed from very modest (economically marginal) families (*i.e.*, having just enough to get by for a few months in case of unemployment of the breadwinner, perhaps finding it necessary on occasion to resort briefly to financial assistance from welfare agencies or relatives for short periods but being quickly able to resume full self-support).

Since we deliberately selected youngsters for the purposes of *Unraveling Juvenile Delinquency* from a low socioeconomic background, we now have the opportunity to examine the *selective* influence of economic dependency on the genesis of delinquency.

In *Unraveling Juvenile Delinquency* it was shown that an excessive proportion of delinquents grew up in indigent families, as reflected in their almost continuous economic dependence. This finding might well lend support to the commonly held notion that poverty, as such, is a cause (if not *the* cause) of crime. But, thus far, our analysis of the origin of traits has not revealed any influence of destitution on the development of any of the delinquency-related traits encompassed in this research. We are therefore forced to look elsewhere for an explanation of how poverty operates on delinquency in present-day American culture.

We have now unearthed some clues as to how rearing in such circumstances contributes to delinquency. It appears from our current findings that children with *low verbal intelligence* who are reared in abject poverty (*i.e.*, in families usually 'on relief') are more likely to become delinquents than are boys of *low verbal intelligence* who grew up in homes where the struggle to make both ends meet was not so great (*i.e.*, the family somehow managed on its own resources with only very occasional outside help).

We also find that youngsters having a *feeling of not being appreciated*, when reared in families needing constant financial aid from welfare agencies, are likewise more likely to become delinquent than boys so characterized who are not surrounded by such stringent economic circumstances.

Management of Family Income (Appendix Tables F-4, F-11, F-43) We turn next to the influence on delinquency of rearing in an atmosphere of carelessness and unconcern as reflected by poor management of the family resources. Negligence in this regard has been found to contribute to the development of certain traits shown in *Unraveling Juvenile Delinquency* to be related to delinquency: namely *destructiveness, destructive-sadistic trends, extroversion of action, lack of conscientiousness* and *receptive trends*. Since all these traits are significantly more characteristic of delinquents than of nondelinquents, it can be said that rearing in a household unconcerned about meeting the family's basic economic needs indirectly enhances the risk of delinquency on the part of the children.

However, there are other ways in which growing up in a home typified by an atmosphere of living from day to day without planful allocation of funds to insure the family's minimal needs contributes to delinquency. These are reflected in the revelation that a greater proportion of delinquents subjected to a hand-to-mouth existence are found among *enuretic* children and children with *low verbal intelligence* and also among children who are *not masochistic* than is the case among those so characterized who grew up in families able to manage their economic resources with care.

PHYSICAL ASPECTS OF HOME

Crowding of Home (Appendix Tables F-33, F-45, F-65). Although delinquency is often ascribed to crowded living quarters (measured by us as the occupancy of a bedroom by more than two persons), the difference in the proportion of delinquents and nondelinquents reared in such conditions, although significant, is not very great according to the findings in *Unraveling Juvenile Delinquency*. (This is, of course

116

in part due to the selection of both groups of boys from areas of low economic status.)

The question before us now is: How do crowded living conditions contribute to delinquency? Is the influence a direct one, flowing entirely from the expulsive effect on a youngster from an overcrowded home which may result in his seeking leisure-time outlets in the streets?

Let us examine the present findings regarding the influence on delinquency of rearing in over-full homes. It has been learned that crowding of the home contributes to the evolution of the trait of *acquisitiveness*, as well as to the development of *destructiveness, destructive-sadistic trends* and *low verbal intelligence*. All these traits are significantly criminogenic according to our findings in *Unraveling Juvenile Delinquency* in that they are more characteristic of delinquents than of nondelinquents. Other traits to the evolution of which rearing in a crowded home contributes are the *feeling of isolation* and *marked suspiciousness*. The relationships between rearing in overcrowded homes and certain character traits thus afford some indication of the indirect influence of growing up in a crowded home on the development of certain traits which, in turn, are associated with delinquency.

How does rearing in crowded quarters, with its lack of opportunity for privacy and for play, contribute more *directly* to delinquency? There are three traits (*emotional lability, poor surface contact with others, emotional conflicts*), all of which are generally more characteristic of delinquents than of nondelinquents, which when present in boys growing up in overcrowded homes contribute more to the impulsion to delinquency than they do when characterizing youngsters not subjected to the corrosive effects of overcrowded homes.

Household Routine (Appendix Tables F-7, F-11, F-67). Careless household routine, like the haphazard use of the family income, bears an association with delinquency; for proportionately more delinquents are products of homes in which the basic affairs of the day (such as specific mealtimes, playtimes, hours for doing homework, bedtime for the children) are left almost entirely to the whim of each family member with resultant confusion in the daily pattern of living.

Since such haphazard routines were found in *Unraveling Juvenile Delinquency* to be common not only in three out of every four homes of the delinquents but also in two in four homes of the nondelinquents, it is evident that this environmental circumstance does not always contribute to delinquency. What, then, is the nature of its selective influence? How does it operate toward impelling some children and not others to delinquency? (The reader is reminded that certain clues have already been derived from *Physique and Delinquency*, where it was learned that a careless household regime is more damaging to mesomorphic youngsters, who are generally extroverted and energetic and for whom a confused household results in the search for recreations outside the home.)[1]

The first clue (other than the varied reaction of boys of different body builds to certain environmental stresses) comes from the discovery that rearing in a careless household evidently contributes to the development of *destructiveness* and *destructive-sadistic trends*, both constitutionally-oriented traits which are (according to our findings in *Unraveling Juvenile Delinquency*) more characteristic of delinquents than of nondelinquents. But, as is true in regard to the impulsion toward delinquency of rearing in homes in which there was so much unconcern on the part of the elders for the welfare of their children that they did not budget for the basic financial needs of the household, so also in regard to the subjection of children to hit-or-miss daily living. Youngsters with *low verbal intelligence* reared in such households are more likely to become delinquent than are children with *low verbal intelligence* who grow up in homes in which there is a reasonable consistency in the household routine (mealtimes, playtimes, study periods, sleep, and so on). These findings suggest that children already delinquency-endangered (so designated because they have certain characteristics that are more common to delinquents than nondelinquents) are more likely to 'go over the brink' if subjected to a haphazard home atmosphere than are youngsters with one or another of the same traits who have not grown up in such an unsettled environment. Obviously, there are many children who withstand such confusion in the daily life of the home; others react to it with antisocial behavior.

Psychopathic children growing up in a carelessly permissive household are also more likely to become delinquent than are such children in homes where there are reasonable limits set for the performance of the daily functions. Such children, characterized as they are by emotional instability, might well become dangerously unmanageable in a highly permissive environment.

There is still another characteristic which appears to add to the delinquency potential of certain children reared in a carelessly functioning household—*absence of dermographia* (skin sensitivity). Readers might ponder the significance of the finding which appears to indicate that 'skin toughness' bears some relationship to the delinquency of boys reared in a haphazard environment.

[1] See S. and E. T. Glueck, *Physique and Delinquency*, New York, Harper & Brothers, 1956, p. 224.

Cleanliness and Orderliness of Home (Appendix Table F-4). Another aspect of the physicial home environment generally looked upon as delinquency-inducing, probably because of its expulsive effect on youngsters as well as for what it reflects about the character and habits of those who are responsible for the management of the home, is uncleanliness and general disorderliness.

In *Unraveling Juvenile Delinquency* it was shown that a significantly excessive proportion of delinquents were reared under such conditions, despite the fact that delinquents and nondelinquents had been matched initially for residence in underprivileged areas. How does bringing up in such homes actually contribute to delinquency? As regards its indirect influence (that is, its effect on the shaping of traits), it would appear that it operates through the development of *destructive-sadistic trends,* of *extroversive trends* and also through its contribution to the development of an *unmethodical approach to problems.* More directly, however, rearing in unclean and disorderly homes appears excessively to influence the delinquency of *enuretic* children. The explanation for this is obscure.

ATMOSPHERE OF HOME

Conduct Standards of Family (Appendix Table F-33). What effect does rearing in families whose behavior standards are low (as reflected in criminality, drunkenness, immorality among its members during the boy's early years) have on a boy's becoming delinquent? It was shown in *Unraveling Juvenile Delinquency* that low behavior standards are in general far more characteristic of the families of delinquents than of nondelinquents.

We have already learned that being brought up in such an antisocial home environment contributes to the development of the trait of *hostility* in a child, so that in this indirect way the poor behavior standards set before a youngster may influence his delinquency. There is only one delinquency-related trait, namely, *poor surface contact with others,* which, when present in youngsters reared in homes of low conduct standards, clearly adds to their delinquency potential. This would appear to mean that, on the whole, a pattern of marked antisocial conduct in members of a boy's family exerts a *direct* influence in impelling him to become a delinquent. In such instances, an intervening set of environmental influences on existing traits (with the exception of *poor surface contact with others*) is evidently not necessary, since the antisocial example gained in the home is so potent, especially when a boy has strongly identified himself with his parents. The classic example of this is in the theft-pattern among gypsy

119

children. There, the superego is delinquent from the point of view of the general society, although normal in the gypsy social group. In other words, a youngster growing up in a home in which he is surrounded by evidences of low conduct standards is more likely to succumb to the influences that immediately surround him in the community than is a youngster in whose home the conduct standards are reasonably decent. It must always be borne in mind, however, that an influence operates *selectively* on children possessing certain traits; and that it is neither exclusively nor necessarily the most powerful among the constituents of the total dynamic set of stimuli to delinquent behavior.

Self-Respect of Family. What is the effect on delinquency of rearing by parents who are not self-respecting, *i.e.*, without pride and without concern about the opinion held of them by neighbors and friends; without a strong desire for self-help; insensitive to any fall from grace on the part of family members?

Lack of family pride was shown in *Unraveling* to be significantly more prevalent among the families of delinquents than of nondelinquents. In the present work, analysis of trait formation has indicated that lack of parental self-respect contributes to the development of two of the delinquency-linked traits included in this inquiry—*impracticality* and *lack of self-criticism*. There is no further evidence in our findings of the role of this factor in the delinquency of children.

Family Ambitiousness (Appendix Table F-11). Lack of ambition in parents, like absence of self-respect, is also more characteristic of the families of delinquents than of nondelinquents and therefore partially criminogenic. Ambitiousness, it will be recalled, has to do with parental desire to improve the status of the family members (higher education for the children, serious intent to move to better neighborhoods and into more adequate homes to enable the children to have better play facilities and more space; saving to buy a house; plans for a small business venture with a view to improving the family's economic status). We have already learned that growing up in a family which lacks the initiative to 'pull itself up by the bootstraps,' if need be, contributes to the development in a youngster of *marked suspiciousness, inadequacy, lack of conscientiousness* and *adventurousness*, all traits that are in general more characteristic of delinquents than of nondelinquents. Thus, it is in part through its contribution to the development of these potentially criminogenic traits that lack of family ambitiousness is involved in delinquent trends. More directly, it is now revealed that one trait—*low verbal intelligence*—influences the delinquency of boys reared in homes in which the parents lacked

120

the drive to better themselves and their children than if present in a boy whose family was ambitious to improve its condition.

In this chapter, as in the prior one, we have noted the intervention of two types of environmental influence in criminogenesis: (*a*) the influence of some aspects of the home environment on the formation of certain traits previously shown, in *Unraveling*, significantly to differentiate delinquents from nondelinquents; (*b*) the influence of some factors of family life either in rendering criminogenic certain traits which had not been previously found to distinguish delinquents from nondelinquents, or in *adding weight* to the antisocial inducement of traits already shown in *Unraveling* to be in themselves criminogenic.

Here again, therefore, we have clear proof of the selective influence of sociocultural stimuli, a characteristic of environmental forces which is too often ignored or undervalued.

XII

FAMILY RELATIONSHIPS, TRAITS AND DELINQUENCY

IN this chapter we pursue further the analysis of the influence on delinquency of various sociocultural factors—largely parent-child relationships—in the case of children possessing certain traits.

PARENTAL RELATIONSHIPS

There are two aspects of parental relationships which are encompassed in our study: one has to do with affection between the parents; the other concerns domination of family affairs by the mother.

Compatibility of Parents (Appendix Table F-3). We know from *Unraveling* that a much higher proportion of delinquents than of nondelinquents are the sons of incompatible parents (as manifested by constant quarreling); and from Chapter IX of the present work it has been learned that rearing in an atmosphere of emotional tension between parents contributed to the development of *extreme restlessness* in children and had a bearing also on limiting their *verbal intelligence*. Evidence has also emerged that rearing in a home in which the psychological atmosphere was one of lack of affection between the parents contributed to the enhancement of the essentially constitutional trait of *destructiveness*, as well as of *destructive-sadistic trends*.

Since all of these traits have been found, in *Unraveling*, to be more significantly characteristic of delinquents than of nondelinquents it becomes evident that it is partly through contributing to the development of these traits that parental incompatibility is involved in delinquency.

It is now found that rearing by parents whose incompatibility has been so great that it actually resulted in open breach (desertion, separation, divorce) gave added force to the delinquency potential of restless youngsters; for a considerably higher proportion of extremely restless delinquents were found to be the sons of parents whose conjugal relations had actually reached a breaking point.

122

Dominance of Mother in Family Affairs (Appendix Tables F-30, F-50). There is much speculation concerning the effect on the delinquency of children of rearing in mother-dominated homes.

In *Unraveling*, it was obvious that in about half the homes of both the delinquents and the nondelinquents the mother rather than the father was the 'head' of the family. Our previous analysis of the origin of traits did not, however, disclose that the domination of the household by the mother contributed to the formation of any of the traits related to delinquency. It is now found that among boys having a *feeling of not being appreciated* a higher proportion of those who were reared in a household in which the mother rather than the father assumed the guidance of family affairs became delinquent than of boys whose fathers were the heads of the household. One can only speculate that a male child already suffering from a sense of inferiority is further emasculated by living in the shadow of a dominating mother, and therefore develops deep hostilities which, together with other influences, propel him into delinquency.

Another possible influence of mother domination on delinquency occurs among youngsters with predominantly *introversive trends* (living more 'within one's self,' having difficulty in relating oneself emotionally to others). Although this trait has not in itself been found to be more characteristic of delinquents than of nondelinquents, it appears that introversive boys are more likely to become delinquent if brought up in a mother-dominated household than if reared in the more normal circumstances of a father-dominated home.

UPROOTINGS FROM HOME AND NEIGHBORHOOD

We turn now to a consideration of those closer aspects of childrearing that are reflective of lack of stability in the home and in neighborhood ties. We shall examine the extent to which the homes of delinquents were broken by the death, desertion, separation, or divorce of parents; the extent of rearing of children by parent substitutes; and the extent of a family's moving about to a degree which generally deprives parents and children of firm roots and attachments in a single neighborhood.

We shall consider these sociocultural influences both in relation to certain traits and as independent contributors to a delinquent tendency.

Broken Homes (Appendix Tables F-45, F-53). We know from *Unraveling* that a greater proportion of delinquents than of nondelinquents stem from broken homes. As to the pathway of influence, this is a factor which would appear on the surface to bear *directly* and permeatively on delinquency, since it has been found to contribute to the development of but a single delinquency-associated trait included in this research, namely, *uninhibited motor responses to stimuli.*

However, it is now found that in instances in which youngsters from broken homes are characterized by *emotional lability* or by a *feeling of inadequacy* exposure to the unsettling effect of a broken home adds to their delinquency potential.

Age at First Breach in Family Life (Appendix Table F-61). Are children whose home life was disrupted before they were five years old more likely to become delinquent than those who did not have this unsettling experience until they were older?

In prior chapters we learned that an early break in the home ties has a bearing on the development of a *tendency to phantasy* and of *marked suspiciousness* in a child and also on his *suggestibility* (all of these traits being more characteristic of delinquents than of nondelinquents); so that through its involvement in the evolution of these potentially criminogenic traits an early break in the home ties may be said to contribute to the delinquency of some children.

We now find evidence that very young children subjected to such uprooting experiences who are *lacking in conventionality* are more likely to be propelled into delinquency than are unconventional youngsters who, though reared in broken homes, were not exposed to such a disruptive experience until they were somewhat older.

Rearing by Parent Substitutes (Appendix Tables F-15, F-31, F-36, F-67). What now of the influence on delinquency of a child's upbringing by parent substitutes (step-parents, foster parents, relatives)? Although such rearing is sometimes regarded as an unmitigated evil, no evidence is found within the compass of the present inquiry to indicate that it contributes to any of the delinquency-related traits we have been studying.

How then does rearing by parent substitutes play its role in delinquency? From a study of the relationships between the social background of delinquents and the traits encompassed in this inquiry, it is revealed that children possessing the following traits are apparently more prone to delinquency if brought up by parent substitutes than if reared by their own parents: *poor power of observation, destructiveness, psychopathic trends, absence of a fear of failure or defeat.*

The dynamic significance of the relationship of rearing by substitute parents to the translation of such characteristics into delinquent behavior deserves systematic clinical observation.

Frequent Moving. We consider next the influence on delinquency of frequent uprooting of children as reflected in the moving about of a family from one home to another, often from one neighborhood to another (a situation more characteristic of the families of delinquents than of nondelinquents).

In analyzing the origin of traits it was found that frequent moving (more often than once a year) was associated with the development of only one of the delinquency-related traits encompassed in the present research, *lack of self-criticism*, which may be an accidental association. It is possible that a strong influence involved in frequent uprootings of home and neighbourhood is the need of making frequent adaptations to varied local cultural patterns.

RELATIONSHIP BETWEEN BOY AND PARENTS

How does the lack of a close relationship between father and son (as reflected in parental indifference or open hostility to the boy), the lack of attachment of a boy to his parents, and a father's unacceptability to the boy as a pattern for emulation influence a child's delinquency potential?

Affection of Father for Boy (Appendix Tables F-11, F-20, F-45, F-49, F-67). First, let us consider the case of a father's lack of affection for his son. Is this a social factor which operates on delinquency directly or through the intermediary of delinquency-related traits?

Of these traits, one—*hostility*—was found to be conditioned by a father's lack of affection for his son.

We now find, in addition, that youngsters of *low verbal intelligence*, as well as *emotionally labile* children, who are unloved by the father are more likely to become delinquent than are boys with these characteristics who are held in warm paternal affection. The same is true regarding a *preponderance of extroversive trends* in the personality; and it may be reasoned that a predominantly extroversive youngster who is rejected by his father is more likely to find ready outlets for his emotional disappointments in 'street society' which could very well embroil him in delinquent activities. We learn also that *psychopathic* youngsters who are ignored or disdained by the father are also more likely to become delinquent than are boys with psychopathic trends who are held in warm paternal affection. This is likewise the case as regards children who *lack a capacity for objective interests*.

Attachment of Boy to Father (Appendix Tables F-33, F-37). We have already learned about the influence of a father's indifference or hostility on his son's antisocial conduct. Now we are concerned with

125

the contribution to delinquency of a boy's lack of attachment to his father. We know from *Unraveling* that an excessive proportion of delinquents have no close emotional ties to the father, a finding which, however direct or indirect may be the connection, justifies an inference that indifference or hostility of a boy to his father is not infrequently criminogenic.

Now it becomes evident that youngsters who are not fond of their fathers and who in addition have *poor surface contact with others* (inability to get along with people regardless of the underlying attitude, which may be one of isolation or even hostility), as well as boys having a *feeling of isolation*, are more likely to become involved in delinquency than are youngsters with the same traits who are buttressed by a warm attachment for the father.

It should be noted that both of the traits involved—*poor surface contact with others* and a *feeling of isolation*—are in themselves more characteristic of delinquents than of nondelinquents.

Acceptability of Father to Boy (Appendix Tables F-54, F-56, F-60). A lower proportion of delinquents than of nondelinquents were shown in *Unraveling* to regard their fathers as acceptable patterns for emulation. The emphasis so often made in psychoanalytic literature need not be labored that the role of the father as a person with whom a child can emotionally identify is of extreme importance in influencing the child's values and conduct.

It does become evident, however, that *stubbornness, uninhibited motor responses to stimuli* and *acquisitiveness* contribute more to the delinquency of boys reared by fathers with whom they do not identify than to those brought up by fathers who were acceptable to them as patterns for emulation.

RELATIONSHIP OF BOY AND MOTHER

Affection of Mother for Boy (Appendix Table F-3). The affectional relationship of mother and son, as that of father and son, plays a vital role in the etiology of delinquency; this, despite the correlative finding that a lower proportion of mothers than of fathers of delinquents had been shown (in *Unraveling*) not to be closely attached to their sons. As regards the evidence of the contribution of a mother's lack of affection, a relationship has been found between maternal indifference or hatred for a child and his *feeling of resentment* and *hostility*.

In addition to this tangential means of contributing to a child's delinquency there may be a more direct route through the presence in a boy of *extreme restlessness*, a trait which, occurring in youngsters who are unloved by the mother, is enhanced in its delinquency-inducing power.

Of course, no one combination of factor and trait operates on delinquency independently of other factors and traits; but it begins to be evident that it is not merely the presence of a particular environmental circumstance which propels some boys into delinquency, *but the influence of particular circumstances on youngsters already possessing certain innate or acquired traits.*

Rank of Boy among Siblings (Appendix Tables F-18, F-37, F-41, F-54). In *Unraveling* it was learned that, contrary to the generally accepted view that a *higher* proportion of especially 'favored' and 'spoiled' children (the only child and the youngest) are to be found among delinquents than among nondelinquents, there was in fact a lesser incidence of children of these birthranks among the delinquents than among the nondelinquents. We learned in *Unraveling* also that there is no greater proportion of firstborn children among the delinquents than among the nondelinquents. Although no characteristics are now found that contribute selectively to the delinquency of first-born children, it must be borne in mind (a fact already ascertained in the present inquiry) that the first child in a family is more likely to be *emotionally unstable* than are children of other birthranks; and since such instability is more characteristic of delinquents than of nondelinquents, the ordinal rank of a boy may be said to contribute to his delinquency in this indirect way.

We must focus our attention on the 'middle' children in the family constellation. The findings indicate that a youngster who is neither an only child, the youngest in the family, nor the firstborn is more likely to become delinquent if he is *lacking in common sense*, if he has a *feeling of isolation*, if he is *narcissistic*, if he is *stubborn*.

As regards the only child, however, it has already been indicated that a somewhat *lower* proportion of children who have no brothers or sisters are found among delinquents than among nondelinquents. In the analysis of the origin of traits, we have been able to isolate only two delinquency-related characteristics that appear to be conditioned by the circumstance of being an only child—*impracticality* and *lack of common sense*. Now we gain a further clue as to why it is that an only child (who is likely to be more protected by his parents than are other children) becomes delinquent.

It is now found that if an only child has a *feeling of not being taken care of* (senses a lack of active interest on the part of others, especially of parents, or lack of help from them in situations in which he feels entitled to such interest and help), he is more likely to become delinquent than if he is a child of 'middle rank' who, being one of two or more children, probably gains some emotional strength from siblings.

The very small number of one-child families in *Unraveling* (24 among the 500 delinquents and 43 among the 500 nondelinquents) suggests that examination of a large group of one-child families would be necessary in order to increase knowledge of the influences that propel the only child into delinquency.

Attachment of Brothers and Sisters to Boy (Appendix Tables F-54, F-64). Moving now from the impact on delinquency of the birthrank of a youngster among his brothers and sisters to the influence of the affectional relationships between him and his siblings, it is found that in the case of *stubborn* boys and also of *impractical* boys, indifference or hostility on the part of brothers and sisters has a more deleterious effect (*i.e.*, is more delinquency-inducing) than if the stubborn or impractical brother is well accepted by his brothers and sisters. In addition, it was noted in Chapter IX that lack of acceptance of a boy by one or another sibling plays some part in limiting his verbal intelligence; and since *low verbal intelligence* is in general more characteristic of delinquents than of nondelinquents, it may be said that indirectly, through its influence on the formation of this trait, the lack of attachment of siblings to a boy may contribute to his pattern of delinquent behavior.

In our discussion of the orientation of traits there were found six other delinquency-related traits that are proportionately more characteristic of youngsters who were not well accepted by siblings—*extreme restlessness, enuresis, emotional conflicts, destructiveness, destructive-sadistic trends* and *unconventionality*. The question is whether lack of acceptance by siblings contributes to the formation of these traits or whether children are initially less friendly to a brother who already possesses one or another such characteristic. Be this as it may, there is certainly an interaction between factor and traits which indirectly adds to the delinquency-proneness of boys who are not well accepted by one or more of their brothers and sisters.

Cohesiveness of Family (Appendix Tables F-4, F-9, F-59). In *Unraveling Juvenile Delinquency* it was learned that lack of family cohesiveness constitutes one of the major and most important differences in the background of delinquents and nondelinquents. It now appears that the influence of family disintegration on delinquency is not uniform, being more potent in the case of *enuretic* children, those who are *sexually underdeveloped*, and *sensuous* boys (than among youngsters having these same characteristics but who were reared in cohesive homes). *Genital underdevelopment* and *sensuousness* are essentially constitutional traits, and *enuresis*

128

possibly so. With the exception of *sexual underdevelopment*, these traits were found in general to be more characteristic of delinquents than of nondelinquents.

It becomes clear, then, that children having one or another of the foregoing characteristics and who are members of a disintegrating family are more likely to become delinquent than are children with the same traits who have, fortunately, been reared in cohesive families. Apart from this, it must be borne in mind that absence of family cohesiveness has been found to contribute to the development of *emotional conflicts,* a *defensive attitude, unconventionality* and *impracticality,* all characteristics that are more prevalent among delinquents than among nondelinquents.

The social factors presented in this chapter are perhaps the most potent influences in the entire complex field of impulsions to anti-social behavior, for they concern the most intimate relationships of the growing child—his emotional ties to parents and siblings.

Once again it has been noted that the criminogenic influence of the factors can be plotted along three dynamic lines:

(*a*) the direct effect which they have on delinquency;

(*b*) their influence on the formation of certain delinquency-related traits;

(*c*) the catalytic influence of certain sociocultural factors in imparting a criminogenic dynamism to certain traits regardless of whether either factor or trait is itself directly related to delinquency.

XIII

PARENTAL UNCONCERN FOR BOY,
TRAITS AND DELINQUENCY

INTRODUCTION

IN prior chapters we have reviewed the influence of social factors and traits on delinquency with particular reference to the pathology of the parents, the atmosphere of the homes in which the delinquents were reared, and the interpersonal family relations. Now we turn to some evidences of lack of parental concern for the boys as reflected in meager provisions for recreation in the home, indifference or inhospitality toward the friends of the son, and a lack of family group recreations. Attention will be given also to the influence of inadequate supervision by the mother and faulty disciplinary practices by mother and father.

What we have several times previously emphasized—that no single environmental influence operates independently to impel children to delinquency—should by now be abundantly clear. If delinquency-inducing influences were unilateral, *all* children in certain families would be delinquents; and all delinquents (and nondelinquents) would have similar environmental circumstances in their background. We have ample evidence already that environmental pressures act *selectively* to induce delinquency in youngsters possessing certain constitutional or acquired traits, while not exerting a criminogenic influence on others, although the reason why particular combinations of social factors and traits are delinquency-inducing is not always clear.

HOME RECREATIONS

Recreational Provisions (Appendix Tables F-11, F-33, F-43, F-50). A reflection of lack of parental interest in a child is the failure to provide recreational facilities in the home. In the crowded neighborhoods in which our delinquents were reared, lack of 'under-the-roof' recreation was bound to have an expulsive effect, forcing them into the streets to find their leisure-time activities. We already know that this kind of neglect on the part of parents contributes to the development of *marked suspiciousness*, to a *feeling of not being appreciated*, to a *feeling of isolation*. We know also that the absence of family solidarity (as expressed in a total lack of family group recreations) contributes to the development of *receptive trends* and *lack of conscientiousness* in children, to a *poor power of observation*, as well as to a *lack of common sense*; that it contributes also to the development of the constitutionally-oriented traits of *destructiveness*, *destructive-sadistic trends* and *acquisitiveness*, and that it *impedes* the development of a *potential capacity for objective interests*. Since all of these traits are more characteristic of delinquents than of nondelinquents, parental unconcern for the well-being of a child may be said to contribute in this indirect way to a boy's delinquency potential.

More directly, however, children deprived of adequate recreational facilities in the home who have *low verbal intelligence*, or *poor surface contact with others*, or *introversive trends* (difficulty in relating themselves emotionally to others), or who are *not masochistic*, are more impelled to delinquency than are boys possessing such traits who, more fortunately, had been reared in households in which adequate provision was made by parents for their leisure hours at home.

Of all the foregoing traits, it is of particular interest to note that *introversiveness* is not, in general, more characteristic of delinquents than of nondelinquents, and can not therefore be regarded as directly criminogenic; however, an *introversive child reared in a deprived home environment may seek expression for piled-up tensions in delinquent activity*.

Hospitality of Parents to Boy's Companions (Appendix Tables F-11, F-43, F-62, F-67). An atmosphere of indifference or inhospitality on the part of parents to the friends of a child is more characteristic of the fathers and mothers of delinquents than of nondelinquents. The lack of parental understanding or concern for a child's well-being which such an attitude reflects has been found to engender certain traits in a youngster. It is to be noted that, with three exceptions (*defiance, narcissistic trends* and a *tendency to phantasy*), the remaining traits are similar to the ones engendered by the parents through failure to provide suitable home recreations for a child: *poor power of observation, feeling of not being appreciated, feeling of isolation, receptive trends, destructiveness, destructive-sadistic trends* and *lack of conscientiousness*. Since it was shown in *Unraveling* that all these traits are more characteristic of delinquents than of nondelinquents, and thereby at least partially involved in criminogenesis, it can be considered that through its role in the development

131

of these traits parental failure to make the home a pleasant place for a child is an indirect contributor to delinquency.

What now of the additional criminogenic influence of certain types of parental neglect on boys with certain specific traits?

As was true of the effect of meager recreational provisions in the home on children of *low verbal intelligence*, so with respect to the effect of parents' inhospitality to their children's friends: youngsters of *low verbal intelligence* as well as those who tend to be independent of others (*i.e., not masochistic*) are propelled in greater measure into delinquency than similarly handicapped boys stemming from homes in which the parents typically welcomed the child's friends to the home. In addition to these traits, boys who are *uncritical of themselves* are more likely to become delinquent if reared in the unfavorable atmosphere of parental inhospitality to their playmates than if brought up in homes where the parents welcome their children's friends. Finally, *psychopathic* boys reared in an atmosphere of parental inattentiveness (as reflected in inhospitality to the boy's friends) are more likely to become delinquent than are such boys growing up in a home in which the parents were sufficiently concerned about a child's well-being to welcome his playmates into the home.

We can readily surmise that it is not merely the inhospitality of parents to a boy's friends which adds to the pressure toward childhood maladjustment but that this is a frequent index of more permeative shortcomings of the parents in relation to their children.

Family Group Recreations (Appendix Table F-11). Parent-child recreational activities were found in *Unraveling* to be far less characteristic of the families of the delinquents than of the nondelinquents. This evidence of a lack of 'family spirit' has been found to be involved in the development in a youngster of *narcissistic* or *receptive trends* and of a *tendency to phantasy*. Since all these traits are more characteristic of delinquents than of nondelinquents, it can be said that in this indirect way the social factor contributes to delinquency.

However, there is a more direct influence on delinquency of a home lacking in 'togetherness,' which occurs through its selective operation on boys with *low verbal intelligence* who are generally more at ease in the approach to meaning through concrete physical things than through intermediate symbols. In the boy's world outside the home there are certainly plenty of opportunities for such expression.

SUPERVISION AND DISCIPLINE BY MOTHER

Supervisory Practices of Mother (Appendix Tables F-40, F-43). We know from *Unraveling* that unsuitable supervision of boys by the mother is far more usual in the background of delinquents than of nondelinquents. Is this a direct influence on delinquency, or does it operate, in part at least, through the development in a child of certain traits which are, in turn, more characteristic of delinquents than of nondelinquents? Or are youngsters with certain personality traits found more frequently among poorly supervised delinquents than among delinquents who had been given adequate oversight?

We have already noted in Chapter IX that boys who are allowed by a mother to run about without oversight are more likely (than are those who are closely supervised) to develop *poor power of observation, lack of common sense, impracticality,* a *feeling of isolation, receptive trends,* and a *lack of conscientiousness.* Since these traits have previously been found to be more characteristic of delinquents than of nondelinquents, they may be presumed to be at least partially criminogenic; and, in this indirect way, unsuitable maternal supervision of the child contributes to delinquency.

Two traits, the *feeling of being able to manage one's own life* and the *absence of masochistic trends,* have now been found clearly to enhance the delinquency potential of boys who are left unsupervised by the mother.

Disciplinary Practices (Appendix Tables F-21, F-23, F-29, F-41, F-43, F-56, F-61). Poor maternal disciplinary practices (extreme permissiveness, or overstrictness or inconsistency) have previously been shown to be more characteristic of mothers of delinquents than of nondelinquents. The very high proportion of delinquents (95·8%) who were subjected to faulty discipline by the mother (in contrast with 34·4% of nondelinquents) raises the question of whether this factor is so penetrating and permeative as to operate on delinquency directly, or exerts its antisocial pressures through the intermediary of certain traits in the child.

From the analysis of trait origins already made, it was learned that the mother's inadequate disciplinary practices do indeed contribute to the development of certain traits found in *Unraveling* to be related to delinquency. Thus, overstrictness on the part of a mother influences the development of *hostility* in a youngster; permissiveness contributes to a child's *feeling of isolation* and to a *feeling of resentment;* erratic discipline (vacillation between laxity and overstrictness) is associated with *impracticality* and also with a *lack of conscientiousness* in the child. Since each of these traits has been found to be more characteristic of delinquents than of nondelinquents, it can be said that maternal discipline which is other than firm but kindly is in this trait-influencing way indirectly involved in developing a boy's tendency to delinquency.

F.E.D.—K 133

What of the more directly influenced delinquency potential of boys who are inappropriately disciplined by the mother, *i.e.*, with complete permissiveness, with overstrictness, or with vacillation on her part between laxity and overstrictness as contrasted with firm but kindly management of disciplinary problems?

It now becomes evident that boys who are *socially assertive*, who are *not submissive*, who do *not* have a *feeling of helplessness*, who do *not fear failure and defeat*, who are *not masochistic* (self-punishing), who are *uninhibited in their motor responses to stimuli*, who are *unconventional*, are the ones who, if not handled with firmness and kindness by the mother, are more likely to become delinquent (*i.e.*, to become actively aggressive) than are youngsters with one or another of these characteristics whose discipline is based on sound reason which the boy clearly understands.

Physical Punishment by Mother. Physical punishment by the mother has been found to be associated with *extreme restlessness* in a youngster. We have in our prior analyses suggested that it is difficult to say whether physical punishment by the mother actually does add to a child's restlessness or the use of physical punishment is an expression of maternal frustration in the management of an already restless child. It was found previously that more delinquents than nondelinquents were extremely restless as children.

Thus, in contributing directly to a child's *restlessness*, physical punishment by the mother may also indirectly contribute to his delinquency.

Threatening and Scolding by Mother. What of the effect of threatening and scolding by the mother on the delinquency of children? A relationship between this method of discipline and the development of any of the traits encompassed in this research has not, in fact, been found; but this does not mean that there may not be an association between such discipline and other traits that are not within the compass of the current study. Apart from its influence on trait formation, however, we now learn that *enuretic* children who are threatened or scolded by the mother are more likely to become delinquent than are enuretics who are not subjected to this form of discipline.

DISCIPLINE BY FATHER

We have noted the influence of the mother's disciplinary practices on the delinquency of her children. What now of the role of ineffectual discipline by the father?

Disciplinary Practices (Appendix Tables F-12, F-50). Discipline

134

that is other than firm and kindly was found, in *Unraveling*, to be more generally resorted to by fathers of delinquents than of non-delinquents. Again our question is whether undesirable disciplinary practices operate on delinquency directly, or through the inter-mediary of, or in conjunction with, certain traits in a boy. Although it is true that almost all delinquents have experienced poor disciplin-ary practices by father (or mother), it is also a fact that almost half of the nondelinquents had been just as inappropriately disciplined.

Permissiveness by the father has previously been found to con-tribute to the development of the delinquency-linked trait of *social assertiveness*. Now it is learned that it contributes to the delinquency potential of boys with *high performance intelligence* and with *introversive trends*.

There is no evidence in our inquiry that overstrict discipline con-tributes to the development of any of the delinquency-related traits encompassed in this research. There is evidence, however, that *high performance intelligence* in a boy who has been overstrictly disciplined by his father is more likely to propel him into delinquency than the same trait in a boy who is managed with firmness and kindness by his father.

Contrary to the findings regarding overstrict and lax discipline, a relationship does exist between *erratic* discipline on the part of the father and three delinquency-related traits encompassed in this research—*hostility, suggestibility, lack of practicality*. In addition, we learn that youngsters who experience this kind of discipline are more likely to become delinquent when characterized by *high per-formance intelligence*, or *introversiveness*.

Physical Punishment by Father (Appendix Tables F-39, F-42). As in regard to the use of physical punishment by a mother, so, too, respecting this form of discipline by the father, it appears to be associated with *extreme restlessness* in a child. Here again, it may be asked whether restlessness *results* from physical punishment, or the use of physical punishment follows *extreme restlessness* in youngsters; there is, perhaps, a reciprocal influence.

However, as regards the impact of physical punishment on delin-quency, it is found to be proportionally greater on boys having *receptive (oral) trends*, and also on boys who are *not markedly depend-ent on others*, than on youngsters thus characterized who are not subjected to physical punishment by the father.

Threatening and Scolding by Father (Appendix Table F-56). As in regard to the use of physical punishment by the father, so with refer-ence to threatening or scolding (actually not found to be more characteristic of fathers of delinquents than of nondelinquents), this

135

method of attempting to control a youngster is also associated with *extreme restlessness* in the child.

There is evidence, also, that youngsters subjected to frequent threatening or scolding by the father, and who are *uninhibited in their motor responses to stimuli*, are more likely to become delinquent than are such youngsters who are not disciplined by the father in this way.

Once again we have found that environmental (interpersonal) factors operate selectively, their action being catalyzed by the presence of one or another psychologic or physiologic trait. To speak of sociocultural influences on behavior without taking account of their selective impact is to gloss over a crucial aspect of the play of environmental forces on human behavior.

XIV

FAMILY ENVIRONMENT, TRAITS, BODY BUILD AND DELINQUENCY: A SUMMARY

INTRODUCTION

IN the four prior chapters we have analyzed the influence of various aspects of family life on the delinquency of children.

In *Unraveling Juvenile Delinquency* we learned that almost all 44 aspects of the family environment under scrutiny were more characteristic of the background of the delinquents than of the nondelinquents. But our more intensive quest for an understanding of crime causation has now revealed that the family environment plays a *selective* role on the delinquency of children; *i.e.*, that children with certain characteristics are far more likely to become delinquent when reared in an inimical family environment than if brought up in a less damaging atmosphere.

SUMMARY BY SOCIAL FACTORS

In Exhibit XIV–1[1] a summary of the findings is presented, factor by factor, so that the reader may easily see which traits in a child tend to enhance his delinquency potential in a given environment.

A word of caution is necessary. We are warranted only in focusing attention on the *positive* findings and would hope that in other investigations the factors about which no conclusion could be drawn will be more intensively explored.

EXHIBIT XIV–1. SOCIAL FACTORS WHICH OPERATE *SELECTIVELY* ON THE DELINQUENCY OF BOYS HAVING SPECIFIED TRAITS

PATHOLOGY OF PARENTS

    F.   *Delinquency of Father*
          30. Feeling of Not Being Appreciated
          33. Poor Surface Contact with Others
          42. Receptive Trends

---

[1] The reader is once again reminded that the designation throughout this work of each factor by a letter (as F, H, L, and so on) and of each trait by number (30, 33, 42, and so on) makes possible ready cross-reference within text and to Appendices.

H. *Alcoholism of Father*
    30. Feeling of Not Being Appreciated
    37. Feeling of Isolation
    50. Preponderance of Introversive Trends
J. *Emotional Disturbance of Father*
    53. Feeling of Inadequacy
L. *Serious Physical Ailment of Father*
    59. Sensuousness
O. *Poor Work Habits of Father*
G. *Delinquency of Mother*
    17. Tendency to Phantasy
    42. Receptive Trends
I. *Alcoholism of Mother*
    16. Intuition
K. *Emotional Disturbance of Mother*
    28. Absence of Feeling of Not Being Taken Seriously
    40. Feeling of Being Able to Manage Own Life
    45. Emotional Lability
    47. Vivacity
    49. Preponderance of Extroversive Trends
M. *Serious Physical Ailment of Mother*
    24. Ambivalence to Authority
    61. Unconventionality
X. *Mother Occasionally Employed Outside Home*
    12. Low Performance Intelligence
    45. Emotional Lability
    65. Emotional Conflicts

SOME ASPECTS OF HOME CLIMATE
E. *One or Both Parents Foreign-Born*
R. *Lack of Cultural Refinement in Home*
    9. Genital Underdevelopment
    19. Unmethodical Approach to Problems
    59. Sensuousness
N. *Financial Dependence of Family*
    11. Low Verbal Intelligence
    30. Feeling of Not Being Appreciated
P. *Poor Management of Family Income*
    4. Enuresis in Early Childhood
    11. Low Verbal Intelligence
    43. Absence of Masochistic Trends
B. *Crowded Home*
    33. Poor Surface Contact with Others
    45. Emotional Lability
    65. Emotional Conflicts
Q. *Careless Household Routine*
    7. Absence of Dermographia
    11. Low Verbal Intelligence
    67. Psychopathy

138

C.   *Unclean and Disorderly Home*
    4. Enuresis in Early Childhood
U.   *Poor Conduct Standards of Family*
    33. Poor Surface Contact with Others
S.   *Lack of Family Self-Respect*
T.   *Lack of Family Ambition*
    11. Low Verbal Intelligence

FAMILY RELATIONSHIPS

V.   *Broken Relationship between Parents*
    3. Extreme Restlessness in Early Childhood
W.   *Dominance of Mother in Family Affairs*
    30. Feeling of Not Being Appreciated
    50. Preponderance of Introversive Trends
EE. *Rearing in Broken Home*
    45. Emotional Lability
    53. Feeling of Inadequacy
FF. *Boy less than Five Years of Age at First Breach in Family Life*
    61. Unconventionality
GG. *Rearing by Parent Substitutes*
    15. Poor Power of Observation
    31. Absence of Fear of Failure and Defeat
    36. Destructiveness
    67. Psychopathy
QQ. *Frequent Moving*
HH. *Indifference or Hostility of Father to Boy*
    11. Low Verbal Intelligence
    20. Lack of Potential Capacity for Objective Interests
    45. Emotional Lability
    49. Preponderance of Extroversive Trends
    67. Psychopathy
RR. *Indifference or Hostility of Boy to Father*
    33. Poor Surface Contact with Others
    37. Feeling of Isolation
SS. *Unacceptability of Father to Boy for Emulation*
    54. Stubbornness
    56. Uninhibited Motor Responses to Stimuli
    60. Acquisitiveness
II. *Indifference or Hostility of Mother to Boy*
    3. Extreme Restlessness in Early Childhood
TT. *Indifference or Hostility of Boy to Mother*
DD. *Middle Child in Family*
    18. Lack of Common Sense
    27. Feeling of Not Being Taken Care Of
    37. Feeling of Isolation
    41. Narcissistic Trends
    54. Stubbornness

139

JJ. *Indifference or Hostility of Siblings to Boy*
    54. Stubbornness
    64. Impracticality
CC. *Lack of Family Cohesiveness*
    4. Enuresis in Early Childhood
    9. Genital Underdevelopment
    59. Sensuousness

PARENTAL CONCERN

BB. *Meager Recreational Facilities for Boy in Home*
    11. Low Verbal Intelligence
    33. Poor Surface Contact with Others
    43. Absence of Masochistic Trends
    50. Preponderance of Introversive Trends
AA. *Parents Indifferent or Inhospitable to Boy's Companions*
    11. Low Verbal Intelligence
    43. Absence of Masochistic Trends
    62. Lack of Self-Criticism
    67. Psychopathy
Z. *Lack of Family Group Recreations*
    11. Low Verbal Intelligence
Y. *Unsuitable Supervision of Boy by Mother*
    40. Feeling of Being Able to Manage Own Life
    43. Absence of Masochistic Trends
LL. *Poor Discipline of Boy by Mother*
    19. Unmethodical Approach to Problems
    21. Social Assertiveness
    23. Nonsubmissiveness to Authority
    29. Absence of Feeling of Helplessness
    31. Absence of Fear of Failure and Defeat
    43. Absence of Masochistic Trends
    56. Uninhibited Motor Responses to Stimuli
    61. Unconventionality
OO. *Physical Punishment of Boy by Mother*
PP. *Threatening or Scolding of Boy by Mother*
    4. Enuresis in Early Childhood
KK. *Poor Discipline of Boy by Father*
    12. High Performance Intelligence
    50. Preponderance of Introversive Trends
MM. *Physical Punishment of Boy by Father*
    39. Lack of Dependence on Others
    42. Receptive Trends
NN. *Threatening or Scolding of Boy by Father*
    56. Uninhibited Motor Responses to Stimuli

SUMMARY BY TRAITS

Before we turn in the next chapter to a consideration of some implications of the findings for the management of juvenile delinquency,

it will be helpful to summarize the findings *trait by trait* in accordance with the origin of each as assigned in Chapter VIII: *Constitutional, Probably Constitutional, Constitutional and Socially Conditioned* and *Socially Conditioned*. A recapitulation of the classification of traits at which we arrived for the purpose of the inquiry may at this point be helpful.

(1) *Constitutional* traits are those which were found in *Physique and Delinquency* to vary in incidence among the body types but not found in the present inquiry to be associated with any, or at most related to only one (very occasionally to two) of the 44 social factors of family environment in a way suggesting a contribution of the factor to the development of the trait.

(2) *Probably Constitutional* traits are those which, although *not* found in *Physique and Delinquency* to vary in incidence among the body types, have also not been found to be related to any social factors or related at most to only one (an association which may have occurred by chance).

It is reasonable to conclude that both these groups of traits are closer to the constitutional than to the conditioned zone of our postulated biosocial continuum.

(3) Traits which are designated as both *Constitutional and Socially Conditioned* are those which were found in *Physique and Delinquency* to vary in incidence among the body types but which in the present study have been found to be related to three or more social factors in a way suggesting a probable influence of the factors on the development of the traits. Such traits are placed in a position toward the center of our postulated biosocial continuum.

(4) The traits which we have designated as *Socially Conditioned* are those which were not found in *Physique and Delinquency* to vary in incidence among the body types[1] but are seen in the present study to be related to three or more social factors.

There is a final group of six traits the orientations of which are *unclear*, making it impossible to assign them to one or another of the above four categories.

In Exhibit XIV-2 are listed, beneath each trait, the inimical factors of the family environment, found in the analyses in Chapters X–XIII to act selectively on the delinquency of children with the given trait. It will be noted that in some instances not one of the 44 social factors was found to operate on delinquency through the

[1] We recognize that there are certain traits or characteristics of genetic origin (such as eye color) which have no greater incidence in one body type than in another; but in respect to the largely psychologic traits of the present study it is reasonable to assume that a significant variation in incidence among the physique types is highly suggestive of constitutional orientation.

intermediary of any of the 66 traits encompassed in the present work. Among such traits are a few which are no more characteristic of delinquents than of nondelinquents (*cyanosis, tremors, sensitivity, irregular reflexes, originality, banality*); and with these we need have no further concern.

EXHIBIT XIV–2. TRAITS *ENHANCING* THE DELINQUENCY POTENTIAL OF BOYS REARED IN DELINQUENCY-RELATED ENVIRONMENTAL CIRCUMSTANCES

I. CONSTITUTIONAL TRAITS

  9. *Genital Underdevelopment**
      R.　Lack of Cultural Refinement in Home
      CC.　Lack of Family Cohesiveness
  10. *Strength of Hand Grip*
  21. *Social Assertiveness*
      LL.　Lax/Erratic Discipline of Boy by Mother
  23. *Nonsubmissiveness to Authority*
      LL.　Lax/Overstrict/Erratic Discipline of Boy by Mother
  31. *Absence of Fear of Failure and Defeat*
      GG.　Rearing by Parent Substitutes
      LL.　Lax/Erratic Discipline of Boy by Mother
  47. *Vivacity*
      K. Emotional Disturbance of Mother
  57. *Emotional Instability*
  58. *Lack of Aestheticism*
  59. *Sensuousness*
      L.　Serious Physical Ailment of Father
      R.　Lack of Cultural Refinement in Home
      CC.　Lack of Family Cohesiveness
  65. *Emotional Conflicts*
      B.　Crowded Home
      X.　Mother Occasionally Employed Outside Home

II. PROBABLY CONSTITUTIONAL TRAITS

  1. *Poor Health in Infancy*
  4. *Enuresis in Early Childhood*
      C.　Unclean and Disorderly Home
      P.　Poor Management of Family Income
      CC.　Lack of Family Cohesiveness
      PP.　Threatening or Scolding of Boy by Mother
  7. *Absence of Dermographia*
      Q.　Careless Household Routine
  16. *Intuition**
      I.　Alcoholism of Mother

142

19. *Unmethodical Approach to Problems*
    R.   Lack of Cultural Refinement in Home
    LL. Overstrict Discipline of Boy by Mother
20. *Lack of Potential Capacity for Objective Interests*
    HH. Indifference or Hostility of Father to Boy
22. *Defiance*
24. *Ambivalence to Authority*
    M.   Serious Physical Ailment of Mother
33. *Poor Surface Contact with Others*
    B.   Crowded Home
    F.   Delinquency of Father
    U.   Poor Conduct Standards of Family
    BB. Meager Recreational Facilities for Boy in Home
    RR. Indifference or Hostility of Boy to Father
45. *Emotional Lability*
    B.   Crowded Home
    K.   Emotional Disturbance of Mother
    X.   Mother Occasionally Employed Outside Home
    EE. Rearing in Broken Home
    HH. Indifference or Hostility of Father to Boy
46. *Lack of Self-Control*
54. *Stubbornness*
    DD. Middle Child in Family
    JJ. Indifference or Hostility of Siblings to Boy
    SS. Unacceptability of Father to Boy for Emulation
55. *Adventurousness*
67. *Psychopathy*
    Q.   Careless Household Routine
    AA. Parents Indifferent to Boy's Companions
    GG. Rearing by Parent Substitutes
    HH. Indifference or Hostility of Father to Boy

III. CONSTITUTIONAL AND SOCIALLY CONDITIONED TRAITS

    17. *Tendency to Phantasy*
        G.   Delinquency of Mother
    36. *Destructiveness*
        GG. Rearing by Parent Substitutes
    39. *Lack of Dependence on Others*
        MM. Physical Punishment of Boy by Father
    43. *Absence of Masochistic Trends*
        P.   Poor Management of Family Income
        Y.   Fair Supervision of Boy by Mother
        AA. Parents Indifferent to Boy's Companions
        BB. Meager Recreational Facilities for Boy in Home
        LL. Lax/Overstrict/Erratic Discipline of Boy by Mother
    44. *Destructive-Sadistic Trends*

53. *Feeling of Inadequacy*
    J.   Emotional Disturbance of Father
    EE. Rearing of Broken Home
56. *Uninhibited Motor Responses to Stimuli*
    LL. Lax Discipline of Boy by Mother
    SS. Unacceptability of Father to Boy for Emulation
60. *Acquisitiveness*
    SS. Unacceptability of Father to Boy for Emulation
61. *Unconventionality*
    M.   Serious Physical Ailment of Mother
    FF. Boy less than Five Years of Age at First Breach in Family Life
    LL. Lax Discipline of Boy by Mother
64. *Impracticality*
    JJ. Indifference or Hostility of Siblings to Boy

IV. SOCIALLY CONDITIONED TRAITS

11. *Low Verbal Intelligence*
    N.   Financial Dependence of Family
    P.   Poor Management of Family Income
    Q.   Careless Household Routine
    T.   Lack of Family Ambition
    Z.   Lack of Family Group Recreations
    AA. Parents Inhospitable or Indifferent to Boy's Companions
    BB. Meager Recreational Facilities for Boy in Home
    HH. Indifference or Hostility of Father to Boy
12. *High Performance Intelligence**
    KK. Lax/Overstrict/Erratic Discipline of Boy by Father
15. *Poor Power of Observation*
    GG. Rearing by Parent Substitutes
18. *Lack of Common Sense*
    DD. Middle Child in Family
25. *Absence of Enhanced Feeling of Insecurity*
26. *Marked Feeling of Not Being Wanted or Loved*
27. *Feeling of Not Being Taken Care Of**
    DD. Middle Child in Family
28. *Absence of Marked Feeling of Not Being Taken Seriously*
    K.   Emotional Disturbance of Mother
29. *Absence of Feeling of Helplessness*
    LL. Lax/Overstrict/Erratic Discipline of Boy by Mother
32. *Feeling of Resentment*
34. *Hostility*
35. *Marked Suspiciousness*
37. *Feeling of Isolation*
    H.   Alcoholism of Father
    DD. Middle Child in Family

RR. Indifference or Hostility of Boy to Father
40. *Feeling of Being Able to Manage Own Life*
    K.   Emotional Disturbance of Mother
    Y.   Unsuitable Supervision of Boy by Mother
42. *Receptive Trends*
    F.   Delinquency of Father
    G.   Delinquency of Mother
    MM. Physical Punishment of Boy by Father
48. *Absence of Compulsory Trends*
49. *Preponderance of Extroversive Trends*
    K.   Emotional Disturbance of Mother
    HH. Indifference or Hostility of Father to Boy
50. *Preponderance of Introversive Trends**
    H.   Alcoholism of Father
    BB. Meager Recreational Facilities for Boy in Home
    KK. Lax Discipline of Boy by Father
62. *Lack of Self-Criticism*
    AA. Parents Inhospitable to Boy's Companions
63. *Lack of Conscientiousness*
66. *Absence of Neuroticism*

V. Traits Not Clearly Constitutional or Socially Conditioned

  3. *Extreme Restlessness in Early Childhood*
    V.   Broken Relationship between Parents
    II.   Indifference or Hostility of Mother to Boy
30. *Feeling of Not Being Appreciated*
    F.   Delinquency of Father
    H.   Alcoholism of Father
    N.   Financial Dependence of Family
38. *Defensive Attitude*
41. *Narcissistic Trends*
    DD. Middle Child in Family
52. *Suggestibility*

---

* These traits were not found to be delinquency-related in *Unraveling Juvenile Delinquency*.

As regards some traits in Exhibit XIV–2 (*poor health in infancy, defiance, lack of self-control, adventurousness, emotional instability, lack of aestheticism, defensive attitude, suggestibility, strength of hand grip, destructive-sadistic trends, feeling of resentment, hostility, marked suspiciousness, absence of compulsory trends, lack of conscientiousness, absence of neuroticism, marked feeling of not being wanted or loved*) as to which no relationship was found to any of the 44 social influences encompassed in this study, it can not be said with assurance that some or all of them act *directly* on a child's involvement in delinquent behavior independently of the influence of some aspects of the *family environment* embraced in this study. However, there appears to be a reasonable likelihood that children with such characteristics more readily fall prey to adverse school, neighborhood and community influences, even though the home atmosphere may not in itself be delinquency-inducing.

PHYSIQUE TYPE, FAMILY ENVIRONMENT, TRAITS AND
DELINQUENCY

There is one further dimension in our analysis of the selective influence of the home environment on the delinquency potential of children with certain traits, and this has to do with the differential impact of specific *factor-trait* combinations on the delinquency of children of the various physique types.

In Chapters VI and VII, where attention was on the home influences contributing to the development of those traits which had been found in *Physique and Delinquency* to vary in incidence among the body types, we gave consideration to the selective impact of certain factors of family environment on trait formation among boys of the different body types.

However, in the discussion in Chapters X–XIII, where the focus is on the impact of the family environment on the delinquency of children possessing certain characteristics, we did not refer to the influence of factor-trait combinations on boys of different body types, in order not to complicate further an already complex presentation. We do, however, provide in Appendix G the detailed findings regarding factors, traits, body build and delinquency. The first column in these tables duplicates the findings in *Physique and Delinquency* regarding the differential impact of a *trait* (not trait-and-factor) on the delinquency of the body types. Next to these are the new findings concerning the selective impact of the trait *plus* factor on the delinquency of the body types.

In Exhibit XIV–3 below, we now draw together the findings regarding the selective influence of the factor-trait combinations on boys of differing body structure (the body types on whom the greater impact occurs are italicized). Their significance for the management of juvenile delinquency is illustrated in Chapter XV; but attention might be drawn to one or two indications of the meaning of the findings. For example, in general, and irrespective of physique type, boys who have a *feeling of not being appreciated* and who at the same time have a father who is himself criminalistic are more

146

ikely to become delinquents than are boys with this characteristic whose father is noncriminalistic. Adding the new dimension
of physique type, it is found that the *combined circumstances* of a
criminalistic father and the feeling on the part of a son that he is
not being appreciated exert a *greater* delinquency-inducing influence
on boys of *mesomorphic* physique (*i.e.*, sturdy, muscular) than on boys
of balanced type (*i.e.*, with equal components in the body structure
of mesomorphy, ectomorphy and endomorphy). Similarly, among
boys with *receptive trends* who are the sons of criminalistic fathers,
mesomorphs, endomorphs and *ectomorphs* are more likely to become
delinquent than are boys of balanced physique.[1]

EXHIBIT XIV–3. FACTORS OPERATING *SELECTIVELY* ON THE
DELINQUENCY OF BOYS OF DIFFERENT PHYSIQUE TYPES

. CONSTITUTIONAL TRAITS

21. Social Assertiveness
    LL. Lax/Erratic Discipline of Boy by Mother (*Meso./Endo.* vs.
        Ecto.)
23. Nonsubmissiveness to Authority
    LL. Lax/Overstrict/Erratic Discipline of Boy by Mother (*Endo.*
        vs. Meso./Ecto.)
59. Sensuousness
    L. Serious Physical Ailment of Father (*Bal.* vs. Ecto.)
    R. Lack of Cultural Refinement in Home (*Bal.* vs. Ecto.)
    CC. Lack of Family Cohesiveness (*Bal.* vs. Ecto.)

I. PROBABLY CONSTITUTIONAL TRAITS

  4. Enuresis in Early Childhood
    C. Unclean and Disorderly Home (*Ecto./Bal.* vs. Meso.)
  7. Absence of Dermographia
    Q. Careless Household Routine (*Meso.* vs. Ecto.)
19. Unmethodical Approach to Problems
    LL. Overstrict Discipline of Boy by Mother (*Meso./Endo./Bal.* vs.
        Ecto.)
24. Ambivalence to Authority
    M. Serious Physical Ailment of Mother (*Endo./Bal.* vs. Meso.)
33. Poor Surface Contact with Others
    B. Crowded Home (*Meso./Endo.* vs. Bal.)
    U. Poor Conduct Standards of Family (*Ecto.* vs. Endo./Bal.)
    RR. Indifference or Hostility of Boy to Father (*Ecto.* vs. Endo.)
45. Emotional Lability
    EE. Rearing in Broken Home (*Meso.* vs. Bal.)

[1] For details of the findings summarized in Exhibit XIV-3, see Appendix G where
the appropriate tables are presented in accordance with the trait numbers (in the above
instance, numbers 30 and 42).

III. Constitutional and Socially Conditioned Traits

17. Tendency to Phantasy
    G. Delinquency of Mother (*Meso.* vs. Bal.)
43. Absence of Masochistic Trends
    AA. Parents Indifferent to Boy's Companions (*Meso./Endo./Ecto.* vs. Bal.)
53. Feeling of Inadequacy
    EE. Rearing in Broken Home (*Meso.* vs. Ecto.)

IV. Socially Conditioned Traits

11. Low Verbal Intelligence
    Q. Careless Household Routine (*Meso.* vs. Ecto.)
    T. Lack of Family Ambition (*Meso.* vs. Ecto.)
    AA. Parents Inhospitable or Indifferent to Boy's Companions (*Meso.* vs. Ecto.)
    HH. Indifference or Hostility of Father to Boy (*Meso.* vs. Ecto.)
25. Absence of Enhanced Feeling of Insecurity
    DD. Only Child in Family (*Endo./Ecto.* vs. Bal.)
27. Feeling of Not Being Taken Care Of
    DD. Middle/Firstborn/Youngest Child in Family (*Meso.* vs. Endo./Bal.)
29. Absence of Feeling of Helplessness
    DD. Only Child in Family (*Endo.* vs. Meso.)
42. Receptive Trends
    F. Delinquency of Father (*Meso./Endo./Ecto.* vs. Bal.)
    G. Delinquency of Mother (*Meso.* vs. Bal.)
49. Preponderance of Extroversive Trends
    K. Emotional Disturbance of Mother (*Meso.* vs. Ecto.)

V. Traits Not Clearly Constitutional or Socially Conditioned

30. Feeling of Not Being Appreciated
    F. Delinquency of Father (*Meso.* vs. Bal.)
    N. Financial Dependence of Family (*Meso.* vs. Endo.)

A further illustration of the selective impact of social factors on boys of different body builds who are characterized by certain *traits* may be clarifying. A boy of *low verbal intelligence* reared in a home in which the daily routines are haphazard, in which the family lacks ambition to improve its status, in which the parents are inhospitable or indifferent to the child's friends, and/or in which the father is indifferent or actually hostile to the boy, is more likely to become delinquent than a boy of low verbal intelligence reared in less inimical circumstances.

Considering, now, the differential impact of these influences on boys of the four body types (see Appendix Table G-11), it becomes evident that *mesomorphs* of low verbal intelligence if reared in one or another of the inimical home surroundings set out above are

148

even *more likely* to become delinquent than are ectomorphs (the thin, linear, fragile type) from such environments. To understand the reason for this selective reaction it is necessary to re-examine the findings initially made in *Physique and Delinquency* regarding the traits that are characteristic of boys of each of the four physique types.[1]

The summary of the findings of Part II of this inquiry dealing with family environment and delinquency is now completed. The findings of Part I, regarding the origin of traits, were summarized in Chapter VIII.

As a result of our analysis, we see the need for further exploration into the role of family environment in the etiology of delinquency, particularly in the direction of inductively, but rationally, guided *clusterings* of the factors and traits that have individually emerged as of significance in what is as yet largely a particularistic analysis.

Like other research criminologists, we are seeking not only the Great Divide between delinquents and nondelinquents but also a *typology* of delinquents emerging from an inductively-arrived-at base. *Unraveling Juvenile Delinquency, Physique and Delinquency* and the present study provide us with many findings and many clues which must be pursued farther. This is an exciting quest; but it must be reserved for later exploration.

Meanwhile we turn to some implications of the findings of the current investigation for the management of delinquency.

[1] See Chapter XI, Mesomorphs and Delinquency; Chapter XII, Endomorphs and Delinquency; Chapter XIII, Ectomorphs and Delinquency; Chapter XIV, Balanced Type and Delinquency; especially the sections in these chapters in which the traits that are characteristic of each body type are contrasted with those distinguishing every other physique type.

CONCLUSION

XV

SOME IMPLICATIONS OF THE FINDINGS FOR MANAGEMENT OF DELINQUENCY

INTRODUCTION

ʙᴇꜰᴏʀᴇ making some suggestions for the practical application of the results of the present work, a few words are in order regarding the development of our thinking in respect to etiology in delinquency.

In *Unraveling Juvenile Delinquency* we tested a number of prevailing views regarding the origins of delinquency by the familiar scientific method of comparing samples of delinquents and nondelinquents in respect to numerous traits and factors derived from anthropologic, psychiatric, psychologic and social investigation. By this method we discovered certain fundamental differences between the two groups, including the fact that among the delinquents there was a significant excess of boys of mesomorphic constitution and a significant deficiency of boys of ectomorphic body build. This raised a causal hypothesis which we explored in *Physique and Delinquency*, with the resultant finding that certain traits associated with delinquency distinguish each of the four body types, while other traits appear to be involved in criminogenesis irrespective of physique.

But among the other original findings of *Unraveling Juvenile Delinquency* was that of a significant variation in the incidence of unwholesome aspects of home life, notably in respect to such factors as family cohesiveness, affectional relations of parents and child, supervision and discipline.

At first glance, the finding of extreme differences in somatotype incidence between delinquents and nondelinquents would appear to contradict the finding of a considerable involvement of family pathology in the etiology of delinquency. But the two insights are in fact not contradictory; for, as Dr. Bernard Glueck, Sr., has put the etiologic issue in a frequently noted formula, 'a factor, whether personal or situational, does not become a cause unless and until it first becomes a motive.' For example, not all mesomorphs become

153

delinquents; many become successful athletes, soldiers and business
men. It is in this connection that the *sociocultural* forces, especially
such under-the-roof influences as parental affection, supervision
discipline and family cohesiveness—all of which, in their unwhole
some aspects, markedly differentiate delinquents from nondelin
quents—come into play to determine the direction in which the
energy, drive, extroversiveness, adventurousness and other such traits
of mesomorphs are channeled.

In the present work we have taken two further steps: (*a*) to test the
reliability of the previous assignment of various criminogenic trait
to an essentially constitutional orientation by examining the relation
ship of sociocultural influences of home and family to the traits
and (*b*) to determine the media through which such influences exert
pressure toward delinquency.

The analysis in Chapters III–VIII deals with the participation o
family influences in the *formation of traits*. In Chapters X–XIII the
analysis is focused on the bearing of the complex materials of the
present work on the exceedingly difficult problem of *criminogenesis*
Certain fundamentals have emerged from this analysis of the in
volvement of constitution, traits of character and personality, and
family influences in the etiology of delinquency.

First, while not denying that it is important that prophylactic and
treatment programs take account of the total person and the total
family (as well as the total community), there is strong evidence in
the foregoing analysis that it is also highly important, and much
more pointed, that those engaged in such endeavors fix their sights on
more specific targets in terms of criminogenic factors and traits. In
treating the child, in aiding the family, and in assessing the aims and
means of general prophylactic endeavor, a greater *specificity* o
interest and action becomes possible on the evidence in the presen
study.

Second, it has been established that certain inimical family in
fluences during the first few years of life can affect the development
of delinquency in one or more of *three ways*.

(*a*) Some sociocultural factors contribute to the formation of traits
which, in *Unraveling Juvenile Delinquency*, were shown to be signi
ficantly associated with antisocial behavioral tendencies in children

(*b*) Certain malign social influences operate to render criminogeni
some traits which are normally neutral.

(*c*) Still other sociocultural factors operate within the total complex
of criminogenic forces quite apart from the influence of the variou
delinquency-linked physiologic, neurologic or psychologic trait
encompassed in this inquiry.

154

Some Implications of the Findings

A third general finding of the analysis is that the influences of the home environment, even when they are criminogenic, operate *selectively* to propel toward maladjustment and delinquency certain children who are characterized by specific traits which enhance their vulnerability. Some of these traits are of an essentially constitutional orientation and are therefore relatively rigid; others are predominantly the product of sociocultural conditioning and are therefore more plastic and modifiable; still others—those for which evidence exists that they are brought about by the considerable influence of both genetic endowment and environmental stimulation—have been referred to the central area of our postulated biosocial continuum and may, in some measure, respond to re-education. Individuals differ in the degree of permeability or affinity to the elements in the social and cultural milieu in which they find themselves and to which they are subjected. It is the *concatenation* in the particular individual of factor-trait interpenetrations of these influences from divergent sources that determines whether, at a certain point of pressure, resistance to antisocial self-expression will break down.

In other words, it is differential *contamination*, rather than differential *association*, that is at the core of the etiologic process; and contamination depends not merely on exposure but also on susceptibility as opposed to immunity.

The focusing of attention in the present volume on family influences should not obscure the biological involvements; and, from the sociologic point of view, the emphasis in this work on factors in the home does not imply that the pressures of the neighborhood, community and more general sociocultural forces are not also involved in criminogenesis. For example, we are not unaware of the probability that despite the original matching of our delinquents and non-delinquents in terms of residence in underprivileged urban regions (as well as by age, global intelligence and ethnic origin), economic deprivation weighs more heavily on the families and homes of most of the delinquents than on those of the nondelinquents. We are aware, also, that such potentially dangerous situations as are involved in problems of physical and mental ill health, or inadequate child care and discipline, or those stemming from a mother working outside the home (especially in cases where her motivation springs from a wish to escape the responsibilities of home-making and child-rearing[1]) involve not merely the family's internal life but also more general external influences over which its members may have little control. But unless it be assumed that the great majority of the families from

[1] See S. and E. T. Glueck, 'Working Mothers and Delinquency,' *Mental Hygiene*, Vol. 41, No. 3, July 1957.

which delinquents come are the victims of 'bad luck' and the great majority of the families of nondelinquents are the special 'favorites of fortune,' we must attribute the behavioral variations between delinquents and controls to demonstrated differences in the makeup and early home conditions of the two groups.

The need for improvement of family life is clear; and about this something can be done. However, to the extent that the general malaise of the times, the pervasive cultural changes, and the growing disharmonies and threats to our civilization may be implicated in the ultimate etiologic background of antisocial behavior, it must be recognized that a wide-ranging, permeative network of forces is involved which can be managed only by society as a whole and through a general economic, social and political policy, the aims and the methods of which are by no means clear.

As researchers close to this problem, the deeper we penetrate the jungle of that form of maladjustment called juvenile delinquency, the more are we convinced of the essential correctness of a view we have already expressed elsewhere:

> . . . In the ultimate analysis, prevention of delinquent careers, as our findings suggest, is also dependent upon something more specific than the manipulation of the general environment. It entails the structuring of integrated personality and wholesome character during the first few formative years of life; and this, fortunately, is accomplished largely in the home. Although basic modifications of the general system of habits and values that permeate our culture are bound to be slow, we can take advantage of the oft-neglected fact that parents are to a great extent not only the bearers, but also the *selective filters*, of the general culture.[1] The same is true of schoolteachers, with whom children spend much of their time during the most impressionable and formative stages of life. Thus, there is both realism and promise in taking more direct and specific steps to improve the *under-the-roof culture* in home and school.[2]

Readers of some of our prior works may recall that we have long sought to define the targets of prophylactic-therapeutic activity in ever more specific terms. For example, in *Delinquents in the Making*[3] we discussed the practical implications of the anthropologic, psychiatric, psychologic and social indications of *Unraveling Juvenile Delinquency* in the following areas: (*a*) traits and characteristics of the delinquent himself; (*b*) family life; (*c*) the school; and (*d*) use

[1] For the selective response to culture, see S. Glueck, 'Ten Years of Unraveling Juvenile Delinquency, An Examination of Criticisms,' 51, *Journal of Criminal Law, Criminology and Police Science*, 1960, pp. 283–308.

[2] S. and E. T. Glueck, *Delinquents in the Making*, New York, Harper & Brothers, 1952, p. 192.

[3] *Op. cit.*

of leisure. And in *Physique and Delinquency*[1] we explored the relevance of variations in body build for preventive and therapeutic effort, by first summarizing the outstanding characteristics of the four physique types:

> *Mesomorphs* (the bone and muscle physique) present a portrait of an essentially sturdy physical and nervous and emotional structure, with a tendency to express impulse in action.
> *Endomorphs* (the soft, round physique) are less sturdy, less energetic, and less dynamic than the mesomorphs, and are more inhibited and conventional in their ideas and behavior.
> *Ectomorphs* (linear, fragile body type) have less sturdiness and are more delicately organized than mesomorphs and present a more sensitive and aesthetic exterior to the world. They are more tense, inhibited, and conflict-ridden, bottling up their impulses and their destructive-sadistic trends.
> The only trait found to distinguish boys of *balanced* physique from all the others is that they are less fearful of failure and defeat. Otherwise, a clear picture does not emerge. They appear to have some characteristics of each physique.[2]

In arriving at these rough sketches of the physique types, we realized that before they could be made more clear, we would have to take into account the role of various elements of *environmental conditioning* in the formation of the characteristic traits of each of the four body types. This would not only confirm or modify the original findings of the constitutional orientation of many traits, but would also reveal the contributory sociocultural influences and throw some light on the question of which criminogenic characteristics are probably modifiable through reconditioning. This would, in turn, influence preventive and therapeutic action, since traits now confirmed as essentially constitutional, and therefore not subject to much modification, would have to be dealt with by directing their possessors into relatively harmless behavioral outlets; while traits having strong environmental components could be systematically approached through such reconditioning techniques as re-education, various forms of individual and group psychotherapy, social case work, religious and ethical teaching and example. With the important added dimension of *sociocultural conditioning* of traits, it now

[1] New York, Harper & Brothers, 1956.
[2] *Ibid.*, p. 251. It might be noted that the balanced type, placed in this category by the physical anthropologists on the basis of anthropometry and trained judgment proved (as a result of *later* correlational analysis of physique types and traits) to have characteristics of each of the other physiques, the traits having been determined by psychologists and a psychiatrist through independent analyses.

becomes possible to suggest more specific targets of preventive and therapeutic effort.

It must always be borne in mind, however, that it is the *total personality* that is involved in behavior; not independent, dissociated fragments or traits. And it is the family *as a whole* that is involved in the most important area of environmental influence, the home—not merely a factor such as a broken home, or lack of affection of a mother for her child, or unsuitability of a father as a pattern for emulation by the son. Yet, despite the interrelationships between the constituents of personality and character, and despite the fact that home and family comprise a more or less unified matrix of influence, it is helpful to disentangle some of the major strands to enable the therapist to note the effect on the total pathologic situation of modifying or redirecting some of its constituent elements.

Without repeating what we have said elsewhere about the role of psychiatrists, social workers, group therapists, educators, clergy and others in preventive and therapeutic effort,[1] we deem it helpful to suggest the relevance for the management of delinquency of the findings of the current inquiry, drawing our illustration from the area of *father-son* interpersonal relations.

ILLUSTRATION OF PRACTICAL APPLICABILITY OF FINDINGS

Under the influence of clinical psychiatry it is generally considered that, until about the age of three, a boy concentrates his affective attention on the mother, the objective figure who feeds, protects and comforts him. After that, however, he tries to imitate his father's most striking characteristics (especially those implying strength) though not without some jealousy of the father's obviously favored role *vis-à-vis* the mother.

As shown by the experience of clinicians and social workers, a warm relationship between father and son is of crucial significance in helping a boy to develop a wholesome set of ideals (assuming the father himself has such a set of ideals), largely through emotional and intellectual *identification* with the father. Should this affective bond not be close because of the sordid or tragic realities of, for example, the father's criminalism, alcoholism or mental illness, the child will be crippled in his character development and may seek substitute satisfactions of an antisocial nature in companionship with delinquents; or he may pass through stages of insecurity, frustration, resentment and other forms of emotional tension, with

---

[1] *Delinquents in the Making, op. cit.*, pp. 195–210; *Physique and Delinquency, op. cit.*, pp. 252–63.

resultant psychoneurotic symptoms. In brief, the process of identification of the growing boy with his father (or father, substitute), whom he consciously and unconsciously tries to emulate, is of prime importance in the moulding of personality and character.[1]

While not attempting to relate disturbances in the 'identification' process directly to delinquency, there are indications in this study that different aspects of a malign father-son association are involved, in varying degrees of directness and in varied influence, on particular physique types.

Let us consider some traits linked to certain aspects of the father-son relationship which have been found to exert an influence on delinquency. First, it should be recalled that a significantly higher proportion of boys to whom the *father was unacceptable as a pattern for emulation* had, in *Unraveling Juvenile Delinquency*, been found among delinquents than among their nondelinquent counterparts. In the present work it is shown that the impact of this emotional deprivation, on which so much of the building of character depends, is heavier among boys who are characterized by the traits of *stubbornness*, and/or *uninhibited motor responses to stimuli* and/or *acquisitiveness*.

The obvious remedial approach is of course to provide a substitute adult model with whom a boy can identify, such as a teacher, Boy Scout leader, Big Brother, clergyman, athletic director. Such a person would be in a better position to deal effectively with a boy if he knew something of his traits and their probable orientation. For instance, it would be useful to know that one of the delinquency-linked traits, *stubbornness*, does *not* vary among boys of the different body builds; so that whether a boy is mesomorphic, at one extreme, or ectomorphic, at the other, makes little difference. But it would also be useful for the parent substitute to know, for example, that while a father's unacceptability as a pattern for emulation does not in itself contribute to the formation of the criminogenic trait of stubbornness in his son, its presence does enhance the boy's delinquency *potential*. It would also be useful to know that stubbornness is *probably constitutional* in orientation although not varying in incidence among the body types. This knowledge would preclude any head-on attempt to modify the trait but would, rather, suggest the need of guiding a stubborn boy into socially acceptable expressions of this characteristic.

Another trait that a father-substitute would have to take into account, for example, is the *tendency to uninhibited motor responses to*

---

[1] There are, of course, various additional influences of both a conscious and subconscious nature involved in father-son relationships.

stimuli. Here, too, it happens not to be a case of an element of social pathology contributing to the formation of a delinquency-linked trait, because the father's unacceptability for emulation has not been found to contribute to the formation of this tendency. But the fact that this trait, like stubbornness, is of constitutional orientation, should serve to encourage a father-substitute to guide his charge into socially acceptable uses of his tendency to uninhibited motor responses to stimuli.

A further illustration of how the findings of the present inquiry might guide preventive action is afforded by considering the influence of a *father's drunkenness* on a child's behavior. Although it has been found that paternal alcoholism does not, in general, have a greater impact on the delinquency of boys of one body build than on those of another, rearing by an alcoholic father is in several ways a malignant influence. First, it contributes to the development of certain traits which, in turn, are generally more common to delinquents than nondelinquents, such as *hostility* and *unconventionality*. Secondly, a father's chronic inebriety, if operative in the life of a boy possessing certain other traits (to the development of which a father's inebriety does not itself contribute)—*feeling of not being appreciated, feeling of isolation*—is now known to enhance the son's delinquency potential. It has also been learned that paternal drunkenness is likely to convert the trait of *introversiveness*, which normally is no more characteristic of delinquents than of nondelinquents, into one directed toward antisocial purposes.

What can a therapist do about a situation in which either a pre-delinquent or delinquent boy lives in a home with an alcoholic father? The problem is especially complex, because such a parent can, in his sober interludes, be a loving and loved father. However, whether or not the child is to remain at home, his character can be influenced, as part of a total preventive or therapeutic strategy, by counteracting or redirecting the traits involved that have been shown to be related to delinquency. To do this, the therapist must diagnose the situation more penetratingly than has heretofore been possible. For example, of the delinquency-related traits mentioned in the foregoing paragraph, only *unconventionality* is probably referable to the central area of our postulated biosocial continuum because it is clearly and substantially influenced both genetically and environmentally. The fact that it is partly the product of several identified sociocultural influences would seem to make it susceptible of planful reconditioning. Such traits as *hostility*, *feeling of isolation* and *introversive trends* are probably modifiable by well-directed, patient and sympathetic effort on the part of a father-surrogate or other adult or youthful associate, and thereby give promise of minimizing the strength and valency[1] of the other elements of the total delinquency pattern as well.

One more illustration of the translation of the findings of this study into the management of delinquency—the effect on a boy of rearing by a *father who is seriously disturbed emotionally*. As was the case in regard to excessive alcoholism, emotional disturbance of the father (psychosis, psychopathy, psychoneuroticism, sexual abnormality, marked instability) was found in *Unraveling Juvenile Delinquency* to be much more frequent among fathers of delinquents than those of nondelinquents. In *Physique and Delinquency* some significant differences in the impact of rearing by an emotionally disturbed father on the delinquency of the son were noted: as might be expected, sensitive ectomorphic boys were found to be more generally affected than the more stolid muscular mesomorphs.

Examining the impact of a social factor on the relevant traits, it has been shown in the present work that rearing by an emotionally disturbed father tends to develop in a son certain characteristics which are themselves related to delinquent behavior: an inclination to escape reality through excessive flight into *phantasy, marked dependency attitudes, preponderance of introversive trends*. The first two traits have been found to distinguish delinquents from nondelinquents to a degree suggestive of their criminogenic involvement. The last, though normally neutral, becomes criminogenic in the presence of paternal emotional disturbance. In addition to these direct linkages of affective abnormality in the father with the dynamics of delinquency in the son, the chances that a boy possessing a *feeling of inadequacy* will become a delinquent are found to be enhanced if he lives in a home with an emotionally disturbed father.

How can these findings guide the therapist? For example, *excessive phantasying*, though discovered in *Physique and Delinquency* to vary among the body types (more prevalent among ectomorphs) and therefore deemed to be oriented constitutionally, is also influenced by four or more sociocultural factors. Thus, the therapist need not despair of being able, through motivated reconditioning, to reduce the marked inclination in a boy to escape into a make-believe world. Regarding the normally noncriminogenic tendency to *introversiveness*, this too (as pointed out in another connection above) can be counteracted by a sympathetic, yet well integrated, father-substitute; for although this trait is constitutional in orientation, there are strong elements of environmental conditioning in it. As for the *feeling of*

---

[1] In the sense of the degree of attractive power existing between the various traits and factors, inclining them to unite or produce a specific effect on one another.

inadequacy, in the presence of which a tendency to maladjustment is enhanced in the case of boys with an emotionally disturbed father, it too is susceptible of reconditioning.

These few illustrations of the implications of our findings for the management of delinquency with reference to father-son relationships are merely suggestive. The clinician, social worker and counsellor interested in predelinquent or delinquent boys should try to obtain information regarding the presence of various traits and sociocultural factors that have been found directly or indirectly relevant to criminogenesis. They are invited to consult Chapter VIII, Exhibits 1 through 12, in which are listed the sociocultural factors contributing to the formation of the various traits; Exhibit IX-1, in which are summarized the *delinquency-related* sociocultural factors that contribute to the formation of the criminogenic traits; Exhibit XIV-1, in which are listed the various *factors* that operate selectively on the delinquency of boys already possessing certain traits; Exhibit XIV-2, in which are indicated the *traits* (listed by their orientations) that enhance the delinquency potential of boys, under the impact of various sociocultural influences; and Exhibit XIV-3, which presents, under appropriate headings from the point of view of our postulated biosocial continuum, various factors in family life that act selectively on the delinquency of boys of different physique types.

It should be repeated that the foregoing illustrations regarding the implication of certain father-son relationships for the management of delinquency are, of course, not intended to imply that the worker in the preventive or therapeutic field can overlook the total complex of interactive relationships in which a child is nurtured; they suggest, rather, that definition of the *therapeutic targets in terms of factor–trait and physique–trait–factor relationships* adds to understanding by taking account of the trees as well as the forest of etiologic influence. If the therapist can keep in mind the specific personality and character traits with which he must deal, their variation among physique types, their relative fixity or plasticity, and their relationship to the more important factors of the *family–home matrix*, he will be more likely to influence entire areas or patterns of interrelated traits and factors which have proved to be, either directly or indirectly, criminogenic. Moreover, consideration of the findings of this inquiry should ever remind the prophylactic and therapeutic specialists of the *selectivity* of various environmental and cultural influences; of the fact that a boy possessing a syndrome of certain traits and reared in certain inimical conditions generates a tendency to 'kick over the traces'; while to a boy of another physique and character structure these very circumstances present a challenge to rise above the handicapping environment.

CONCLUSION

We have seen that there are many sociocultural aspects of family life that have a bearing on the propulsion of children in the direction of delinquency. But we trust that the few illustrations of their application in a more direct pinpointing of therapeutic effort will be sufficient to stir the imagination of ingenious therapists (whether they be psychiatrists, psychologists, educators, social workers, clergymen) to bring to bear on our findings their own experience in the management of children with severe behavioral aberrations.

Perhaps it will now be more clearly evident why present efforts to cope with delinquency have met with such little success. They have as a rule been neither pointed nor continuous enough to influence the criminogenic traits and their chief matrix in home and family. In the light of the present study, the problem of controlling delinquency may seem to many to be disappointingly complex. But nothing is gained by ignoring the difficulties involved; this will not cause them to disappear.

We should like to have presented the reader with a simple frame of reference that would neatly categorize the influences converging on the act of delinquency—constitutional, those of home and family life, those of the 'delinquency subculture' and those of the general culture. We doubt that such a neat packaging of a highly complex personal–situational phenomenon will ever be possible. But, as stated in the prior chapter, we plan, in a later volume, to make more penetrating and elaborate intercorrelations of the various aspects of our data.

Some readers will no doubt gain the impression that by demonstrating the probable origins of the various traits linked to delinquency, we have taken a 'too deterministic' attitude. We do not believe that by showing causal linkages in segments of human experience we are any more deterministic than is the physician or the researcher in the biologic disciplines. Determinism should not be confused with fatalism. Our view is that causal connections should be explored in those areas of human experience where this is possible. While the extent to which individuals possess the capacity for conscious purposive freedom of choice can not be measured, to some extent at least it is possible to analyze certain *interferences* with that capacity set up by the forces of Nature and Nurture.

And with regard to therapeutic and educative effort, we believe the only promise of even relative success in changing aberrant conduct is to remove as many as possible of the deterministic ashes of family and individual life that stifle the quantum of capacity for free choice with which the particular individual has been endowed by nature. By setting more acceptable social standards for him and helping to remove obstacles in his path to wholesome development, he will be the better able to exercise his particular gift of free-choosing capacity. This is in effect what the physician does when he tries to get at the roots of the particular illness presented by the patient. To the extent that he is able to intervene successfully in the relevant etiologic chain that leads from internal and external causes to symptoms, he is able to restore the patient to his particular limits of health and self-management.

We hope this study furnishes information of aid to doctors of family life and of individual character, in focusing attention on criminogenic traits in terms of their relative fixity or plasticity and their relationship to social factors. By planful choice of re-educative and psychotherapeutic measures in the light of such information, the possibility should be enhanced of changing the destination of many vulnerable youngsters.

It must be remembered that the various traits and factors found linked to delinquency do not always exist in an individual instance; the method we have pursued is the statistical path of probabilities, and this has shown that the influences in question are frequent enough to warrant their serious consideration in prevention and therapy.

It must also be borne in mind in this connection that some of the traits and factors we have called criminogenic because of their significantly higher incidence among delinquents than among non-delinquents are to be found, though far less frequently, among boys who do *not* become delinquent. Yet, as has been indicated, commonly and typically they are linked, on the one hand, to various expression of delinquent behavior and, on the other, to physique type and to deprivations of parental affection and care and other forms of familial unwholesomeness.

In the detailed analysis of traits and factors we trust we have sufficiently emphasized the fact that, just as the good physician does not consider his patient merely a heart, or a liver, or a stomach so the wise social- and psychotherapist does not consider his patient and his patient's family only as agglomerates of conditioned reflexes

We are also not unaware that some of the causes of antisocial behavior are deep-seated stirrings of an essentially subconscious

164

nature; but subconscious motivation is not the only kind. Motivation is a two-way channel; while much of it is the subconscious dynamism of previously repressed painful experiences, much of it begins at the conscious level and works downward. At all events, it is time that the therapeutic professions which are concerned with aberrant behavior in children undertake a many-sided attack on the family influences and character traits which have been shown in this research to be enmeshed in predelinquent and delinquent behavior.

A final word about a current of thought that has recently become prominent in the wake of the disappointing results of the clinical method of dealing with predelinquent and delinquent youngsters. There is a growing feeling among many worthy and intelligent citizens, including judges, that delinquency is largely 'lack of will power.' With respect, we submit that this attitude goes little beyond the discredited explanation that antisocial behavior is the product of the devil operating in the minds and hearts of persons particularly open to satanic enticements. This sort of explanation long held sway in the field of mental aberration; it simply does not explain.

On the other hand, etiologic study need not eliminate a recognition of the moral accountability of the individual offender to the extent that he could have chosen to behave otherwise, unmeasurable though this may be; nor need it nor should it eliminate the disciplined requirement of sincere effort, on the part of the delinquent under treatment, to 'mend his ways.'

The impatient attribution of most wrong-doing to failure of the offender to 'control his will' springs from an overemphasis and oversimplification of the human dilemma. There is much more profound wisdom, both from a scientific and humanitarian viewpoint, in the attitude of Victor Hugo's good Bishop in *Les Misèrables* who 'condemned nothing in haste and without taking circumstances into account. He said, "Examine the road over which the fault has passed." '

This is what we have attempted to do in this work.

APPENDIX A

CASE OF HENRY W

Prepared by George F. McGrath and Mildred P. Cunningham

(*Edited by Virginia Atchley*)

INTRODUCTORY NOTE

The case of Henry W, although prepared prior to the publication of *Unraveling Juvenile Delinquency* (New York, The Commonwealth Fund: 1950), is only now being published. The method of constructing the social histories of 500 delinquent boys and 500 nondelinquents, reported by us in *Unraveling Juvenile Delinquency*, is exemplified in the case of Henry W. Students of social research techniques will benefit from an examination of this case not only in conjunction with the present work but also with Chapter V of *Unraveling Juvenile Delinquency*, 'Exploring Family and Personal Background,' which describes the procedures utilized in the gathering and verification of the necessary data. Several field investigators and three different case collators, all of whom were subject to the same methodological instructions, participated at one stage or another in constructing the case histories of the 1,000 cases. This particular case was prepared by George F. McGrath (now Massachusetts Commissioner of Correction) and Mildred P. Cunningham. Mr. McGrath conducted the interview with Henry's mother and Mrs. Cunningham was responsible for gathering and verifying already-recorded sources of information. Names and places in the case history have been disguised as well as certain details of the family and personal background of the boy, in order to assure against identification. Each one of the 1,000 cases reported in *Unraveling Juvenile Delinquency* is the product of similarly intensive and thorough exploration.

Note: The following key to the abbreviations used in the Case History and in the tabular summary which follows it may be helpful: *BCW*, Boston Child Welfare Agency No. 1; *B. Hosp.*, Boston Hospital; *BSA*, Boston Social Agency No. 1; MH & H, Maternity Home and Hospital No. 1; *Bradwood CWA*, Child Welfare Agency; *Bradwood SA*, Social Agency; *BPD*, Boys' Parole Division; *BVS*, Bureau of Vital Statistics; *CPA*, Child Placing Agency No. 1; *DMH*, Dept. of Mental Health; *FM*, Feeble-Minded; *H of C*, House of Correction; *PO*, Probation Office; *RA*, Relief Agency No. 1; *SSI*, Social Service Index; *SH*, Settlement House.

CASE OF HENRY W

(Illustrating Method of Social Investigation)

Initial Consultation of Social Service Index

Henry was selected at a Correctional School in January 1941. The investigation was begun by securing from the school the boy's birthdate, names of parents and siblings, and their approximate birthdates and last address. It was learned that Henry had a stepfather and three half-brothers, and that his real father was a man about whom nothing was known, except that he was thought to have been a machinist named James S. J, who had never married the boy's mother.

With this meager identifying data, inquiry was made of the Social Service Index in Boston for contacts of the boy, his mother, and his stepfather with social welfare agencies, and for any data available on the maternal and paternal grandparents and their children. Attention was also drawn to Henry's alleged father in the hope that the Index could throw more light on the boy's paternity. Photostatic copies of the Index's file cards on several family members were soon received.

Appendix A

These revealed that Henry's mother, Rose P. W, and stepfather, Leo W, had been known to twenty agencies either before or after their marriage:

A Red Cross Agency, 10/22/19
A Red Cross Supervisors' Office, 1/5/21
A Welfare Committee for Men, 1/4/22
A U.S. Veterans' Clinic, 2/8/22
Mental Hospital No. 1, OPD, 3/2/22, 8/4/32 and 4/1/34
Social Service Department of Maternity Home and Hospital No. 1, 1/5/24
Social Service Department of a Boston Hospital, 1/6/26
Boston Social Agency No. 1, 5/27/26
A Vocational Aid Society, 6/18/26
Relief Agency No. 1, 10/15/27
Relief Agency No. 2, 7/1/28
Boston Child Welfare Agency No. 1, 7/13/28, 1/15/34 and 6/10/36
A Veterans' Agency, N. P. Section, 7/13/28
Relief Agency No. 3, 8/1/28
A Boston Health Agency, 9/16/28
A Church Relief Society, 10/28/28
Legal Assistance Bureau, 12/26/32
Child Placing Agency No. 1, 3/5/33
A Welfare Agency for Transients, 11/30/33
A State Child Placing Agency, 2/9/36

Addresses of the family in the years 1919, 1921, 1926, 1928, 1936, 1938, and 1940 were given, plus the information that the mother was born in 1906 in Everett, Mass., and worked in a factory; that the father (whom we knew to be the step-father) was born in 1890 and was a teamster; and that Henry's siblings (whom we knew to be half-siblings) were Arthur, born in 1927, Kenneth, born in 1934, and Charles, born in 1937. The name of James S. J, born in 1901, of Stoughton, Mass., was given as a reference, but there was no indication that he was Henry's father.

The maternal aunt, Florence P, was reported by the Index to be known to three agencies:

Girl Welfare Agency No. 1, 12/16/19
Boston Social Agency No. 1, 3/4/38
Relief Agency No. 1, 8/30/40

Addresses of the maternal aunt were also listed, and a comparison of these with the addresses of the boy's family indicated that the aunt frequently lived with them. In addition, it was learned that the aunt was born in Everett, Mass., in 1908, and was single.

The maternal grandparents were found to have been known to ten agencies:

Boston Child Welfare Agency No. 1, 6/5/10
A State School for Feeble-Minded, 12/28/18
Maternity Home and Hospital No. 2, 1/15/19
Child Placing Agency No. 2, foster home, 2/28/20
Relief Agency No. 1, 4/14/27 and 5/2/33
Veterans' Relief Agency No. 1, 2/5/28
Boston Social Agency No. 1, 10/26/30
Boston Social Agency No. 2, 7/10/33
Relief Agency No. 3, 9/17/33
Mental Hospital No. 1, 3/31/34

Case of Henry W

Addresses of the maternal grandparents between the years 1910 and 1934 were given, plus the information that the maternal grandmother was born in New Hampshire in 1879, the maternal grandfather in Connecticut in 1873, and that they had two children: Florence, born in 1908, and Rose (the mother of Henry), born in 1906.

The paternal step-grandparents and step-relatives were also shown to be known to several agencies, but as they were not Henry's blood relatives these data were not of interest to us.

A couple named Mr. and Mrs. W, cross-indexed with the boy's stepfather, was known to a number of agencies. The stepfather was listed as a reference, but no details were given. The contents of this card were regarded as probably irrelevant for the inquiry, but were kept available for possible use later.

Initial Clearance through the Massachusetts Board of Probation

The court records of Henry, his mother, stepfather, and older half-brother were secured by mail from the Massachusetts Board of Probation. (The court records of the two other half-siblings were not checked, as they were only about six and three years old, respectively.) Neither the mother nor the older half-brother, Arthur, had a court record; but a possible record of the stepfather was found, containing insufficient identifying data. Further investigation showed that this was not his record.

Henry himself had the following record:

2/9/36 Larceny, 2 counts, W District Court. Correctional School on each count, appealed. 4/11/36, C Superior Court, probation 2 years on each count.

9/28/36 Assault and battery, D District Court. Adjudged delinquent. Filed. 10/3/36, surrendered on probation of 4/11/36, C Superior Court. Committed to Correctional School. Paroled, 10/2/37; expiration of sentence, 1/16/46.

12/1/38 Breaking and entering nighttime, Y Court. Adjudged delinquent. Filed. Parole revoked, returned to Correctional School. Paroled, 12/28/39; expiration of sentence, 1/16/46.

8/18/40 Larceny, W District Court. Filed. 8/24/40, parole revoked, returned to Correctional School.

Home Interview

On 2/10/41, the home investigator went to 17 P Street, Dorchester, the home address for Henry's family given in the records at the Correctional School. Here the family interview was carried out with Henry's mother. It lasted about two hours, during which the investigator took no notes except for recording the boy's health history toward the close of the interview. The information obtained was recorded as follows:

(1) a running account of the interview was dictated; (2) data were entered in red ink on the social investigation schedule (to distinguish them from data obtained from other sources); and (3) a memorandum was prepared for the case collator indicating which factors needed to be verified, amplified or initially secured.

Following is the dictated report of the interview with the boy's mother.

In the late afternoon of 2/10/41, the home investigator called at 17 P Street, Dorchester. This address turned out to be an old wooden tenement house. The investigator did not know on which floor the family lived, and after trying all bells and getting no response, he went into the front hallway and knocked on

171

a door on the second floor. A woman, who proved to be the boy's mother, answered the door, and the investigator explained that he wished to talk with her about her son, Henry. Without any hesitation or questioning, she invited him into the home and preceded him through the length of the apartment to the kitchen in the rear. Coming into the kitchen, he observed that she was slicing apples for applesauce. Throughout the first part of the interview she continued her work, finally sitting down at the kitchen table when the sauce was on the stove. The interview was carried out in the kitchen and there were no interruptions or distractions.

In appearance the boy's mother is tall and strongly built, with a dark complexion and dark brown hair. Her hands showed no evidence of hard work and were well kept, with brightly polished nails. Her attitude was one of grudging cooperation. She volunteered little in the discussion and had to be questioned closely; though not unfriendly, she was more or less indifferent. The investigator got the impression that she is an 'old hand' at being interviewed by social workers and others and has cultivated an attitude of appearing to be cooperative but at the same time giving only the barest amount of information. He felt that her statements could not be accepted as completely reliable, as she resisted giving any information derogatory to the family.

In the course of the discussion, Mrs. W allowed the investigator to infer that her husband was Henry's father. After the investigator informed her that he knew Henry was adopted by her husband, she readily admitted that he was not the real father. Under questioning she stated that Henry's true father, Mr. J, was so adjudged in B District Court, and later in C Superior Court, and was ordered to pay $6.00 a week for the boy's support. This he did for two or three years through the Probation Office of the C Superior Court. Regular payments continued until Henry was about three years old, when his father made a settlement of $250 in a lump sum, and the case was closed. Mrs. W stated that this arrangement, which was entirely agreeable to her, was suggested by Mr. J because he was making plans to marry.

According to the mother, Henry's father had always been a resident of Randolph, Mass., and was employed there in a shoe factory. In discussing her association with him, she said that they 'kept company' for some time, although forbidden to do so by her father (no reason for this parental disapproval was proffered). Henry's father has not seen him and has taken no interest in him other than sending the financial support ordered by the Court. Mrs. W herself has not seen Mr. J since the court proceedings and has no idea where he is now living. He was an only child, four years older than herself, and came of 'nice people.' The paternal grandfather, when she knew him, had been injured and was unable to work. He got some sort of compensation at the time she kept company with Henry's father.

Mrs. W, first in a family of two children, was born in Everett, Mass., in 1906. Asked about her nationality, she said her parents were born in this country, one in New Hampshire and one in Connecticut. Leaving school in the eighth grade, she did factory work until her marriage to Mr. W.

Since her mother's death in 1932, her sister, Florence, who is a year and a half younger, has been living in the W household. Florence was described as being unable to work because she is an epileptic. Before coming to live with the W's, she had spent much time at the Q State Infirmary, the P State Hospital and a State School for the Feeble-Minded.

The investigator was unable to get a very clear picture of Henry's stepfather as Mrs. W obviously did not wish to talk about him. When they were first married, he was a factory worker; but after he lost his job, they were obliged to apply for relief. For nearly fourteen years, according to her, he has worked steadily for the X Public Utility Company as a laborer, earning almost $30 a week. She claims that during this period they have never received any public aid. (This seems doubtful in view of the information already received from the Social Service Index.) Mrs. W said that he was born in Jamaica Plain, Mass., but she constantly referred to Pennsylvania and Delaware, giving the impression that her husband spent most of his youth in these two states. When asked if this was true, however, she said that it was not, that he was brought up in Boston. He was aware of Henry's presence at the time of their marriage and shortly thereafter legally adopted him. Until recently, she said, her husband had been quite a heavy drinker who would 'drink anything,' but now contents himself with buying a small bottle of wine every pay day. He was never abusive, she said, to her or the children: 'I've got no kick coming. He's been a good provider.' This statement was made without a great deal of conviction, however, and the investigator got the impression that there is considerable friction in the home.

Mrs. W said that she had seen her father-in-law only a few times when he paid visits to her home; and she would say nothing about his personal or family history, or, as she called it, 'his personal affairs,' which she said she does not 'pry into.' When she last heard, he was living in Michigan. Her father-in-law owns his own business, she said, although she would not admit any knowledge of its nature or size.

All three of Henry's half-brothers are attending school and are living at home.

Henry's chief interests seem to have been in group athletics. He was a member of Settlement House No. 1, and, according to his mother, spent most of his leisure time there. His hobby has been making model airplanes and he hopes some day to become an airplane pilot. Toward that end he intends to complete a high school education and then make application to join the U.S. Army in the Air Corps section. Mrs. W visits Henry regularly at the Correctional School and is hopeful that he will be home before Easter time.

Most of the above information, as well as other specific data gathered in the home interview, was recorded in the social investigation schedule.

The investigator's memorandum to the case collator read as follows:

1. Obtain stepfather's court record at Board of Probation. The one sent to us previously is not that of stepfather. He probably has a long court record for drunkenness.

2. Get further identifying data on the boy's true father and clear through the Board of Probation for his court record.

3. What is true father's nationality or descent? Mother is 'Old American.'

4. Obtain true father's birthplace and date. Is he still living? Did he marry?

5. What is the religion of the boy and his parents? Interviewer did not get this information.

6. Correctional School records may be incomplete on the boy's half-brothers. Send requests for court records on any additional half-siblings. Stepfather seems to have been married previously. Were there any children of this marriage?

7. Mother says her sister has been in the Q State Infirmary, the P State Hospital, and a State School for the Feeble-Minded; and that she is an epileptic. Suggest this be verified.

8. Data concerning delinquency, alcoholism, mental dullness, mental disease,

and education of the boy's true father and his family largely unknown to the boy's mother.

9. Why was the boy first placed out in a foster home?

10. Was the boy's parole to the same foster home on his second as on his first parole from Correctional School?

11. Exact length of time the family has been living at the present address needs to be determined.

12. Health history is unreliable. Verify the boy's mild attack of epilepsy in 1928.

Verifying and Amplifying Data Obtained and Securing New Data

With the results of the home visit in hand, the case collator mapped out the next steps with a view to amplifying and verifying the data thus derived and securing additional information on Henry and his family. Many clues had already been provided by consulting the Massachusetts Board of Probation and the Social Service Index.

Boys' Parole Division. First, Henry's record at the Boys' Parole Division in Boston was consulted. A field investigator summarized the information in the boy's folder, omitting data previously obtained at the Correctional School. He found a copy of a home investigation report made by a parole agent following Henry's first commitment to the Correctional School in 1936. The address visited by the agent at this time was noted. (New addresses were constantly being discovered, so that by the time the field work was finished, a complete record had been obtained of all the addresses where Henry had lived from birth to the time he was taken on for study.) There was a report of another home visit in September 1938, when conditions were described as much better than before. However, on a later visit in December 1939, the agent stated that home conditions were not improved: 'The mother was still in bed near noon. She claimed to be sick but a plate of cigarette butts by her side shows she must be an excessive smoker.' (This statement tended to support the home visitor's observation that the household routine was not well planned.) As a result, the parole agent recommended foster home placement, but Henry was allowed to return home, and it was from home that he was sent back to the Correctional School for the term during which we examined him on 1/5/41. Henry was then in the graduating class at the F School and had expected to enter high school in the fall.

The Boys' Parole Division record also contained a statement from Mental Hospital No. 1 to the effect that Henry had no physical abnormalities; that blood tests for syphilis were negative; and that one of his lungs was weak. (The mother had told the home visitor that Henry had had pneumonia at three years of age and that one lung had been weak ever since.) The hospital psychiatrist added that he felt Henry's irregularities of behavior were probably the result of unhealthy family atmosphere or heredity.

While taking these notes, the field investigator copied the name, approximate birthdates and birthplaces of Henry's mother and stepfather; their address in August 1940; the names of their children; and so on. He noted that there was much less family information in the folder than was usually the case.

State Bureau of Vital Statistics. At this point the case collator felt it advisable to verify certain names, birthplaces, and so on, and to seek additional data. A field investigator therefore checked the birth of Henry's true father at the State Bureau of Vital Statistics. His approximate age and place of birth being already known, the record was readily found, and as there was only one of that name and ge, it was, without doubt, that of the father. He was born 5/16/01 in Spencer, Mass. The birth certificate provided the names and birthplaces of the paternal grandparents, and the information that the paternal grandfather was born in Norwell, Mass., and the paternal grandmother in Spencer. As it had already been determined that the maternal grandparents were native-born, and it was now confirmed that both the parents were native-born, the factor, dominant stock (#5 on the schedule), was established as Old American. This information answered in part questions 2, 3, and 4 of the home visitor's memorandum to the collator.

The birth of Henry himself was also verified. It was recorded under his mother's maiden name. Residence of mother was given as 12 A Street, Roxbury. (The mother had told the home visitor that she had been living at 120 A Street, Roxbury, with her parents at that time.) Such slight inaccuracies in a mother's statements were frequent throughout the study and usually indicated lapse of memory rather than any attempt to falsify.

Massachusetts Board of Probation. There was now enough identifying information for an investigator to obtain from the files of the Massachusetts Board of Probation the court record of Henry's true father and stepfather. Following is that of the true father:

> 10/3/24 Bastardy, B District Court. Adjudged father, appealed. 3/13/25, illegitimate child, C Superior Court. Probation two years.
> 2/30/26 Illegal parking, B District Court. $5.00 paid.
> 3/14/29 Nonsupport of child, H District Court. Probation, 7/10/29. Defaulted.

The Board of Probation also provided the additional information that in 1929, when last arrested, James S. J had a wife, Helen, and was living in Stoughton, Mass. All this information was now inserted under items previously recorded by the home investigator as *unknown*.

The court record of the stepfather included twenty arrests for drunkenness and one conviction for grand larceny. Two weeks before Henry was returned to the Correctional School on 7/3/40 (the particular term of confinement during which he was selected for inclusion in the study), his stepfather was surrendered on a suspended sentence and sent to the C House of Correction for one month. (This information was recorded in the schedule, not under factor #31, family background, as the stepfather was not a blood relative of the boy, but under factor #A17, moral standards of home, because the stepfather was living in the household of which Henry had been a part.)

Boston Social Service Index. Now that so much information on the true father had been secured, the Boston Social Service Index was again consulted concerning him and his wife, Helen. A photostatic copy of the Index card indicated that the couple was known to the Bradwood Social Service Index (3/8/33) and a Bradwood Child Welfare Agency (10/10/39); that they had a daughter, Anne, born in 1928; and were living in Bradwood in March 1933. This information added a new half-sister to the list. Attached to this photostat was a card on Henry, questioning his connection with the J family and indicating that he was known to Mental Hospital No. 1, as a house patient. It also gave Henry's addresses in 1935 and 1939.

Relief Agency. Reference to the data derived initially from the Social Service Index in Boston concerning Henry's mother and stepfather indicated that the agencies most likely to have the fullest records for our purposes were Relief Agency No. 1, Boston Child Welfare Agency No. 1, and Boston Social Agency No. 1.

From the records of Relief Agency No. 1, the field investigator learned that Mr. and Mrs. W were first referred to this agency in October 1927. There were two children in the home at that time, Henry and his half-brother, Arthur W, born 6/12/27 in Boston. The stepfather was receiving veterans' compensation of about $30 a month for a disability. He had been laid off one month before from a factory. Grocery orders for $3 a week were given until November 1927, when he secured work. In December 1927 he was again laid off and again received $3 grocery orders until January 1928, when he was re-employed. He was aided again, off and on, between June 1928 and October 1928; and then was not heard from again until 1940 when the mother reapplied, because he had just been committed to the House of Correction. There were now three children in the home (Henry had just been sent to the Correctional School). In addition to Arthur, there were Kenneth, born 7/5/34 in Boston, and William, born 6/5/37 in Boston (who had been incorrectly recorded as Charles at the Index). The stepfather now had a permanent job as a laborer at the X Public Utility Company and last worked there 8/10/40. The maternal aunt, Florence, was living in the home. Emergency aid was given until the stepfather's release from the House of Correction and his return to his job with the utility company. A list of addresses in the record extending from 1924 through 1928 and for the year 1940 were noted for inclusion in the final listing of places of residence of Henry.

Though Henry's mother had not indicated to the home investigator the extent to which she had had relief, the periods during which the family received aid, according to Relief Agency No. 1, were not long enough to change the *marginal* economic status of the family as recorded by the home investigator. The records of this agency also supported the mother's statement that her husband was a permanent employee of the X Public Utility Company.

While at Relief Agency No. 1, the field worker secured information about the maternal grandparents, who were known to that agency in 1928 and 1933. He learned that the maternal grandfather was Arnold P, born in Bridgeport, Conn., 9/1/72; and that the maternal grandmother was Margaret C, born in Keene, N.H. She had died 1/16/32 (verified) at the M. C. Hospital of 'aortic stenosis.' This confirmed the mother's statement about her mother's death. There was a maternal aunt, Florence, born 12/3/08, in Everett, Mass., who was living with the maternal grandfather. This grandfather had not received aid, according to this particular record, until July 1933, and was last assisted in January 1934, to the extent of $8 a week. He had worked for the City of Boston as a janitor and was discharged for drunkenness. This information supported the mother's statement to the home visitor that the status of her parents had been *marginal* with occasional dependence (factor #40, economic status of maternal family).

Massachusetts Board of Probation. With the above definite information on the maternal grandparents and aunt, the case collator sent for their court records at the Massachusetts Board of Probation which revealed the following information.

The maternal aunt had been committed to jail on 4/5/33 for fornication from the N District Court. She was listed as single and was living with the W's at this time. The fact of her criminal misbehavior helped to confirm the home visitor's judgment that the moral standards of Henry's home were poor.

The maternal grandfather had the following court record:

10/1/29 Drunk, B District Court. Filed.
5/19/32 Drunk, V District Court. Released.

Case of Henry W

The names of his parents were listed in the record as well as his address and birthdate as 9/1/72.

The maternal grandmother had no court record in Massachusetts.

This information from the Board of Probation corroborated the mother's statement to the home visitor that her father had been arrested for drunkenness (factor #32). The maternal aunt's conviction for fornication provided data for the factor, Delinquency in Maternal Family, which was previously *unknown*.

Boston Child Welfare Agency. A field investigator now visited Boston Child Welfare Agency No. 1 and summarized its long record on the family, keeping in mind those factors especially needed for the social schedule. The complainant to this agency, in July 1928, was Henry's true father who felt that the mother and stepfather were neglecting his son. The BCW agent made frequent visits to the boy's home between 1928 and 1935, when final arrangements were effected for Henry's placement in a foster home away from the unfavorable environment of his own home. The BCW record revealed early-morning drinking parties, entertainment of men at all hours by the mother and the aunt, brief separations of the mother and the stepfather, the birth of a child, Kenneth, whose paternity the stepfather denied, and abuse of the children. It was clear from the BCW record that Henry was fully aware of what was going on.

The following data derived from the BCW record were used in the social investigation schedule.

The mother's statement that she never married the true father of the boy was confirmed by the BCW (factors #19-21). The circumstances surrounding the birth of the half-brother, Kenneth, on 7/5/34 in Boston, were recorded. Mrs. W had given the home investigator the impression that this child was legitimate, but the BCW record stated not only that the stepfather denied the paternity of this child, but that the mother had admitted it was not his. Moreover, Henry had vividly described to the BCW worker the frequent visits of men to the home around the time that Kenneth was conceived. The landlady, who wished to evict the family, made similar complaints. Though the mother had no court record, according to the Board of Probation, it was now clear that she had been delinquent (factor #31). She had one illegitimate child at least (Henry), and probably another as a result of adultery. She had been brought into court with her husband for neglect of her children on 5/31/35 through the efforts of the BCW but, after several continuances, was found not guilty. There was no indication in the BCW record that she was an excessive drinker (factor #32). The BCW noted that Henry's half-brother, Arthur, was guilty of considerable petty stealing (factor #31).

The BCW record confirmed the mother's statement that the maternal aunt, Florence, was epileptic and had been at P State Hospital. It further stated that the mother had been treated for gonorrhea in 1933 at a Boston hospital (factors #35-36). The mother herself had made no mention of this in discussing her own health. The BCW record also contributed to the list of addresses at which Henry had lived, clarified with whom he had lived, and why the family had to move so frequently—for example, because the mother and stepfather separated and the mother returned to maternal relatives, or because the landlady evicted the family for misconduct.

The mother had told the home visitor that Henry shared a room with his half-brother. Though this was a fact at the time of Henry's admission to the Correctional School, it was clear from the BCW record that he had often slept in the same bed with his mother, mainly to keep the stepfather out of it, or with his

177

aunt (factor #62). The aunt in this way introduced Henry to bad sex practices at the age of ten years, according to the stepfather. This item was noted in the schedule under sex habits of boy (factor #A42). The mother had not mentioned this.

The BCW record supplemented the description of the home and of the mother's housekeeping habits (factors #65–67). It contained statements that in 1928 the home was well furnished, upset but not untidy; that in 1931 it was untidy and neglected-looking and that the children were brought to school in very unkempt condition; that in 1934, however, the home was cleaner than usual (factors #65–66). On the whole, the mother was not a good manager, according to the district nurse's report to the BCW. The nurse felt her main difficulty was laziness. This corroborated the home investigator's impression that she was not planful (factor #A10). According to the BCW record, in addition to poor moral standards (factor #A17), as already indicated, the family showed little self-respect (factor #A18) by allowing a 'steady stream' of men callers at all hours regardless of the protests of neighbors and landlords and the comments of their own children. The stepfather did protest at times but his own behavior gave this action little weight.

As to the methods of control and discipline (factors #A24, A26), the BCW reported that the stepfather knocked the children about rather brutally when in a half-drunken condition; that he tried to discipline Henry but that his wife opposed it. She had stated that the father took little or no part in control of the children.

Though Mrs. W told the home investigator that she and her husband had never separated (factor #A29, conjugal relations of parents), the BCW record stated that they had separated once; that the stepfather was planning to divorce his wife; and that she had returned to her mother's home with Henry, complaining that her husband was boorish and uninteresting and became quarrelsome when she refused to have sex relations with him. As for affection for the boy (factor #A30), she had told the home investigator that the stepfather was indifferent; he accepted the boy in the home, but had no affection for him. The BCW felt that the stepfather was inclined to 'pick' on the boy, but that Henry's relationship with his half-brother, Arthur, was good—Henry was fond of him (factor #A32).

From the BCW record some data about Henry's health were gleaned: he had his tonsils and adenoids removed at the P Q Hospital in 1934, though his mother had said that he had not had any operations (factor #A38). She also stated that Henry had never had scarlet fever, but the BCW had learned from school that he was home with this contagious disease in 1934 (factor #A39).

As for bad habits of the boy (factors #A42–A43), Henry's mother had apparently withheld or not recalled information at the time of the home investigator's visit, for she had revealed to the BCW a much earlier onset of bad habits. These old records have often been found to be far more valuable and reliable than a mother's memory in ascertaining such important items as the earliest misbehavior of a boy. For example: Mrs. W told the home investigator that Henry started smoking when he was about thirteen or fourteen years old; but, according to the BCW record, he was smoking at ten years. By her account, Henry began to steal rides and hop trucks at twelve or thirteen years; according to the BCW, he began at ten years. The BCW record shows that he used vile language at ten years; in the interview his mother did not acknowledge any. She said she did not consider him pugnacious but, according to the BCW record, he was complained of for striking girls on the street at nine years; at eight years he was guilty of destructive mischief (which consisted of breaking many windows in houses and automobiles). At this age, he also snatched things from store counters and set small fires. The last alarmed the landlady, and the stepfather became 'panic-struck,' but the mother minimized the matter, according to the BCW. She had not mentioned the fire-setting at all to the home investigator, though he specifically questioned her about this.

When she had been asked for her explanation of why Henry became delinquent, she tended to place the blame on the particular circumstances surrounding each of his delinquencies rather than on the boy himself or home conditions; but to the BCW in 1935 she said that Henry did not seem to be able to withstand temptation (factors #A53–A54).

The BCW record also contained digests of records of other agencies which were sufficiently full and mutually corroborative to eliminate the need for seeking the original sources. The advantage of this is obvious when one recalls that the mother and stepfather alone were known to at least twenty agencies. For example:

The BCW had made a contact with a Veterans' Clinic that had known the stepfather and was told that his statements regarding his wife were unreliable.

A Legal Assistance Bureau had stated that the stepfather was so drunk when he asked for a divorce in 1933 that he could hardly walk; yet he vowed he never drank. This organization had reported that both the stepfather and mother were low grade mentally and the children in danger of becoming neglected.

A worker from Settlement House No. 2 had reported in 1933 that Henry was stealing from other boys at the club (factor #A43) and that he had begun to attend this settlement club at the age of seven years (factor #A46).

The out-patient department of Mental Hospital No. 1, to which Henry was taken by the BCW worker in 1934, had reported that an intelligence test had been given him (intelligence quotient of 96) and that, following the test, he stole a fountain pen from the psychologist (factor #A43). On 9/13/34, the chief of the out-patient department at this hospital had reported that Henry's history indicated a mild form of epilepsy (factor #A38). 'If allowed to remain longer with parents, he will undoubtedly develop into a delinquent boy.' The mother had denied convulsions or any other epileptic symptoms or extreme nervousness in the boy in her interview with the home investigator. Henry had been a house patient at this same hospital from 2/22/36 to 4/11/36 after appearing in the W District Court and was found to be 'not psychotic.' The stepfather had also been examined at the out-patient department of this hospital in 1933, where it was noted that he had a mental age of only nine years and where he was diagnosed as a neurosyphilitic. As he was not a blood relative, this significant information had no place in the social investigation schedule except as it threw light on the home atmosphere.

A Children's Clinic had also reported to the BCW in February 1934 that Henry's physical examination was negative except that he seemed nervous (factors #A40–41).

A Boston Hospital had reported to the BCW that the mother was seen there in August 1932, because of 'fainting spells.' The diagnosis was 'question of neurasthenia.' This was recorded (factor #34) with the hope of getting further evidence of psychoneurosis from some other agency to help in making a judgment on the mental health of the mother.

A State School for the Feeble-Minded had reported to the BCW that Henry's maternal aunt had been an inmate there for three years and had an intelligence quotient of 55 (factor #33). The mother had not mentioned this serious mental defect in her family to the home interviewer.

179

Appendix A

While securing information on the immediate family at the BCW, the field investigator also examined the record of the maternal grandparents, dating back to 1910. This revealed the alcoholism of the grandfather; also the adultery of the grandmother, for which offense she was committed on 6/30/10 to a House of Correction. Their children, including Henry's mother, were committed to the care of the state but returned to their parents in 1911. There was now no doubt that both delinquency and alcoholism existed in the maternal family (factors #31–32). (The court record of the maternal grandmother was obtained from an old social service record and not from the Board of Probation which was not functioning for all Boston until 1916, and for the rest of the state until 1924.)

In 1927, the BCW had again received a complaint that the family was degenerate, that the maternal aunt was teaching neighborhood children perversions. Investigation at that time had revealed that the maternal aunt had epileptic fits and could not work (factors #35–36); but that the maternal grandfather was now working steadily as a janitor for the city (factor #40).

Boston Social Agency. The field investigator now consulted the records on Henry's mother and stepfather and his maternal grandparents at the central office of Boston Agency No. 1. Mr. and Mrs. W had asked for aid occasionally between 1927 and 1940, receiving a few grocery orders from time to time and a pair of trousers for Henry. No intensive work was done with the family, however, because after learning of the previous experiences of other agencies, the agency decided for the most part to refer the family back to Relief Agency No. 1.

The BSA folder contained the answer to the home investigator's questions about a possible earlier marriage of the stepfather and whether there were any children by this marriage. He had been previously married and divorced; there were no children.

The following data derived from the BSA records were used for the social investigation schedule:

To the BSA, Mrs. W quite readily revealed occasional adultery (factor #31); and she was also considered by them to be 'low grade mentally' (factor #33). Besides the BCW record of petty stealing by the half-brother, Arthur, the BSA mentioned his habit of truancy (factor #31); he could thus be considered an incipient delinquent, though his actual court record did not begin until after the completion of Henry's social investigation. The BSA also verified Henry's adoption by his stepfather on 12/1/26, when his surname was changed. The addresses mentioned in this record were added to the list of Henry's places of residence. The BSA augmented the home visitor's description of Henry's home (factors #65–66) by stating in 1934 that it was an untidy, badly-cared-for tenement; and in 1935 that the mother was in bed at all hours and 'not always alone in bed,' the baby was filthy, and so on. As to work habits of the stepfather (factor #A4), he was laid off jobs from time to time, probably because of drinking, until in 1931 he got a job on a public utility truck. This gave Mr. W at most nine years of steady employment rather than fourteen years, as his wife had said. Even from this job he had temporary layoffs. He frequently came to the BSA office with a 'strong odor of liquor about him.'

Henry's mother had told the home investigator that the family had no savings (factor #A9). This was confirmed by the BSA, which said that, in the past at least, they had no credit, were behind in the rent, and were generally hard up. The stepfather complained of the way his wife spent the income, but he drank a lot of it up himself. This tended to confirm the home visitor's observation (factor #A10) that the family 'lived from day to day.'

180

Case of Henry W

Under moral standards of the home (factor #A17), it was noted from the BSA record that the immoral, alcoholic maternal aunt had lived a great deal with the family and was a bad influence on Henry. The BSA substantiated the home visitor's feeling that the family had little if any self-respect (factor #A18): Mrs. W had begged aid of the agency just after collecting her husband's pay in 1939; and he had asked aid of Relief Agency No. 3 in 1933 when he was earning $29 a week. Though the home investigator had recorded Mrs. W's statement that her husband was uninterested in disciplining Henry (factor #A26), the BSA told of a neighbor's complaint that he sometimes beat Henry severely.

Besides having a summary of the BCW records, the BSA had information from the Veterans' Clinic and the Red Cross about the stepfather's early history. Relief Agency No. 3 had reported to the BSA that they had aided the family in 1928 with food and clothes. Child Placing Agency No. 1 also had talked the problem over with the BSA; but the field investigator decided to get the details from that agency directly as specific information about the foster home placements was especially needed.

The maternal grandparents' record at the BSA mostly concerned Henry's aunt, Florence, who went to live with Henry's mother and stepfather after the maternal grandmother had died, 1/16/32 (verified). This was a second confirmation of Mrs. W's statement that her mother had died of heart trouble in 1932 (factor #35). The aunt at this time, according to Henry's mother who took her in, was 'tearing around with men and drinking and picking up strange men and bringing them home.' The mother made clear to the BSA that she also was having 'a good time' and leaving her husband home to take care of the children.

Bradwood Social Service Index. While the above information was being secured in the Boston area, information was sought from agencies with whom contact was best made by correspondence. Consultation of the Bradwood Social Service Index revealed that Henry's real father and his legal wife had been known to a Bradwood Social Agency and a Bradwood Child Welfare Agency.

The brief report of the Bradwood Social Agency was received with the Bradwood SSI card. James S. J's wife had come to the office in 1933 to ask for some clothing for their child, Anne (half-sister of Henry). Her husband had deserted her four and a half years before, in 1929, and she had returned to her parents in Bradwood. She received the clothing but never returned to the agency.

Bradwood Child Welfare Agency. A letter was sent to the Bradwood Child Welfare Agency asking for a summary of their contact, in the hope of learning Mr. J's present whereabouts. Unfortunately, their record was mostly concerned with the behavior of his wife, Helen, with whom the inquiry was not concerned. However, the record did mention the 'wild' behavior of Henry's half-sister, Anne J, and gave her exact birthdate as 4/15/27 in Bradwood. Also it contained the verified date of James J's marriage to Helen (factor #22) and the date of her divorce from him (1934), at which time she was given the care and custody of Anne. It stated in 1941 that the father had never been located. As search in Bradwood, Stoughton, Randolph and Boston directories and in Massachusetts death records proved unavailing, the case collator had to content herself for factors #6 and #23 with the fact that, though it was known that Henry's father was living in Stoughton in 1929 when he defaulted in H District Court, it had not been determined whether he was alive or dead in 1940. Henry's mother did not know either, according to her statement to the home investigator.

Maternity Home and Hospital No. 1, which had known Henry's mother in 1924, was also consulted by letter. The hospital report confirmed her birthdate and her religion as Protestant (factor #18), and her delivery of a male child there, Henry, on 1/16/25 ('normal delivery and no complications'). The mother had also told the home investigator that delivery was normal (factor #A38). She was said to be 'willing and easy to manage.' Over a year later she wrote to the hospital that she had married Leo W.

Superior Court. Further information about Henry's true father was sought from his probation record in C Superior Court. (As an example of the specific instructions given by the collator to the field investigators, the following are typical: 'We know very little about Henry's real father, James S. J, so please get all you can about him, his parents and siblings, if any; habits; comments on intelligence, personality, and so on.')

At the probation office of the C Superior Court, the field investigator learned that James S. J had pleaded not guilty to the charge of bastardy in B District Court on 10/3/24, but was adjudged to be the father of the mother's unborn child and appealed the case. The mother, interviewed by the probation officer in C Superior Court in March 1925, said that Mr. J claimed he could not marry her because he was already married; but he proved to the court that he had been divorced from his first wife in Chicago, Illinois, on 5/5/21 (verified). According to the probation officer, Henry definitely resembled the defendant, who on 3/13/25 (about two months after Henry was born) was ordered to pay $5 a week for the boy's support and the confinement expenses, and was placed on two years' probation on an illegitimate child charge. At that time Mr. J was living in Stoughton and earning $26 a week in a machine shop, but he worked very irregularly during his probation and was soon in arrears. The probation officer said he never was inclined to work, kept his jobs only a short time, and that although the mother wanted to marry him, he was in no financial condition to do so. On 5/10/26 the mother married Leo W, and they and Henry continued to live with her parents. Mr. W was earning $27 a week and was anxious to adopt Henry. Shortly after this, on 6/2/26, Mr. J married Helen B in Bradwood. In October 1925, very little money having been paid by him to Henry's mother, the probation officer persuaded the paternal grandmother ('a respectable woman' —factor #31) to advance the father some money to cover all payments. On 2/12/27 the adjudication was vacated and the complaint dismissed.

The early addresses of Henry, his mother, and stepfather as contained in the C Superior Court record were noted.

Lower Court. At this point a copy of the Y Court probation record on Henry himself was received. Henry had made only one appearance in this court, on 12/1/38, for breaking and entering a variety store. He was found delinquent and the case was filed, since he was turned over to his parole officer for return to the Correctional School. Even this brief record added a few items to the social investigation schedule: according to the Y Court, Henry was a Methodist (factor #3) and his mother a 'Protestant' (factor #18). His stepfather was employed as a laborer by a public utility company at $29.50 a week (factor #A7), and had been in court with Henry, resentful that the boy was causing so much trouble (factor #A30). Henry was convicted of stealing at thirteen years of age (factor #A43). He was attending Settlement House No. 1 in 1938 when thirteen years old (factor #A46); in fact, he stated that the reason he went into town and got into trouble was because there were no activities at the Settlement House that day.

Child Placing Agency. A field investigator then went to Child Placing Agency No. 1 and consulted their long record on Henry.

On 6/18/35, the BCW asked CPA No. 1 to place Henry in a foster home, as his mother and stepfather were not well adjusted to each other and could not control the boy, who had a tendency to petty theft, truanted, was on the street at all hours, and had also set a fire. A charge of neglect against the parents had been dismissed with a warning by the judge. The CPA was assured, however, that Henry's intelligence quotient was fairly high. After some hesitation because of the family background, and upon receipt of a second request from the BCW, the CPA finally agreed to place him, particularly since his examination at the PQ Hospital was negative; the doctor had found him in fine condition except for his teeth. Henry was back and forth in CPA foster homes from 11/6/35 until he was committed to the Correctional School in 1936.

The following data derived from the CPA records were used for the social investigation schedule:

The record indicated grave doubt as to the paternity of Mrs. W's last child, William, born 6/5/37, because during 1936 the neighbors considered her 'everybody's wife,' and Mr. W himself doubted that the expected baby was his (factors #28, 31).

Mrs. W told the CPA in 1935 that Henry's true father was alcoholic; he 'worked one day and drank the next' (factor #32). She herself did not appear 'bright' to the CPA visitor (factor #33), to whom she gave a lively description of her attempt at suicide. She said she took poison and was saved when her sister called a doctor. This item, added to those already listed under factor #34 on the mother, indicated emotional instability. On one call the CPA found the home clean and neat; on another, not very clean (factor #65). When the worker called to take Henry to his foster home, as planned with his mother, she not only did not have him dressed but had not given him any breakfast; while the social worker waited, she gave the boy (ten years old) three doughnuts and two cups of coffee (factor #66). It was clear that she had not been supervising him adequately, as he was on the street at all hours (factors #A6, A27). Her method of punishing him was to whip him or deprive him of supper or the movies (factor #A25). The stepfather also resorted to these methods, but he was usually drunk when home weekends, and alternately quiet and noisy, erratic and unpredictable in his handling of Henry (factor #A26).

The mother and stepfather had separated several times (factor #A29). She told the CPA that she returned to her husband following these periods of separation only for financial reasons. (She had apparently chosen to forget these incidents when talking to our home investigator in 1941.) According to the CPA, Henry knew he was adopted but knew nothing of his father. The stepfather's favorite child was Arthur, the only one he felt sure was his own (factor #A30). The mother, too, considered Arthur her favorite, and Henry felt this. But she also showed considerable fondness for Henry, giving him a bicycle in 1935 (factor #A31); and she avoided court action against her husband for fear the children might be taken from her. As to household duties of the boy (factor #A33), the CPA confirmed her statement that they were not regular. She sent Henry to the store occasionally on errands and considered him quite reliable on such jobs. 'He rarely stole more than a few pennies from me.' The CPA record illustrated the disunity in the family (factor #A37), for besides considerable evidence of the parents' neglect of their children and their lack of affection for each other, Henry's stepfather and maternal aunt, Florence, 'fought like cats and dogs' (factor #A37). Mrs. W insisted, however, on keeping Florence in the home as it was her mother's 'dying wish.'

At the time of Henry's foster home placement in 1935, the CPA gave him a physical examination, in connection with which some of the early health information was probably supplied by his mother. It confirmed her statement to our home investigator that Henry was a full-term baby, normally delivered, and not a late walker or talker (thirteen months and fifteen months, respectively) (factor #A38). However, though she denied any history of convulsions to the home investigator, it was here recorded that he had had two convulsions, one at six months and the other at one year (factor #A38). He had had his tonsils and adenoids removed in 1935 (factor #A38); and had had pneumonia and frequent colds (factors #A40–A41). His mother also denied to the home visitor that he had recurrent headaches, though Mental Hospital No. 1 reported infrequent headaches and dizziness to the CPA; and although she denied enuresis, his foster mother complained of it in 1936 when he was eleven years old (factors #A40–A41). Henry's mother could give no evidence of extreme nervousness, though the P Q Hospital reported to the CPA that at ten years of age he was nervous, had nightmares after seeing thrilling movies, and didn't sleep well (factors #A40–A41).

According to the CPA, Henry was already a problem as a truant at ten years of age, though his mother told the home visitor that he had truanted 'once or twice' since he was fourteen. She also told the CPA that Henry was 'truck hopping' and keeping late hours at ten years, and that he had been unmanageable since infancy (factors #A42–A43).

Mrs. W had not said much to the home visitor about Henry's foster home placements, but an accurate account was obtained from the CPA, which revealed that on 11/6/35 Henry was placed with Mrs. M. Q in Canton, Mass. On 1/15/36, Henry was returned to his own mother at her request (the stepfather was paying his board), and Mrs. M. Q stated that she did not want him back, as he had been stealing. He remained at home in Roxbury with his stepfather, mother, maternal aunt, and half-brothers until he was arrested and appeared in W District Court on 2/9/36 for larceny from a department store, for which offense he was committed to the Correctional School. The sentence was appealed, and while awaiting a hearing in C Superior Court, he was kept in a State Child Placing Agency temporary home until 2/22/36. At this time the Court placed him in Mental Hospital No. 1 for a period of observation, because the out-patient department examination had indicated that there was some question of psychotic tendencies. On 4/10/36, the hospital reported that the boy was restless and emotionally unstable, with violent outbreaks of temper if he could not have his own way (factors #A40–A41); that he had an intelligence quotient of 103 (an I.Q. of 96 had been reported in 1934), and a mental age of 12 yrs., 8 mos.; and that he was not insane or feeble-minded. Re-placement in a foster home was recommended. (The fact that this full report had been secured from Mental Hospital No. 1 by the CPA, plus previous summaries, made a separate visit by a field worker to the hospital unnecessary.)

On 4/11/36, Henry was given two years' probation in the C Superior Court and placed by the CPA. After five days in a temporary home, he went to live with a Mr. and Mrs. J. F, on the outskirts of Medway, Mass. (his stepfather paying the board). The CPA was enthusiastic about these foster parents but indicated that the foster mother was a rather rigid disciplinarian. They had a farm of several acres with pigs, cows and chickens, and a large garden (factor #51). After an enjoyable summer of swimming, fishing, and small chores,

Case of Henry W

Henry's behavior began to deteriorate on return to school in the fall. He was rude to the teachers, exhibited a violent temper, stole bicycle fixtures from a store, and ran away several times. Finally he attacked a boy with a knife, seriously injuring him. In consequence of the assault, Henry was sent to the Correctional School. Henry showed no concern over the condition of the boy, nor did he seem to realize the seriousness of what he had done, according to the CPA. The CPA then closed the case and future placements were made by the Boys' Parole Division.

State Department of Mental Health. With the vital statistics now complete on all members of the boy's family, both on the paternal and maternal side, a field investigator checked through the files of the Massachusetts State Department of Mental Health, finding a record only for Henry's aunt, Florence, who, while a patient at one of the state mental hospitals, had been diagnosed as suffering from 'psychoneurosis.' This diagnosis provided data for factor #34.

School History

The gathering of Henry's school history was a task largely separate from the rest of the social investigation.

From Henry himself and from the Correctional School records, it was learned that he had last attended the F Intermediate School in Roxbury, being in the eighth grade (the graduating class) in June 1940, when he was arrested and returned to the Correctional School, just before examination for this study. A school investigator went to the F School to obtain Henry's record there and as much of his previous school record as possible. The ADP card (see *Unraveling Juvenile Delinquency*, Chapter VII) was available but incomplete, beginning only with his experience in the F School. He had attended here twice: first, in the seventh grade from October 1938 to December 1938, when he was returned to the Correctional School; and again, when paroled from the Correctional School, in the eighth grade from January 2, 1940 to the end of June 1940, when he was again returned to the Correctional School. His scholarship record in the last term of the eighth grade was as follows: A in Physical Education and Hygiene; B's and C's in Reading, Literature, English, Spelling, Penmanship, Arithmetic, Geography, and History; D's or E's in Music, Drawing, and Conduct (factors #A64–A65).

The school investigator then interviewed Henry's eighth grade teacher, who checked the following characteristics as applying to him (factors #A71–A74, #A76): stealing, obscene notes and talk, truancy, cheating, unreliableness, lack of interest in work, laziness, smoking, unhappiness, depression, easy discouragement, carelessness in work, inattention, slovenliness in appearance, suspiciousness, and thoughtlessness. The investigator also had a conversation with the Principal, who felt that Henry's behavior difficulties resulted from a combination of home conditions and his own attitude toward life. The family was careless and inadequate; the boy was 'slippery,' untrustworthy, and had poor associations; and, the Principal understood, the stepfather was a drinker. He gave as the reason for retardation (factor #A77) 'lack of interest plus many changes of schools'; as the reason for truancy (factor #A78) 'influence of bad companions plus lack of interest in school.' As for adjustment to schoolmates (factor #A29), he said Henry tended to bad associations. The boy, he said, did not participate in extracurricular activities (factor #A80).

The investigator now needed to complete the history of Henry's earlier schooling. Noting that on his original commitment to the Correctional School Henry had come from a Medway, Mass., elementary school, he wrote to the superintendent of schools in that town, enclosing a questionnaire. The prompt reply happily included an ADP card listing the schools attended by the boy from kindergarten to his first Correctional School commitment, as follows:

School Year	School	Grade
1/17/31 to 12/31	N School, Boston	1, 1
12/31 to 6/33	D School, Boston	1, 2
9/33 to 3/34	P School, Boston	3
3/34 to 6/35	S School, Boston	3, 4
9/35 to 11/35	B School, Boston	5
11/35 to 1/36	F School, Canton	5
1/36 to 2/36*	B School, Boston	5
4/36 to 10/36	R School, Medway	5, 5

* Between 2/36 and 4/36 Henry was in a temporary foster home and in Mental Hospital No. 1 for observation and did not attend school.

Data on scholarship were not included in the reply; but Henry's conduct was given as 'fair to poor.' There were no absences, no tardiness, no truancy. His intelligence quotient was 112 on a Binet-Simon Test, but his school achievement was one to three years below his chronological age. As the boy's outstanding problem (factor #A80) the Superintendent had commented 'obedience and dependability were both subaverage.'

The investigator next wrote to the F School in Canton, and received an identical ADP card covering all experiences through that school. A copy of Henry's fifth-grade report card was enclosed with his marks for the 1935–36 period, ranging from A to D. His mark in conduct was D.

From these ADP cards it was clear that, except for these two out-of-town experiences, all the schools Henry had attended before his commitment to the Correctional School were in Boston. The investigator therefore consulted the B and P Schools in Roxbury and the South End district of Boston and learned that Henry's school misbehavior began in the fifth grade at ten years of age, in the B School. He was unruly, truanted on at least three occasions, and stole. There was no record of misconduct at the P School and the investigator therefore did not consult any previous schools.

At this point the case collator observed a gap between the date 10/36 when Henry left the R School in Medway and 10/38 when he entered the F School. This period was found in the Boys' Parole Division records to be covered as follows: 10/36 to 10/37 at the Correctional School; 10/37 to 2/38 on parole in a foster home, attending the sixth grade in South Holyoke, Mass.; 2/38 to 10/38 at the Correctional School.

There was now available a complete chronological list of Henry's school experiences, from which the following facts were gleaned. He started the first grade at just six years of age (factor #A56). He had between nine and ten years of schooling (factor #A57). He attained the eighth grade in school (omitting the Correctional School) at fifteen years (factor #A58). He repeated grade one and grade five (factor #A59). He was retarded two years at the time he left school (factor #A61). He did not attend any special class or the Disciplinary Day School (factor #A62). He had ten school experiences in all, not counting the Correctional School (factor #A63). His first serious misbehavior (factor #A66) was recorded as truancy, unruliness in class, and stealing. The age and the grade in which his first serious misbehavior was evident (factors #A67–A68) were given as ten years in grade five. The age truancy started (factor #A69) was

Case of Henry W

recorded as ten years; the frequency of truancy (factor #A70) was recorded as occasional at first, but persistent in his last year.

Completing the Investigation

During the course of gathering Henry's family and personal history, the collator frequently reviewed the progress of the case, mapping out new sources of information and redirecting the field investigators to old sources as the need became evident. When it appeared that all the data were in hand, she reread the home interviewer's suggestions for further exploration and found that they had been successfully completed. She then reviewed the detailed schedule, into which the results of the investigations had been entered, to make certain that every factor was accounted for and that there were no contradictions between factors (except in instances where she felt that the authors of *Unraveling Juvenile Delinquency* would have to resolve them, there being no additional data available). After this final check, the social investigation schedule on Henry was ready to be reviewed by the authors and prepared for statistical treatment.

SUMMARY OF INFORMATION AS RECORDED IN THE SOCIAL INVESTIGATION SCHEDULE

Below are presented: (A) a detailed statement of Henry's places of residence, entered on the schedule under the heading *Chronological Summary of Boy's Whereabouts from Birth to Present* (which provided the basis for completing factors #42–56); (B) a summary, factor by factor, of all data derived from the home interview and from the field investigations, as they were finally assembled in the schedule.

A. CHRONOLOGICAL SUMMARY OF BOY'S WHEREABOUTS FROM BIRTH TO PRESENT

(Including breaks in home life and departures from home)

Deteriorated Area	Whereabouts	With Whom	Dates	Reason for Change
Yes	12 A Court, Dorchester	Mother, maternal grandparents, occasionally maternal aunt	1/16/25–4/3/26*	Maternal grandparents moved
Yes	209 B St., Roxbury	Mother, maternal grandparents, occasionally aunt and, after 5/26, stepfather	4/3/26–8/26	Mother and stepfather moved to own place
No	10 Y Street, Dorchester	Mother and stepfather	8/26–11/26	Mother and stepfather returned to maternal grandparents
Yes	209 B St., Roxbury	Mother, stepfather, maternal grandparents, occasionally aunt and, after 6/27, halfbrother	11/26–1928	Mother and stepfather moved to own place

* Actually boy and mother at Maternity Home and Hospital No. 1 (1/16/25–2/4/25),

187

Deteri-orated Area	Whereabouts	With Whom	Dates	Reason for Change
Yes	211 B St., Roxbury	Mother, stepfather and half-brother	1928–30	Unknown
Yes	213 B St., Roxbury	Mother, stepfather and half-brother	1930–32	Unknown
Yes	211 B St., Roxbury	Mother, stepfather, half-brother and aunt	1932–12/11/32	Mother left stepfather
Yes	29 S Street, Dorchester	Mother, half-brother, and maternal relatives (maternal grand-mother had died)	12/11/32–6/33	Mother and step-father reunited
No	81 N St., Boston	Mother, stepfather, half-brother and aunt	6/33–12/12/33	Unknown
Yes	67 C St., Boston	Mother, stepfather, half-brother and aunt	12/12/33–3/25/34	Family put out for disorderly con-duct
Yes	539 M Street, Roxbury	Mother, stepfather, half-brothers and aunt	3/25/34–10/21/34	Unknown
Yes	286 J St., Roxbury	Mother, stepfather, half-brothers and aunt	10/21/34–7/35	Unknown
Yes	13 L St., Roxbury	Mother, stepfather, half-brothers, aunt and boarder (stepfather out of home part of time)	7/35–11/6/35	Placed in foster home by Child Placing Agency No. 1
No	66 S Street, Canton	Foster mother, Mrs. M. Q	11/6/35–1/15/36	Stole, and foster mother did not want him back
Yes	13 L St., Roxbury	Mother, stepfather, half-brothers and aunt	1/15/36–2/9/36	Arrested and appealed
	Temporary home of State Child Placing Agency		2/9/36–2/22/36	Sent by court to Mental Hospital No. 1 for ob-servation
	Mental Hospital No. 1 as patient		2/22/36–4/11/36	Placed in temporary home by Child Placing Agency No. 1
	Temporary home of Child Placing Agency No. 1		4/11/36–4/16/36	Placed in foster home by CPA No. 1
No	J Street, Medway	Foster parents, Mr. and Mrs. J. F	4/16/36–9/27/36	Assaulted a boy and ran home
Yes	21 Y St., Roxbury	Mother, stepfather, half-brothers and aunt	9/27/36–10/3/36	Arrested and com-mitted

188

Case of Henry W

Deteriorated Area	Whereabouts	With Whom	Dates	Reason for Change
	Correctional School	Confined	10/3/36– 10/2/37	Placed out by Boys' Parole Division
No	S Ave., South Holyoke	Foster mother, Mrs. M	10/2/37/ 2/6/38	Ran away
	Bunking out		2/6/38– 2/7/38	Caught and returned to Correctional School
	Correctional School	Confined	2/7/38– 10/9/38	Paroled to mother and stepfather
Yes	17 P Street, Dorchester	Mother, stepfather, half-brothers and aunt	10/9/38– 12/1/38	Returned to Correctional School
	Correctional School	Confined	12/1/38– 12/28/39	Paroled to mother and stepfather
Yes	17 P Street, Dorchester	Mother, stepfather, half-brothers and aunt	12/28/39– 8/18/40	Arrested, but got away
	Bunking out on runaway		8/18/40– 8/24/40	Caught and returned to Correctional School
	Correctional School	Confined	8/24/40	

B. FACTOR-BY-FACTOR PRESENTATION OF DATA FROM HOME INTERVIEW AND FROM FIELD INVESTIGATIONS

FAMILY BACKGROUND

Factor	Home Interview	Field Investigation*
1. Birthplace	Boston	Boston (verified by BPD in 1936; verified in detail by field worker at BVS).
2. Legitimacy	Conceived out of wedlock, parents never married	Illegitimate (BPD in 1936, BSA, BCW, CPA).
3. Religion	Not determined	Protestant (BPD); Methodist (Y Court).
4. Age (at date of examination)	16 years	16 yrs. Calculated on the basis of verified birthdate 1/16/25 (BVS) and date of examination 1/5/41.
5. Dominant stock	Parents native-born; maternal grandparents native-born (N.H. and Conn.)	Old American. Father native-born (verified at BVS). Paternal grandparents native-born (stated on birth certificate of father, BVS). Mother native-born (SSI, RA, BCW, BSA, etc.). Maternal grandmother

*Includes correspondence.

Factor	Home Interview	Field Investigation*
		native-born (verified on death certificate, BVS). Maternal grandfather native-born (SSI, RA, B of Prob).
6. Whereabouts of father	Unknown; never lived with boy	When he defaulted, according to H District Court in 1929, he was living in Stoughton, Mass. (B of Prob). Whereabouts unknown (BPD, 1936, 1940). Whereabouts unknown (Bradwood SA, 1933). Father had deserted true wife in 1929 (Bradwood SA, 1933). Whereabouts unknown, as never located (Bradwood CWA in 1940). No trace of father in 1940 directories or telephone books of Randolph, Bradwood, Stoughton, and Boston, Mass.
7. Whereabouts of mother	With boy	With boy (BPD).
8. Birthplace of father	Spencer, Mass.	Spencer, Mass. (verified at BVS).
9. Birthplace of mother	Everett, Mass.	Everett, Mass. (SSI, RA, BCW, BSA).
10. Disparity in age of parents	Birthdate of father, 1901; of mother, 1906	4 yrs., 7 mos., 18 days. Birthdate of mother 1/4/06 (verified MH & H) minus birthdate of father 5/16/01 (verified BVS).
11. Age of father at birth of boy	Not calculated because date unverified	23 yrs., 7 mos.; birthdate of boy 1/16/25 (verified at BVS by BPD) minus birthdate of father (see #10).
12. Age of mother at birth of boy	Not calculated because date unverified	19 yrs., 12 days. Birthdate of boy (see #11) minus birthdate of mother (see #10).
13. Nativity of parents	Native-born (see #8 and #9)	Both native-born (see #8 and #9).
14. Nativity of parents and boy	Native-born (see #1, #8 and #9)	Parents and boy native-born (see #1, #8 and #9).
15. Date of arrival of boy in U.S.	Native-born (see #1)	Native-born (see #1).
16. Date of arrival in U.S. of father	Native-born (see #8)	Native-born (see #8).
17. Date of arrival in U.S. of mother	Native-born (see #9)	Native-born (see #9).
18. Religion of parents	Not determined	Father Protestant? (divorced twice, C Superior Court and Bradwood CWA); Mother Protestant (MH & H, Y Court).

Case of Henry W

Factor	Home Interview	Field Investigation*
19, 20. Date and place of marriage of parents	Never married	Parents never married (BCW, BSA). Y Court assumed step-father was true father but made no investigation on this brief case.
21. Civil condition	Parents never married	Parents never married.
22. Date of remarriage of parent with whom living	Not determined, but both parents have remarried	Mother married for first time 5/17/26 (verified, BCW) when the boy was under 5 yrs. of age.
23. Date of death of father	Unknown if living or dead	Unknown whether dead or alive (Bradwood CWA, 1940). No record of father's death in Mass. (BVS).
24. Date of death of mother	Still living	Living (BPD, Correctional School).
25. Size of father's family	Only child	No information.
26. Size of mother's family	Mother one of two children	Mother one of two children (SSI, BCW, BSA).
27, 28. Siblings of boy	Three half-siblings by mother	Four living: 3 half-siblings by mother (SSI, BSA, BCW) and one half-sibling by father and his second legal wife (Bradwood CWA). Father had no children by his first legal wife (C Superior Court).
29. Rank of boy among siblings	First child	First child (SSI, BCW, BSA).
30. Time between birth of boy and next older child	Boy is oldest	Boy is the oldest child (SSI, BCW, BSA).
31. Delinquency in paternal family	Negative, as far as mother knows; father came from 'nice people'	Paternal grandparents were respectable (social agencies by implication). Paternal grandmother respectable woman (C Sup. Ct. PO). Paternal grandparents were too old for clearance through the B of Prob for court records as their town did not report till 1924. There were no aunts and uncles.
Delinquency of father	Placed on probation when adjudged father of boy at time of his birth; otherwise unknown	Father convicted of offense of illegitimate child and nonsupport of child (B of Prob).
Delinquency in maternal family	Negative, according to mother	Maternal grandmother was committed to H of C for adultery in 1910 (BCW). Maternal aunt convicted of fornication (BCW, B of Prob).
Delinquency of mother	Boy is illegitimate	Mother had illegitimate child (boy, and possibly two of her

191

Factor	Home Interview	Field Investigation*
		children allegedly by step father were illegitimate (BCW CPA). Mother admits occa sional adultery (BSA). Mothe in court 5/31/33 for neglect o children but found not guilt (BCW).
Delinquency among siblings of boy	Negative, according to mother	Half-brother, Arthur, engaged i petty stealing (BCW); a fre quent truant (BSA); no cour record (B of Prob). Half sister, Anne, 'wild' and stay out late (Bradwood CWA) Other half-siblings too youn to have court records.
32. Alcoholism in paternal family	Negative, as far as mother knows	Unknown. Court records befor 1924 for Randolph, Mass., no available at B of Prob.
Alcoholism of father	Negative, according to mother	Father alcoholic, according t the mother: 'He worked on day and drank the next (CPA).
Alcoholism in maternal family	Mother admits her father has been arrested for drunkenness	Maternal grandfather in cour for drunkenness at least twic and convicted once (B o Prob.). Maternal grandfathe alcoholic (BCW).
Alcoholism of mother	Mother claims she does not drink to excess	No agencies record that mothe drank to excess, though BCW describes early morning drink ing parties in mother' home.
Alcoholism among siblings of boy	Half-siblings too young	Half-siblings too young to drin to excess.
33. Mental dullness in paternal family	Mother considered pater nal grandparents 'normal'	Unknown (no comment by an agency).
Mental dullness of father	Father was of average in telligence, according to mother	Unknown, but probably withi normal range, judging by hi schooling and by the C Sup Ct. size-up of him.
Mental dullness in maternal family	Question about Aunt Florence (see dictated report)	Maternal aunt's I.Q. 55 (Stat School for FM to BCW).
Mental dullness of mother	Impressed investigator as low average	Mother 'low grade mentally (BSA). Appears mentally 'lo grade' (BCW). Not brigh (CPA).
Mental dullness among siblings of boy	No information	Half-siblings appear mentall retarded; their father moron (CPA).
34. Mental disease in paternal family	Negative, as far as mother knows	No mental disease or distortio indicated by agency records Paternal grandparents no known to Mass. DMH.

Factor	Home Interview	Field Investigation*
Mental disease of father	Considered normal by mother	Father not known to DMH. No mental examination at C Sup. Ct., but PO commented that behavior was rather irresponsible. He made a good superficial impression, however.
Mental disease in maternal family	Aunt Florence epileptic; has been in state institution (see dictated report)	Maternal aunt: diagnosis, 'psychoneurosis' (DMH). Maternal aunt had epileptic fits (BCW).
Mental disease of mother	Seems quite normal	Mother had fainting spells. Diagnosis was 'question of neurasthenia' (B Hosp. to BCW). Mother said she attempted suicide in 1933 (CPA).
Mental disease among siblings of boy	Negative, according to mother	Half-siblings not known to DMH.
35, 36. Health of paternal family	Grandfather had been injured and unable to work	No information from agencies.
Health of father	Had always been good, according to mother	Father's health negative in 1925 according to the C Sup. Ct. Unknown since then.
Health of maternal family	Maternal grandmother had heart trouble prior to her death in 1932; maternal aunt had epileptic fits	Maternal grandmother died of 'aortic stenosis' at 53 (BVS to BSA). Maternal aunt had epileptic fits (BCW).
Health of mother	Negative	No illnesses mentioned by agencies except gonorrhea in 1934 (B Hosp. to BCW).
Health of siblings	Negative	No illnesses mentioned except deafness of half-brother, Arthur (CPA).
37. Education of paternal grandparents	Unknown; were literate	Unknown, although undoubtedly both paternal grandparents had some common schooling, as born and grew up in Mass.
Education of maternal grandparents	Grandparents had few years of schooling	No information.
38. Education of father	Went to H. S.; unknown if graduated	No information.
Education of mother	Went through the seventh grade	No information.
39. (Dropped from study)		
40. Economic status of paternal grandparents	Grandparents received 'some kind of compensation' at time of boy's birth as grandfather unable to work	Paternal grandfather a shoe worker (directory and BVS). Paternal grandparents could afford to pay enough to cancel debt of their son in 1926 (C

Factor	Home Interview	Field Investigation*
		Sup. Ct.). Bradwood SSI has no registration for paternal grandparents.
Economic status of maternal grandparents	Marginal, occasionally dependent, according to mother	Maternal grandfather on a pension (RA about 1933); drank and gambled his money away (BCW, 1911); formerly a teamster and janitor who got 'relief' for only a few months in 1933 (RA). Mother and her sister cared for by the state 1910–1911, when maternal grandmother in jail (BCW).
41. (Dropped from study)		
42. Age first left home	11 yrs., 3 mos.	10 yrs., 10 mos. (CPA, BCW).
43. Reason first left home	Not determined	Delinquency of boy, and home considered unsuitable by agency (BCW, CPA).
44. Nature of first departure from home	To foster home	To foster home (BCW, CPA).
45. Summary of abnormal environmental experiences	Foster homes and correctional school; family moved many times	Correctional School, three times (BPD). Foster homes, not relatives (CPA, BPD). Running away and bunking out (CPA and BPD). Excessive moving (RA, BSA, BCW, CPA, school records, directories).
46. Nature of first break in family life	Boy illegitimate, no father in home	Boy illegitimate, father not in home since before birth of the boy.
47. Age of boy at first break	Before birth of boy	Before birth of boy.
48. Summary of breaks in family life	Parents not married and did not live together since before boy's birth	Parents not married and did not live together since before birth of boy. Mother and stepfather separated on and off (BCW, CPA).
49. Household changes	Not determined	5 (all agencies).
50. Parent substitutes	One step-parent and foster parents	Stepfather (BCW) and foster parents (nonrelatives) (CPA).
51. Length of time lived in urban area	Predominantly urban	Predominantly urban (agencies and directories).
52. Age at change from rural to urban area	Usually lived in city	Predominantly urban (agencies and directories).
53a. Frequency of moving	Not determined	More often than once a year (summary of agencies, BPD, schools, and directories).

Case of Henry W

Factor	Home Interview	Field Investigation*
53b. Frequency of moving (number of times)	Not determined	19 moves (summary of agencies, schools, BPD, directories).
54. Nature of mobility	Not determined	Excessive moving to different parts of one city (agencies, schools, BPD, directories).
55. Length of time in slum areas	Not determined	On and off throughout (agencies, schools, etc.).
56. Length of time family lived at present address	Nearly 3 yrs.	2½ years (CPA and directories).
57, 58. Composition of household	Boy, mother, stepfather, maternal aunt and three half-siblings	Boy, mother, stepfather, 3 half-siblings, maternal aunt (BPD, 1940 directory, RA).
59. Type of house	Old 6-family house	Old 6-family house (BPD).
60. Crowding of home	4 rooms, 3 bedrooms, 7 occupants	7 occupants (BPD, 1940 directory, RA).
61. Rental (monthly average per room)	$5.00	No information.
62. Sleeping arrangements for boy	Shares room with half-brother, Arthur	Had slept in same bed with mother or aunt when 9 yrs. old; boy and half-brother sleep with stepfather (BCW, 1933).
63. Sanitary facilities	All but central heat	No information.
64. Furnishing of home	Radio, some books, pictures, lamps; fairly well furnished	Home well furnished (BCW, 1928).
65. Orderliness of home	Rather disorderly; mother seems careless in housekeeping habits	Upset but not untidy (BCW, 1928); untidy and neglected home (BCW, 1931); untidy, badly-cared-for tenement (BSA, 1934); cleaner than usual (BCW, 1934); clean and neat (CPA, 1935); not very clean (CPA, later in 1935).
66. Household routine	Some semblance of routine; not a well ordered household, however	Children brought to school very unkempt (BCW, 1932). Mother in bed all hours. Baby in filthy condition (BSA, 1935). Boy not dressed and hadn't breakfasted when called for by social worker, by appointment; then mother gave him three doughnuts and 2 cups of coffee (CPA, 1935). Mother in bed near noon with plateful of cigarette stubs beside her (BPD, 1939).

195

Factor	Home Interview	Field Investigation*
67. Summary of physical home	(to be filled in by coder)	
68. Neighborhood type	Second-class tenement district, one block removed from a business artery	Fairly good location. Family ha~ moved frequently but gene~ ally in this same neighborhoo~ (BPD, 1936).
69. Street life	Crowds hang around nearby corners	No information.
Barrooms	2 or 3 within 2 blocks of home	No information.
Empty lots	On street near home	No information
Supervised indoor recreational facilities	Boys' club, and Settlement House No. 1 in neighborhood	Settlement House No. 1 in con~ tact with boy (Y Ct., 1938).
A1. Breadwinners	Stepfather	Stepfather (BPD). (His commi~ ment to H of C two week~ before boy's commitment no~ counted.)
A2. Present occupation of father or substitute	Stepfather a laborer for X Public Utility Co.	Stepfather a laborer for X Publi~ Utility Company (BPD, 1940~ RA). (See # A1.)
A3. Usual occupation of father or substitute	Stepfather working on same job for past 15 yrs., according to mother	Stepfather a laborer (1940 Bos~ ton directory, BPD); a team~ ster for X Public Utility Co~ (Y Ct., 1938); employed b~ X Public Utility Co. sinc~ 1932 (BSA).
A4. Work habits of father or substitute	Stepfather has worked for X Public Utility Co. for past 15 yrs.; boy's mother states that his drinking has not interfered with his work	Stepfather working last 8 yrs. a~ laborer for X Public Utilit~ Co. (BSA, RA, Y Ct.); ha~ been laid off occasionally~ probably for drunkennes~ (BSA); works steadily (CPA~ 1935); employment recor~ very irregular between 192~ and 1928 (RA).
A5. Usual occupation of mother or substitutes	Housewife; did factory work after birth of boy and before marriage; no work outside the home since then	Housewife (all agencies).
A6. Supervision of children	Mother says she supervised closely (this may be questioned)	Boy on street at all hours (CPA, 1935).
A7. Sources of family income	Stepfather's wages $28 a week	Stepfather's earnings plus hi~ veterans' compensation. Step~ father in 1934 paid $30 a week~ by X Public Utility Co~ (BCW); receiving veterans~ compensation of about $30 a~ month for mental disabilit~ (RA, BCW); earns $25.95 a~ week and gets $30 a mont~

196

Factor	Home Interview	Field Investigation*
		from the Veterans' Clinic for 'shell shock' (CPA, 1935).
A8. Average weekly income of household per person	Not determined	\$4.44 (\$28 a week plus \$7.50 a week from veterans' compensation).
A9. Family savings	None	Family has no credit, behind in rent, and generally hard up (BSA, 1927).
A10. Planfulness in management of family income	No savings (see #A9); live from day to day; mother admits she uses very little 'system' in her management of her income	Mother is lazy (Veterans' Clinic to BCW, 1933). Stepfather complains of way mother spends income, but drinks a lot of it up himself (BSA, 1935).
A11. Economic condition of family at present	Marginal	Marginal. Stepfather permanent employee of X Public Utility Co. (RA, 1940).
A12. Usual economic condition of family	Marginal; received aid in early married life but none for 15 yrs. according to mother	Marginal. Family received public welfare aid only for short periods in 1927 and 1928 and not again till 1940 when emergency aid received for 3 weeks while stepfather at H of C (RA, 1927–1940). Supplementary aid granted of clothing and very occasionally a grocery order between 1926 and 1940 (BSA). Relief Agency No. 2 aided family in 1928 only, with food and clothing (BSA).
A13. Reasons for dependency of family	Not dependent (see #A12)	Family not usually dependent (see #A12).
A14. Number of agencies knowing family since marriage of parents	Not determined	At least 16 agencies, since conception of boy, as parents never married (SSI).
A15. Type of social agencies interested in family	Not determined	Straight relief, public and private (RA, BSA); family welfare (BSA, Relief Agency No. 1); child welfare (CPA, BCW); physical health (MH & H, CPA, BCW); mental health (Ment. Hosp. No. 1, to agencies); recreational (Y Ct., BCW); vocational (Voc. Aid Soc.).
A16. Age of boy at first social service contact with family	Not determined	Before birth of boy (MH & H).

F.E.D.—O

197

Factor	Home Interview	Field Investigation*
A17. Moral standards of home	Stepfather a heavy drinker until recently, according to mother	Stepfather has long record for B & E, drunkenness, etc.; was committed to the H of C in August 1940 (B of Prob). Stepfather also in court for A & B on wife, and he and wife in court for neglecting the children (BCW). (See #31 on delinquency of mother and half-brother). Immoral, alcoholic maternal aunt lives with family and is a bad influence on boy (BSA, B of Prob).
A18. Self-respect of family	Mother not greatly concerned about family reputation or boy's delinquency	A steady stream of men callers at all hours according to neighbors, landlady and stepfather (BCW, 1935). Mother begged for aid when she had just collected the stepfather's pay (BSA, 1939). Stepfather asked for aid of Relief Agency No. 2 while being paid wages by the X Public Utility Co. (BSA). Mother says the stepfather has told boy to 'pick up things,' *i.e.*, steal (BCW, 1934). Neighbors considered mother 'everybody's wife' (CPA).
A19. Ambition of family	Mother has no ambition; seems resigned to living from day to day without thought of the future; is making no effort to improve the home situation	No indication in agency records that family had ambition.
A20. Plans of family for boy's future	Stepfather and mother willing to allow boy to follow through his own plans but have decided nothing for him; boy wants to complete high school education and join the Air Corps of the U.S. Army	No information.
A21. Recreational facilities for children in the home	Facilities confined to a few 'funny books' and toys; mother admits making no special effort to encourage children to spend their leisure time at home	Mother says boy has toys of his own but that even so he steals toys from others (CPA, 1935).
A22. Provision for children to entertain friends at home	Children are allowed to have friends in the home but no special efforts made in this direction	No information.

198

Factor	Home Interview	Field Investigation*
A23. Family group recreations	Mother states that she and boy often go to the movies together	Stepfather sometimes takes boy and half-brother to the movies, but apt to be too drunk to be a companion (BCW).
A24. Method of control of children by father or substitute	Stepfather takes very little part in the rearing of the children, leaving the discipline of them to mother, according to her	Stepfather knocks the children about rather brutally. Boy states stepfather hit him and made him do what he wanted (BCW, 1932). Stepfather whips or deprives of supper or movies (CPA, 1935).
A25. Method of control of children by mother or substitute	Physical punishment when boy younger; later, deprivation of privileges and threat of law	Mother also whips or deprives of supper or movies (CPA, 1935).
A26. Discipline of boy by father or substitute	Stepfather uninterested in boy's welfare, on the whole; feels little sense of responsibility for his actions, according to mother	Stepfather beats boy till he screams all over the neighborhood (BSA, 1934). Stepfather alternately quiet and noisy, erratic and unpredictable, in his handling of boy (CPA, 1935).
A27. Discipline of boy by mother or substitute	Mother says she may not have been firm enough in disciplining boy	Boy on street at all hours (CPA, 1935). Mother can't control boy (BCW to CPA, 1935).
A28. Dominant parent	Stepfather's role in home seems to be little more than bringing home the pay check; mother makes all the decisions and assumes the responsibility; she seems more dominant	Stepfather believes three of the children are not his and refuses to feel responsible for them (BCW, 1934 and CPA, 1935). Mother insisted on keeping the maternal aunt in the home against the stepfather's wishes (CPA).
A29. Conjugal relations of parents or substitute	Mother has 'no kick coming'; the stepfather a good provider and never abused her; this statement, however, was made without any enthusiasm	Mother says she and stepfather quarrel but seldom fight (BCW, 1928). Separated from Dec. 1932 to May 1933, in 1935 and again later. Mother says she returned to stepfather for financial reasons only. Both contemplated divorce from time to time (CPA, BCW, BSA). Stepfather says mother drove him to drink (BCW, 1934).
A30. Affection of father or substitute for boy	Stepfather is indifferent; has little interest in him, takes no responsibility for his actions, has never shown boy any affection, according to mother	Stepfather really fond only of half-brother, Arthur. Stepfather resentful that boy is causing trouble (Y Ct., 1938); abusive to boy (BSA, 1934); inclined to 'pick' on the boy (BCW, 1932). Stepfather willing to and did contribute to boy's board (CPA, 1935).

199

Factor	Home Interview	Field Investigation*
A31. Affection of mother or substitute for boy	Seems genuine; is boy's regular visitor and correspondent at the Correctional School; finds excuses for his misbehavior	Half-brother, Arthur, is mother's favorite also and boy feels this. Mother fears having her children taken from her; gave boy a bicycle; requested boy be returned to her from foster home (CPA, 1935).
A32. Relations of siblings to boy	Younger brother looks up to boy; no antagonism, according to mother	Boy is fond of half-brother, Arthur (BCW, 1935).
A33. Household duties of boy	Only occasional duties, no regularly assigned tasks; boy has not had to feel responsible for anything at home	Mother sends boy to store occasionally (CPA).
A34. Potentials for culture conflict in home	Inapplicable, because parents and boy native-born	Inapplicable as parents and boy native-born.
A35. Culture conflict in home	Inapplicable (see #A34)	Inapplicable (see #A34).
A36. Evidences of cultural refinement	Home lacks evidence of good taste or love of beauty; stepfather and mother show no indication of aesthetic appreciation	None (see #64, #65, #66).
A37. Cohesiveness of family group	Stepfather is chief factor in family's lack of unity because of his drinking habits and lack of affection for the children; home is more than 'just a place to hang your hat' chiefly because of the mutual attachment between mother and the children	Stepfather and maternal aunt fight 'like cats and dogs,' yet mother insists on keeping aunt in the home (CPA). Stepfather and mother in court for neglecting children, but children were left in their care after a warning by the judge (BCW, 1935). Stepfather believes two of the other children are not his and refuses to feel responsible for them (CPA, BCW). Mother does not want to lose any of the children; no indication of hostility between the children (all agencies).
A38. Birth and infancy of boy	Weighed 6 lbs. at birth; good health in first 2 yrs.; all other items negative, according to mother	A full-term baby (CPA). Normal delivery, no complications (MH & H, 1925; CPA). Breast-fed till 7 mos. Convulsions twice, one at 6 mos. and one at 1 yr. (CPA). Treated for a mild form of epilepsy in OPD of Ment. Hosp. No. 1 in 1930 (BPD). Had tonsils and adenoids removed in 1935 (PQ Hosp. to CPA). Walked at 13 mos. and talked at 15 mos. (CPA).

Factor	Home Interview	Field Investigation*
A39. Contagious diseases	Only contagious disease was a mild case of measles at 10 yrs. according to mother	Scarlet fever in 1934 (school, BCW).
A40, Specific A41. susceptibilities	Frequent chest colds since recovery from pneumonia at 3 yrs. 'One lung weak since'; has had boils at the Correctional School, none at home; all other items negative, according to mother	Frequent colds, croup, and pneumonia once before 10 yrs. (CPA, 1935). Infrequent headaches and dizziness, sometimes refuses breakfast (Ment. Hosp. No. 1 to CPA). Enuresis at 11 yrs. in foster home (CPA, 1936). Boy nervous, has nightmares after seeing thrilling movies and doesn't sleep well (PQ Hosp. to CPA, 1935). Nervous, smokes a lot; complete physical examination negative except for nervousness (RS Hosp. to BCW, 1934). History indicates mild form of epilepsy (Ment. Hosp. No. 1 to BCW, 1934). Restless and very emotional with violent outbursts of temper (Ment. Hosp. No. 1 to BPD, 1936). One lung 'weak' (BPD, 1940). Mother says boy started school late because of ill health (BCW, 1932).
A42, Bad habits (and A43. age began)	*Smoking:* since 13 or 14 yrs.—at home since 14 yrs; *Truanting:* 'once or twice' since 14 yrs.; *Stealing rides and truck hopping:* since 12–13 yrs.; *Stubbornness:* often disobedient and argumentative with parents; *Impulsive stealing* (when arrested)	Mother says boy unmanageable since infancy (CPA). Mother says boy set fire in the house only once, age 8 (BCW, 1933). Stepfather complains that maternal aunt has taught boy (age 9) bad sex practices (BCW, 1935). Mother says boy stole a bus ride to Wellesley (BCW, 1935). *Smoking:* age 10 (RS Hosp. to BCW, police to BCW). *Runaway from foster home:* age 11 (CPA). *Truanting:* age 10 (CPA, school). *Impulsive lying:* age 8 (school to BCW). *Vile language:* age 10 (neighbors to BCW). *Pugnacity:* struck girls on street, age 9 (BCW); threatened schoolmate with knife, age 12 (CPA); attacked boy with a knife, age 11 (BPD). *Destructive mischief:* broke many windows in houses and autos, age 8 (landlady to BCW).

Factor	Home Interview	Field Investigation*
		Tantrums: wild outbursts of temper, age 10 (Ment. Hosp. No. 1 to BPD). *Late hours:* on the street at all hrs., age 10 (CPA). *Impulsive stealing:* from stores, age 8 (school to BCW); stealing from other boys in club, age 8 (S.H. No. 2 to BCW). *Planful stealing:* age 9 (Ment. Hosp. No. 1 to BCW); age 13 (Y Ct.). *Indecent exposure:* age 10 (girl accused boy, BCW).
A44. Agreement between statement of boy and parents	(to be filled in by coder)	
A45. Frequency of movie attendance	Once or twice a week	No information.
A46. Play places	Own neighborhood, distant neighborhood streets, settlement house; mother states boy spent most of his leisure time at Settlement House No. 1	Began to attend S.H. No. 2 toward end of 1932 (BCW, 1933). Attending S.H. No. 1 (Y Ct., 1938).
A47. Church or Sunday School	Occasionally	No information.
A48. Nature of companionships	Few friends; delinquent, younger boys	Boy tended to bad associations (school, age 15).
A49–A52. Agreement between statement of boy and parents	(to be filled in by coder	
A53, A54. Family's reason for boy's conduct	Although boy has been stubborn and hard to handle at times, mother is quite satisfied with his behavior at home; she blames circumstances surrounding each of his delinquencies rather than boy himself or home conditions; does not consider boy in need of correction or adjustment and finds excuses for all the trouble he has gotten into in the community	Mother says boy can't withstand temptation; he is sorry after he misbehaves (BCW, 1935).

Case of Henry W

SCHOOL HISTORY*

Factor	Field Investigation†
A56. Age started school	6 yrs. (chronological list of school experiences based on ADP card from Medway, Mass.).
A57. Number of years in school	Between 9 and 10 yrs. (chronological list of school experiences based on record cards from Medway, Canton, F School and BPD).
A58. Grade attained	Grade 8 (F School records).
A59. Grades repeated	Grade 1 and grade 5 (sources same as #A57).
A60. Grades skipped	None (sources same as #A57).
A61. Amount of retardation	2 yrs. (see Boston Public Schools Scale).
A62. Attendance in special classes	None (sources same as #A57).
Attendance in Disciplinary Day School	None (sources same as #A57).
A63. Number of school experiences	10 (sources same as #A57), not counting correctional school.
A64, Scholarship in last full year A65.	A in Physical Education and Hygiene; B's or C's in Reading, Literature, English, Spelling, Penmanship, Arithmetic, Geography and History; D's or E's in Music, Drawing, Conduct (yellow sheet school records).
A66. Nature of first misbehavior in school	Truancy, unruliness in class, and stealing (records of B School, Boston).
A67. Age at which first school misbehavior occurred	10 yrs. (records of B School, Boston).
A68. Grade in which first misbehavior occurred	Grade 5 (records of B School, Boston).
A69. Age truancy started	Grade 5 (records of B School, Boston).
A70. Frequency of truancy	Occasional at first, later persistent (sources same as #A57).
A71– Teacher's estimate of characteristics of boy A74.	Stealing, obscene notes and talk, truancy, cheating, unreliableness, lack of interest in work, laziness, smoking, unhappiness, depression, easy discouragement, carelessness in work, inattention, slovenliness in appearance, suspiciousness, thoughtlessness (8th grade teacher of F School).
A75, Summary of school behavior A76.	(to be filled in by coder).
A77. Reasons for retardation	Lack of interest plus many changes of schools (Principal of F School).
A78. Reasons for truancy	Influence of bad companions and lack of interest in school (Principal of F School).

* The home interviewer obtained no information on school history. This was done entirely through field investigation.
† Includes correspondence.

Factor	*Field Investigation†*
A79. Adjustment to schoolmates	Tended to bad associations (Principal of F School).
A80. Participation in extracurricular activities	Did not participate (Principal of F School).
Boy's outstanding problems	Boy's problems result from home conditions plus his own attitude toward life; family careless and inadequate; stepfather drinks; boy is slippery, untrustworthy, and has poor associations (Principal of F School).

APPENDIX B

TRAITS

1. DEFINITIONS OF TRAITS
2. INCIDENCE OF 66 TRAITS AMONG DELINQUENTS AND NONDELINQUENTS

EXHIBIT B-1

DEFINITIONS OF TRAITS

Listed in accordance with the table numbers originally assigned in *Physique and Delinquency* and repeated in this volume to facilitate cross-reference)

Developmental Health History
1. Poor Health in Infancy—a pathological condition which interferes with normal physical activity, growth, or response to environment and social stimuli.
3. Extreme Restlessness in Early Childhood—the inability to 'sit still' (*i.e.*, always wanting to be 'on the go') according to parents, teachers and family physicians.
4. Enuresis in Early Childhood—bedwetting persisting beyond the years of normal expectancy.

Neurologic Findings
5. Irregular Reflexes—any marked deviation from the accepted norm of deep or superficial reflexes, the presence of which might or might not, in itself, be of diagnostic significance; includes the pupillary, abdominal, cremasteric (testicular), patellar (knee-jerk) reflexes.
6. Cyanosis—a neurologic trait manifested by a blue discoloration of the skin resulting from inadequate oxygenization of the blood.
7. Dermographia—a condition indicated by reddish tracings on the skin made by light stroking with the nail.
8. Tremors—a neurologically-induced tendency to involuntary trembling.

Other Physical Findings
9. Genital Underdevelopment—undersized or hypofunction of genital organs in relation to average development and function for the specific age.
10. Strong Hand Grip (75 kilograms and over)—as measured by a standard hand dynamometer.

Some Aspects of Intelligence
11. Low Verbal Intelligence (Wechsler Verbal I.Q. below 80)—essentially the lack of capacity to do intellectual tasks requiring the use of abstract reasoning and memory, in which the approach to meaning tends to be through a structure of intermediate symbols rather than through concrete physical things.
12. High Performance Intelligence (Wechsler Performance I.Q. 101 and over)—the aspect of intelligence in which the approach to meaning tends to be by way of direct physical relationships, with a minimum dependence on intermediary symbols and abstractions.
13. Originality—resulting from an unconventional way of perception, experience, or thought; and, in its positive aspect, a genuine and often productive expression of the personality, while, in its negative aspect, leading to estrangement from the community, to a lack of common sense, to 'queerness,' and the like.
14. Banality—the complete or comparative inability to think in other than the most commonplace terms and concepts; often found to be a consequence of conventionality.

207

15. Marked Power of Observation—includes both the ability to observe accurately and the ability to maintain such accuracy of observation at a fairly constant level; requiring a fairly accurate visual memory and a certain amount of attentive concentration.
16. Intuition—the ability to penetrate quickly some or all of the factors in a given situation, experience, or task, not by conscious deductive or inductive reasoning, but by sensing the quality of the factors involved or at least one aspect of their quality; not necessarily leading to constructive results. (For instance, if intuition is combined with a lack of mental control or with flightiness, it may lead to an entirely distorted mental picture of a situation or to a quite inadequate solution of a problem.)
17. Tendency to Phantasy—refers to the invention of something which is not taken from reality, or to a combination of elements taken from reality in a way which does not conform to that reality; may be productive or receptive. (Actually, there are many intermediate states and combinations of these two extremes. In either case, phantasy may lead to a merely arbitrary neglect of certain elements in reality or to a consistent elaboration of well-perceived elements into a product of phantasy.)
18. Common Sense—the faculty of thinking and acting in the ways of the community; may be present even if some acts of the individual run counter to accepted mores. (There may, for instance, be a conflict between common sense and a phantasy-induced thirst for adventure.)
19. Unmethodical Approach to Problems—pertaining to the way in which an intellectual problem or some task is typically attacked in an attempt to master it.
20. Potential Capacity for Objective Interests—self-explanatory.

Basic Attitudes to Authority and Society
21. Social Assertiveness—the rather superficial quality of asserting one's will and ambitions; unlike *self-assertion*, which usually implies a genuine, spontaneous self.
22. Defiance—aggressive self-assertion born out of deep insecurity or weakness; therefore, often indiscriminate in its aims and means and usually directed *against* somebody or something rather than toward a positive goal.
23. Marked Submissiveness to Authority—the abandonment of self-assertion in an attempt to gain security by submitting to others, especially to those believed stronger (originally one or both of the parents, and later, also, the more anonymous power of institutions, public opinion, conventional usage, and the like).
24. Ambivalence to Authority—the result of contradictory or conflicting feelings, such as co-existence of defiant and submissive strivings, of assertive and dependent attitudes.

Feelings of Resentment, Anxiety, Inferiority and Frustration
25. Enhanced Feeling of Insecurity—a state in which these feelings exert a decidedly stronger influence within the personality dynamics—either quantitatively or qualitatively—than is usual in the average person; may, however, remain largely unconscious.
26. Marked Feeling of Not Being Wanted or Loved—the feeling that one is not accepted, not included, or even rejected by others; a sense of a lack of positive human relationship to a particular group or person, especially to parents and other members of the family, in early childhood. (This feeling is very often

repressed and becomes unconscious. It may lead to an exaggerated need for affection, recognition and success.)

27. Feeling of Not Being Taken Care Of—the feeling that there is no active interest on the part of others (especially of parents), or help from them, in situations in which one deems himself entitled to such interest and help. (Once this feeling is established it may outlast the particular situation which produced it.)

28. Marked Feeling of Not Being Taken Seriously—the feeling that one's own person, interests, ideas, and wishes are not acknowledged and not treated as deserving of respect and consideration for their own sake. (This is frequently produced in childhood, often inadvertently, by making a child feel that whatever he does is 'child's play'—especially if his wishes and interests do not coincide with those of his parents.)

29. Feeling of Helplessness—a particularly frequent, important, and very often unconscious kind of insecurity in which the individual feels himself incompetent, especially as regards changing or influencing anything, and most particularly the course of his own life.

30. Feeling of Not Being Appreciated—refers especially to the impression that one's qualities, gifts, intentions, and achievements are not sufficiently thought of or valued; often occurring in association with conscious as well as unconscious grandiose ideas and opinions about one's self.

31. Fear of Failure and Defeat—a frequent consequence of anxiety especially in persons with an overcompetitive attitude; possibly permeating every sphere of life (not only work or play, but relations with others); leading either to greater effort or to inhibitions, aloofness, and a recoiling from competition.

32. Feeling of Resentment—the feeling of frustration, envy, or dissatisfaction, with particular emphasis on the negative wish that others be denied satisfactions or enjoyments that one has himself lacked, rather than the positive hope or attempt to better one's own situation.

Feelings of Kindliness and Hostility

33. Good Surface Contact with Others—the ability to get along with people regardless of the underlying attitude, which may be, for instance, one of isolation or even hostility; sometimes manifesting itself in a surface attitude of 'keep smiling,' without any real friendliness or kindness. (This need not be merely simulated or acted; the individual may sincerely believe that he is very friendly and sociable and appears to be so, whereas unconsciously he may be intensely hostile.)

34. Hostility—conscious or unconscious impulses against others, without good reason, usually accompanying a fear that the person against whom it is directed is, in turn, hostile.

35. Marked Suspiciousness—indiscriminate or exaggerated feeling, unwarranted by the situation. (The person is usually not aware that he is unduly mistrustful; he thinks rather he is being merely cautious or realistic or that he is being persecuted.)

36. Destructiveness—the tendency to destroy, to hurt, to be negativistic, directed against others or against one's self. (Usually both trends run parallel, one often being more manifest, the other more suppressed. Destructiveness is not to be confused with destructive-sadistic trends, which pertain to goals of drives.)

37. Feeling of Isolation—a feeling of being alone (often combined with a sense of helplessness), and of not being sufficiently capable of giving and receiving

love and affection, possibly accompanied by an appearance and a subjective conviction of being very sociable. (This is illustrated, for instance. by the person who is constantly 'on the go' and always 'making friends,' merely to escape awareness of extreme emotional isolation.)

38. Defensive Attitude—either exaggerated in proportion to the attack or directed against an imaginary attack; the means of defense are varied, sometimes consisting of a 'shell-like' attitude of 'warding off' every approach and erecting a wall around oneself and sometimes taking a more aggressive form (as, for instance, in persons who are very sensitive to any criticism and are provoked by it to defiant or obstinate or opinionated behavior).

Dependence and Independence

39. Marked Dependence on Others—the tendency to cling to others rather than to stand on one's own feet, evidenced in relations to loved ones, to employers, or to others who in one way or another furnish protection. (Often, the need for dependence is directed indiscriminately toward anyone who appears strong and who may be a potential protector.)

40. Feeling of Being Able to Manage Own Life—a deep-seated confidence of being able to handle the problems and tasks of life without leaning unduly on others.

Goals of Strivings

41. Narcissistic Trends—reflect love of self, resulting in increased need for power, superiority, prestige, status and admiration.

42. Receptive Trends—reflect a more or less unconscious expectation that one will somehow be taken care of by others, the individual not feeling obliged to make any effort to assume his responsibilities; this tendency may take a passive form (waiting for someone else to provide what one desires); or it may take a more active form leading to outwardly expressed greed, or an attempt to secure the desired object without effort (*e.g.*, by stealing), or without assuming any obligations.

43. Masochistic Trends—the tendency to suffer and to be dependent on others.

44. Destructive-Sadistic Trends—the tendency to destroy, to hurt, to be negativistic.

Some General Qualities of Personality

45. Emotional Lability—refers to the way in which affect (emotion) is discharged and manifested and not to the general fluidity or stability of a person; pertains to qualities in the affective reactions of an individual which permit his inner drives, feelings and urges to take their course and which allow tensions to explode, thus leading to certain emotions and moods which are more or less independent of consequences and of the objective requirements of a situation.

46. Lack of Self-Control—the inability to control the discharge and expression of affectivity.

47. Vivacity—'liveliness' of behavior.

48. Compulsory Trends—reflect attempts to defend the self against conscious or, more often, unconscious anxiety, and includes not only typical neurotic compulsions but the less evident cases of a rigidity not permitting of flexible adaptation to changing situations.

49. Preponderance of Extroversive Trends—the tendency to discharge tensions in emotion or in motoric action.

50. Preponderance of Introversive Trends—the tendency to pile up tensions by an emphasis on the creative mental processes (a living more 'within one's self') and by difficulty in relating emotionally to others.

Deep-Rooted Emotional Dynamisms
51. Sensitivity—the acute awareness of conflicting situations and stimuli and of their implications, resulting in some inhibition of action.
52. Suggestibility—the easy swaying by an appeal to one's feelings, despite one's better judgment.
53. Feeling of Inadequacy—inability to express or conduct oneself, in most aspects of life, with a fair degree of efficiency.
54. Stubbornness—probably largely the result of thwarted dynamic qualities.
55. Adventurousness—exceptional need for change, excitement or risk.
56. Uninhibited Motor Responses to Stimuli—direct behavioral resolution of tension.
57. Emotional Instability—lack of harmonious, integrated, and appropriate feelings and reactions.

Appetitive-Aesthetic Tendencies
58. Aestheticism—impulse for the more refined, discriminating and artistic.
59. Sensuousness—the inclination to free indulgence of appetites.
60. Acquisitiveness—the inclination to acquire material things, money or objects, over and above any desire for their immediate use.

Personality Orientation
61. Conventionality—preference for the safe and familiar.
62. Lack of Self-Criticism—an inability and unwillingness to assay one's own faults and virtues, abilities and liabilities.
63. Conscientiousness—scrupulousness about achieving one's aims.
64. Impracticality—the absence of inclination to consider the feasibility of any contemplated course.

Some Aspects of Mental Pathology
65. Emotional Conflicts—inability to reconcile opposing feelings or attitudes (or contradictory goals), not only in respect to a person's immediate circle but also as regards more generalized emotion-arousing objects or institutions (*e.g.*, sexual conventions); noted only if it could be established that they resulted in a change in conduct.
66. Neuroticism—*marked neuroticism* is a condition in which the individual suffers from more than average insecurity and anxiety (conscious or unconscious) against which he develops protective devices differing quantitatively or qualitatively from the culturally-accepted ones and leading to conflicts which are, as a rule, not solvable by him for the time being; *mild neuroticism* is a condition that does not prevent the individual from relatively efficient adaptation.
67. Psychopathy—refers to 'all marked mental and emotional deviations that do not clearly belong in any one of the other diagnostic groupings.' (The psychopath is less ill than the psychotic, more ill than the neurotic, and usually less amiable than the neurotic.)

Appendix B

EXHIBIT B-2

INCIDENCE OF 66 TRAITS AMONG DELINQUENTS AND NONDELINQUENTS

(From *Unraveling Juvenile Delinquency*)

Trait Identification*	Traits and Subcategories†	Percentages of the Respective Trait Totals			
		Delinquents	Nondelinquents	Differences	P
1. (XIV-1)	Poor Health in Infancy	14·6%	9·6%	5·0%	·02
3. (XIV-2)	Extreme Restlessness in Early Childhood	59·6	30·0	29·6	·01
4. (XIV-2)	Enuresis in Early Childhood	28·2	13·6	14·6	·01
5. (XIV-6)	Irregular Reflexes	34·1	38·6	−4·5	—
6. (XIV-13)	Cyanosis (Marked or Slight)	41·5	43·5	−2·0	—
7. (XIV-13)	Dermographia (Marked or Slight)	45·1	58·3	−13·2	·01
8. (XIV-13)	Tremors (Marked or Slight)	18·4	20·4	−2·0	—
9. (XIV-9)	Genital Underdevelopment (Marked or Slight)	11·6	13·3	−1·7	—
10. (XIV-4)	Strength of Hand Grip (Dynamometric Strength—75 Kilograms and Over)	51·5	43·9	7·6	·02
11. (App. D-11)	Low Verbal Intelligence (Wechsler Verbal I.Q.—below 80)	28·4	16·2	12·2	·01
12. (App. D-12)	High Performance Intelligence (Wechsler Performance I.Q.—101 and Over)	39·6	42·2	−2·6	—
13. (XVII-1)	Originality (Marked or Slight)	27·6	25·5	2·1	—
14. (XVII-3)	Banality (Marked or Slight)	26·3	31·2	−4·9	—
15. (XVII-4)	Marked Power of Observation	63·7	70·7	−7·0	·02
16. (XVII-7)	Intuition (Marked or Slight)	16·6	15·4	1·2	—
17. (XVII-8)	Tendency to Phantasy (Marked or Slight)	39·1	32·4	6·7	·05
18. (XVII-6)	Common Sense (Marked or Slight)	75·0	80·9	−5·9	·05
19. (XVII-10)	Unmethodical Approach to Problems	79·1	65·0	14·1	·01
20. (XVII-11)	Potential Capacity for Objective Interests (Marked or Slight)	44·4	54·4	−10·0	·01
21. (XVIII-2)	Social Assertiveness (Marked or Slight)	45·2	20·5	24·7	·01
22. (XVIII-3)	Defiance (Marked or Slight)	50·4	11·5	38·9	·01
23. (XVIII-4)	Marked Submissiveness to Authority	26·6	79·5	−52·9	·01
24. (XVIII-5)	Ambivalence to Authority (Marked or Slight)	40·9	19·6	21·3	·01
25. (XVIII-7)	Enhanced Feeling of Insecurity (Marked or Slight)	18·4	28·8	−10·4	·01
26. (XVIII-8)	Marked Feeling of Not Being Wanted or Loved	84·3	88·0	−3·7	—

* Numbers in parentheses refer to table numbers in *Unraveling Juvenile Delinquency*. Some of the figures in this table do not agree with those published in *Unraveling Juvenile Delinquency*; all the changes in percentages are small and in no way affect the analysis of the traits made in *Unraveling Juvenile Delinquency*; the differences in the P's are usually the result of the subcategory combinations.

† The subcategories or combinations of subcategories are indicated in parentheses.

Trait Identification*	Traits and Subcategories†	Percentages of the Respective Trait Totals			
		Delinquents	Nondelinquents	Differences	P
27. (XVIII-9)	Feeling of Not Being Taken Care Of (Marked or Slight)	28·8%	24·2%	4·6%	—
28. (XVIII-10)	Marked Feeling of Not Being Taken Seriously	44·2	51·6	−7·4	·05
29. (XVIII-12)	Feeling of Helplessness (Marked or Slight)	42·0	54·4	−12·4	·01
30. (XVIII-11)	Feeling of Not Being Appreciated (Marked or Slight)	36·1	24·5	11·6	·01
31. (XVIII-13)	Fear of Failure and Defeat (Marked or Slight)	43·8	63·0	−19·2	·01
32. (XVIII-14)	Feeling of Resentment (Marked or Slight)	74·0	50·8	23·2	·01
33. (XVIII-17)	Poor Surface Contact with Others	8·3	3·3	5·0	·01
34. (XVIII-22)	Hostility (Marked or Slight)	79·6	55·9	23·7	·01
35. (XVIII-23)	Marked Suspiciousness	51·2	26·5	24·7	·01
36. (XVIII-24)	Destructiveness (Marked or Slight)	48·4	15·4	33·0	·01
37. (XVIII-25)	Feeling of Isolation (Marked or Slight)	45·1	36·3	8·8	·02
38. (XVIII-26)	Defensive Attitude (Marked or Slight)	56·1	44·4	11·7	·01
39. (XVIII-27)	Marked Dependence on Others	68·9	85·6	−16·7	·01
40. (XVIII-32)	Feeling of Being Able to Manage Own Life (Marked or Slight)	73·2	63·7	9·5	·01
41. (XVIII-33)	Narcissistic Trends (Marked or Slight)	23·1	14·3	8·8	·01
42. (XVIII-35)	Receptive Trends (Marked or Slight)	30·0	13·6	16·4	·01
43. (XVIII-34)	Masochistic Trends (Marked or Slight)	15·2	36·7	−21·5	·01
44. (XVIII-36)	Destructive-Sadistic Trends (Marked or Slight)	48·7	15·8	32·9	·01
45. (XVIII-37)	Emotional Lability (Marked or Slight)	43·5	18·6	24·9	·01
46. (XVIII-38)	Self-Control (Marked or Slight)	38·5	65·7	−27·2	·01
47. (XVIII-39)	Vivacity (Marked or Slight)	50·7	23·2	27·5	·01
48. (XVIII-40)	Compulsory Trends (Marked or Slight)	20·6	30·1	−9·5	·01
49. (XVIII-41)	Preponderance of Extroversive Trends (Marked or Slight)	54·6	35·1	19·5	·01
50. (XVIII-42)	Preponderance of Introversive Trends (Marked or Slight)	27·3	24·5	2·8	—
51. (XIX-1)	Sensitivity	31·7	35·7	−4·0	—
52. (XIX-1)	Suggestibility	59·6	26·3	33·3	·01
53. (XIX-1)	Feeling of Inadequacy	84·9	69·3	15·6	·01
54. (XIX-1)	Stubbornness	41·4	8·2	33·2	·01
55. (XIX-1)	Adventurousness	55·2	18·0	37·2	·01
56. (XIX-1)	Uninhibited Motor Responses to Stimuli	56·6	28·5	28·1	·01
57. (XIX-1)	Emotional Instability	81·7	50·1	31·6	·01
58. (XIX-2)	Aestheticism	17·3	38·5	−21·2	·01
59. (XIX-2)	Sensuousness	19·9	6·0	13·9	·01
60. (XIX-2)	Acquisititiveness	20·7	14·0	6·7	·01
61. (XIX-3)	Conventionality	24·7	48·5	−23·8	·01

Appendix B

Trait Identification*	Traits and Subcategories†	Percentages of the Respective Trait Totals			
		Delin-quents	Non-delin-quents	Differ-ences	P
62. (XIX-3)	Lack of Self-Criticism	28·7%	10·6%	18·1%	·01
63. (XIX-3)	Conscientiousness	8·8	54·3	−45·5	·01
64. (XIX-3)	Practicality	19·5	34·9	−15·4	·01
65. (XIX-4)	Emotional Conflicts	74·7	37·6	37·1	·01
66. (XVIII-43)	Neuroticism (Marked, Mild, Trends)	24·6	35·8	−11·2	·01
67. (XVIII-43)	Psychopathy	24.2	6·3	17·9	·01

APPENDIX C

SOCIAL FACTORS

EXHIBIT C-1

DEFINITIONS OF SOCIAL FACTORS

Listed in accordance with letters assigned in the text of the current work to facilitate cross-reference)

. Crowding of Home—considered *overcrowded* if the number of occupants averaged more than two per bedroom (excluding infants).

. Cleanliness and Orderliness of Home—refers to the usual or typical condition of the home; *i.e.*, whether the home was normally neat and clean, reflecting evidence of systematic housekeeping.

. Nativity of Parents—the concern here was to determine whether the parents were both born in the United States; one born in the United States, the other in a foreign country; both parents born outside the continental United States.

. Delinquency of Father

. Delinquency of Mother—determined by past or present official record of arrests and/or proven juvenile delinquency or adult criminality, prior or subsequent to birth of boy, for which not arrested (excluding drunkenness and minor auto violations or violations of license laws).

. Alcoholism of Father

, Alcoholism of Mother—refers to intoxication and includes frequent or regular or chronic addiction to alcohol, and not to very occasional episodes of overdrinking in an atmosphere of conviviality (as at a celebration).

. Emotional Disturbance of Father

. Emotional Disturbance of Mother—refers particularly to the presence of emotional disturbances in a parent since birth of boy, as judged by psychoses, psychoneuroses, psychopathies, epilepsies, sex perversions, delirium tremens, marked liabilities of personality (such as self-indulgence, ego-centricity).

. Serious Physical Ailment of Father

. Serious Physical Ailment of Mother—refers to debilitating illnesses that interfered with a father's earning capacity or with a mother's home duties (such as tuberculosis, cancer, Bright's disease, severe cardiovascular diseases, diseases of the nervous system, rheumatoid arthritis).

. Usual Economic Condition of Family—judged: *comfortable*, if there were sufficient resources for at least four months in the event of a sudden reduction of the usual weekly income; *marginal*, if living on daily earnings and accumulating little or nothing, resorting to temporary aid to supplement income during seasonal unemployment or illness of breadwinners; *dependent*, if continuously receiving outside aid.

. Usual Work Habits of Father—rated: *good*, if he was reliable, and industrious, an asset to his employer; *fair*, if (although having the capacity of a good worker) permitted his work to be interrupted by drunkenness, drug

217

addiction, occasional loafing, or vagabondage; *poor*, if lazy, dishonest, unstable, ambitionless, a liability to his employer.

P.　Management of Family Income—regarded as: *entirely planned*, if basic needs were regularly provided for in the budget (such as rent, food, medical care, insurance, clothing, payment for installment purchases); *partially planned*, if some but not all the fixed obligations were budgeted, but never theless living within the family's financial resources; *haphazard*, if the family did not confine its expenditures to income, borrowing money from friends, relatives, or employers without concern for their ability to repay.

Q.　Household Routine—designated as: *well planned*, if there was a daily pattern in the life of the family (providing for mealtimes, family chores, the children's playtime, home lessons, bedtime), so that the atmosphere of the home was secure and serene; *partially planned*, if there were some fixed points in the daily life of the family (such as mealtimes and bedtimes), but other necessary routines were not clearly established; *haphazard*, if there were practically no fixed points in the running of the household (each member following his own bent as to chores, meals, home lessons, recreations, bedtime, and so on).

R.　Cultural Refinement in Home—reflects an appreciation of the 'finer things of life' on the part of one or more family members, as evidenced by love of classical music (record collections, playing an instrument), of art, of literature, of tasteful home furnishings.

S.　Self-Respect of Family—reflects a strong desire to protect the family name, embarrassment about any irregularity in the behavior or status of any member of the family, and in efforts at self-help in times of crisis.

T.　Ambitiousness of Parents—reflects a desire to improve the status of the family such as higher education for the children, plans to move to better neighborhoods or into more adequate housing, saving to buy a home in order to stabilize living conditions, careful planning to improve economic status, and so on.

U.　Conduct Standards of Family—regarded as: *poor*, if there was immorality and/or drunkenness, and/or criminality (exclusive of minor auto violations or violations of license laws) in one or more members of the immediate family group (excluding the boy being studied); *fair*, if there was a lack of positive and wholesome ideals or conduct even though none of the above were present; *good*, if the family had positive and wholesome ideals (respect for law and order and for the Ten Commandments).

V.　Conjugal Relations of Parents—judged as: *good*, if parents loved each other; *fair*, if they were indifferent or hostile to one another but no open breach had occurred; *poor*, if parents had separated, were divorced, or one had deserted.

W.　Dominant Parent in Family Affairs—refers to the parent who assumed the major guidance of the family affairs (disciplining the children, controlling the purse strings, planning for the children's future).

X.　Usual Occupation of Mother—refers to own, step-, or foster-mother with whom the boy lived for the major part of his life. Classified as: *housewife*, if she had not worked outside the home since the birth of the boy; a *erratic worker*, if her employment pattern was not consistent (flitted from job to job, working now and then to meet an immediate and often selfish financial need or to escape from household routine or responsibility); *employed regularly*, if she showed a consistent pattern of either full-time or part-time work with interruptions because of personal family crises, and not because of her own whims.

Y. Supervision of Boy by Mother—considered: *suitable*, if she personally kept close watch over boy's activities at home or in the neighborhood, or provided for his leisure hours in clubs or in playgrounds (if she was for good reason unable to supervise boy's activities, she made provision for a responsible adult to do so); *fair*, if mother (although not working and not incapacitated) gave or provided only limited supervision to boy; *unsuitable*, if mother left boy to his own devices, without guidance, or in the care of an irresponsible person.

Z. Family Group Recreations—at least some planned activities which include both parents and all the children (except infants), such as church attendance, picnics, excursions, bowling, ice skating, beach parties, visiting relatives, auto rides.

AA. Parents' Attitude to Boy's Companions—considered: *warm*, if boy was encouraged to bring his friends to the home and some provision was made for their entertainment; *indifferent*, if parents did not actually prohibit visits of playmates; *inhospitable*, if parents did not permit boy to invite even those friends considered suitable playmates.

BB. Recreational Facilities for Boy in Home—considered: *adequate*, if they were diversified (such as constructive games, books, toys, materials for hobbies, musical instruments); *meager*, if only an occasional book or toy was provided without any planning for the boy's home use of leisure.

CC. Family Cohesiveness—rated as: *marked*, if there was a strong 'we' feeling among the members of the immediate family as evidenced by warm affection for each other; *some*, if despite pulling away from the family circle by one parent, the remaining parent and the children had warm close ties; *none*, if home was 'just a place to hang your hat,' self-interest of members exceeding the group interest.

DD. Rank of Boy among Siblings—refers to boy's order of birth among living siblings, including half- and step-siblings (only child, firstborn, youngest, or occupying a position between the firstborn and the youngest—*i.e.*, a middle child).

EE. Rearing in Broken Home—a *broken home* is one from which one or both parents were absent by reason of death, desertion, separation or divorce, or were away from the home for at least a year because of imprisonment, illness, or distant employment.

FF. Age of Boy at First Breach in Family Life—refers to age at which the normal family pattern of life with both own parents was first disrupted by desertion, separation, divorce, or death of a parent, or absence of a parent from the home for at least a year by reason of imprisonment, illness, or distant employment.

GG. Rearing by Parent Substitutes—includes rearing by step-parent, foster parent, or relative (grandparent, aunt, older sibling), but does not include instances in which a boy spent brief periods away from his own parents (or parent) in foster home or with relatives.

HH. Affection of Father for Boy

II.   Affection of Mother for Boy—regarded as: *warm*, if parent was outwardly sympathetic, kind, attached, even overprotective; *indifferent*, if parent did not give the child much attention but was not outwardly hostile; *hostile*, if parent openly rejected the child.

JJ.   Affection of Siblings for Boy—concerns itself with whether the boy was loved by all his brothers and sisters (own, half, step) or regarded with indifference or even hostility by one or more of them.

KK. Discipline of Boy by Father

LL.   Discipline of Boy by Mother—refers to usual or typical discipline of the boy on the part of the parent or of a parent surrogate (if he has lived with the latter at least since he was three years old). Regarded as: *lax*, if parent was negligent, indifferent, let boy do what he liked; *overstrict*, if parent was harsh, unreasoning, demanding obedience through fear; *erratic*, if parent vacillated between strictness and laxity, was not consistent in control; *firm but kindly*, if discipline was based on sound reason which the boy understood and accepted as fair.

MM. Physical Punishment of Boy by Father

OO. Physical Punishment of Boy by Mother—refers to rough handling, strappings, and beatings eliciting fear and resentment in a boy and not to casual or occasional slapping, which was not accompanied by rage or hostility.

NN. Threatening or Scolding of Boy by Father

PP.   Threatening or Scolding of Boy by Mother—refers to threats that elicited fear in the boy.

QQ. Number of Moves—refers to the number of moves from one address to another within a given period of time.

RR. Emotional Ties of Boy to Father

TT.   Emotional Ties of Boy to Mother—considered: *attached*, if boy had a warm emotional bond to the father and/or mother as reflected in a close association with the parent and in wanting to be helpful to the parent, in expressions of admiration for the parent, and so on.

SS.   Acceptability of Father to Boy for Emulation—judged by a boy's respect for his father and a desire to pattern himself on his father even though the pattern was not necessarily a good one.

Social Factors

EXHIBIT C-2

SOCIAL FACTOR INCIDENCE AMONG DELINQUENTS AND NONDELINQUENTS

(From *Unraveling Juvenile Delinquency*)

Factor Identification*	Factors and Subcategories†	Delinquents	Nondelinquents	Differences	P
		Percentages of the Respective Factor Totals			
B. (VIII-7)	Crowded Home (More than Two Occupants per Bedroom)	32·7%	24·8%	7·9%	·01
C. (VIII-8)	Unclean and Disorderly Home (Sporadically or Habitually)	51·3	34·5	16·8	·01
E. (IX-2)	One or Both Parents Foreign-Born	58·0	61·1	−3·1	—
F. (IX-10)	Delinquency of Father	66·2	32·0	34·2	·01
G. (IX-10)	Delinquency of Mother	44·8	15·0	29·8	·01
H. (IX-10)	Alcoholism of Father	62·8	39·0	23·8	·01
I. (IX-10)	Alcoholism of Mother	23·0	7·0	16·0	·01
J. (IX-10)	Emotional Disturbance of Father	44·0	18·0	26·0	·01
K. (IX-10)	Emotional Disturbance of Mother	40·2	17·6	22·6	·01
L. (IX-10)	Serious Physical Ailment of Father	39·6	28·6	11·0	·01
M. (IX-10)	Serious Physical Ailment of Mother	48·6	33·0	15·6	·01
N. (IX-14)	Financial Dependence of Family (Usually Dependent)	36·2	14·6	21·6	·01
O. (IX-18)	Poor Work Habits of Father (Fair or Poor)	62·4	28·9	33·5	·01
P. (X-1)	Poor Management of Family Income (Partially Planned or Haphazard)	66·3	43·8	22·5	·01
Q. (X-2)	Careless Household Routine (Partially Planned or Haphazard)	75·6	50·9	24·7	·01
R. (X-3)	Lack of Cultural Refinement in Home	91·7	81·9	9·8	·01
S. (X-4)	Lack of Family Self-Respect	43·2	10·1	33·1	·01
T. (X-5)	Lack of Family Ambition	89·4	69·9	19·5	·01
U. (X-6)	Poor Conduct Standards of Family	90·4	54·0	36·4	·01
V. (X-7)	Incompatibility of Parents (Fair or Poor)	63·2	34·7	28·5	·01
W. (X-8)	Dominance of Mother in Family Affairs	49·6	49·7	−0·1	—
X. (X-9)	Gainful Employment of Mother	47·0	33·0	14·0	·01
Y. (X-10)	Unsuitable Supervision of Boy by Mother	63·9	13·0	50·9	·01
Z. (X-11)	Lack of Family Group Recreations	67·4	37·9	29·5	·01
AA. (X-12)	Parents Uninterested in Boy's Companions	79·6	61·9	17·7	·01
BB. (X-13)	Meager Recreational Facilities for Boy in Home	53·3	35·9	17·4	·01

* Numbers in parentheses refer to table numbers in *Unraveling Juvenile Delinquency*. Some of the figures in this table do not agree with those published in *Unraveling Juvenile Delinquency*; all the changes in percentages are small and in no way affect the analysis of the factors made in *Unraveling Juvenile Delinquency*; the difference in the P's are usually the result of the subcategory combinations.

† The subcategories or combinations of subcategories are indicated in parentheses.

221

Factor Identification*	Factors and Subcategories†	Percentages of the Respective Factor Totals			
		Delin-quents	Non-delin-quents	Differ-ences	P
CC. (X-14)	Lack of Family Cohesiveness (Some or None)	84·0%	38·3%	45·7%	·01
DD. (XI-5)	Rank of Boy among Siblings (Middle Child)	60·0	48·2	11·8	·01
EE. (XI-8)	Rearing in Broken Home	60·6	34·2	26·4	·01
FF. (XI-9)	Boy less than Five Years of Age at First Breach in Family Life	56·8	47·3	9·5	·05
GG. (XI-12)	Rearing by Parent Substitutes	46·0	12·0	34·0	·01
HH. (XI-13)	Indifference or Hostility of Father to Boy	59·8	19·4	40·4	·01
II. (XI-14)	Indifference or Hostility of Mother to Boy	27·9	4·5	23·4	·01
JJ. (XI-18)	Indifference or Hostility of Siblings to Boy	28·2	7·2	21·0	·01
KK. (XI-22)	Unsuitable Discipline of Boy by Father (Lax, Overstrict or Erratic)	94·3	44·5	49·8	·01
LL. (XI-22)	Unsuitable Discipline of Boy by Mother (Lax, Overstrict or Erratic)	95·8	34·4	61·4	·01
MM. (XI-23)	Physical Punishment of Boy by Father	67·8	34·7	33·1	·01
NN. (XI-23)	Threatening or Scolding of Boy by Father	32·2	31·5	0·7	—
OO. (XI-22)	Physical Punishment of Boy by Mother	55·6	34·6	21·0	·01
PP. (XI-23)	Threatening or Scolding of Boy by Mother	46·9	37·0	9·9	·01
QQ. (XIII-2)	Frequent Moving (Eight or More Times)	53·6	18·6	35·0	·01
RR. (XI-15)	Indifference or Hostility of Boy to Father	67·3	34·9	32·4	·01
SS. (XI-16)	Unacceptability of Father to Boy for Emulation	30·6	7·0	23·6	·01
TT. (XI-17)	Indifference or Hostility of Boy to Mother	35·1	10·2	24·9	·01

APPENDIX D

DATA FOR ANALYSIS OF TRAIT FORMATION BASED ON NON-DELINQUENTS OF *UNRAVELING JUVENILE DELINQUENCY*

TABLE D-1. POOR HEALTH IN INFANCY

Factor and Subcategories	Number of Non-delin-quents	Percentages of Respective Subcategory Totals	Significance of Variation between Subcategories	Probable Nature of Relationship between Factor and Trait
Serious Physical Ailment of Father				
Present	23	16·1%	] ·05	Not Clear
Absent	23	7·0		

TABLE D-3. EXTREME RESTLESSNESS IN EARLY CHILDHOOD

Factors and Subcategories	Number of Non-delin-quents	Percentages of Respective Subcategory Totals	Significance of Variations between Subcategories	Probable Nature of Relationships between Factors and Trait
Emotional Disturbance of Mother				
Present	35	39·8%	] ·05	Contributory
Absent	115	27·9		
Conjugal Relations of Parents				
Broken Relationship	16	21·6%	] ·05	Contributory
Incompatible	42	42·9	] ·05	
Compatible	90	27·9		
Recreational Facilities for Boy in Home				
Meager	38	21·2%	] ·02	Reactive
Adequate or Some	112	35·0		
Affection of Siblings for Boy				
Indifferent or Hostile	17	53·1%	] ·05	Not Clear
Warm	111	27·0		
Discipline of Boy by Father				
Lax	25	30·5%		Reactive
Overstrict	14	35·0		
Erratic	34	41·5	] ·10	
Firm but Kindly	66	25·9		
Physical Punishment of Boy by Father				
Used	60	38·7%	] ·05	Not Clear
Not Used	75	25·7		

TABLE D-3. EXTREME RESTLESSNESS IN EARLY CHILDHOOD (*Continued*)

Factors and Subcategories	Number of Non-delin-quents	Percentages of Respective Subcategory Totals	Significance of Variations between Subcategories	Probable Nature of Relationship between Factor and Trait
NN. *Threatening or Scolding of Boy by Father*				
Used	53	37·6%	} ·05	Not Clear
Not Used	82	26·8		
OO. *Physical Punishment of Boy by Mother*				
Used	63	37·3%	} ·05	Not Clear
Not Used	84	26·3		

TABLE D-4. ENURESIS IN EARLY CHILDHOOD

Factor and Subcategories	Number of Non-delin-quents	Percentages of Respective Subcategory Totals	Significance of Variation between Subcategories	Probable Nature of Relationship between Factor and Trait
JJ. *Affection of Siblings for Boy*				
Indifferent or Hostile	10	31·3%	} ·05	Not Clear
Warm	50	12·2		

TABLE D-6. CYANOSIS

Factors and Subcategories	Number of Non-delin-quents	Percentages of Respective Subcategory Totals	Significance of Variations between Subcategories	Probable Nature of Relationship between Factor and Trait
MM. *Physical Punishment of Boy by Father*				
Used	78	50·3%	} ·05	Reactive
Not Used	114	39·2		
TT. *Emotional Ties of Boy to Mother*				
Indifferent or Hostile or Noncommittal	33	64·7%	} ·02	Reactive
Attached	184	41·1		

Analysis of Trait Formation

TABLE D-7. DERMOGRAPHIA

Factors and Subcategories	Number of Non-delinquents	Percentages of Respective Subcategory Totals	Significance of Variations between Subcategories	Probable Nature of Relationships between Factors and Trait
F. *Delinquency of Father*				
Present	80	50·0%	} ·05	Not Clear
Absent	211	62·2		
G. *Delinquency of Mother*				
Present	31	41·3%	} ·02	Not Clear
Absent	260	61·3		
S. *Self-Respect of Family*				
None	19	38·8%	} ·05	Not Clear
Marked	141	60·3		
Y. *Supervision of Boy by Mother*				
Unsuitable	28	43·8%		Not Clear
Fair	60	56·1	} ·05	
Suitable	198	62·1		
AA. *Parents' Attitude to Boy's Companions*				
Inhospitable	51	46·8%		Not Clear
Indifferent	119	60·1	} ·05	
Warm	119	63·3		
BB. *Recreational Facilities for Boy in Home*				
Meager	91	50·8%	} ·05	Not Clear
Adequate or Some	200	62·7		
OO. *Physical Punishment of Boy by Mother*				
Used	80	47·3%	} ·02	Not Clear
Not Used	203	63·6		

TABLE D-9. GENITAL UNDERDEVELOPMENT

Factor and Subcategories	Number of Non-delinquents	Percentages of Respective Subcategory Totals	Significance of Variation between Subcategories	Probable Nature of Relationship between Factor and Trait
RR. *Emotional Ties of Boy to Father*				
Indifferent or Hostile or Noncommittal	16	9·2%	} ·05	Reactive
Attached	50	15·5		

Appendix D

TABLE D-10. STRENGTH OF HAND GRIP
(Dynamometric Strength—75 Kilograms and Over)

Factors and Subcategories	Number of Non-delinquents	Percentages of Respective Subcategory Totals	Significance of Variations between Subcategories	Probable Nature of Relationships between Factors and Trait
V. Conjugal Relations of Parents				
Broken Relationship	30	42·2%		Contributory
Incompatible	33	34·0	] ·05	
Compatible	154	48·0		
Y. Supervision of Boy by Mother				
Unsuitable	20	31·7%		Reactive
Fair	45	42·9	·10	
Suitable	148	46·7		
BB. Recreational Facilities for Boy in Home				
Meager	64	36·2%	] ·05	Reactive
Adequate or Some	153	48·3		
FF. Age of Boy at First Breach in Family Life				
Less than Five Years	29	36·2%		Contributory
Five to Ten Years	25	50·0	·05	
Ten Years or Older	23	60·5		
LL. Discipline of Boy by Mother				
Lax	18	31·0%		Reactive
Overstrict	3	37·5		
Erratic	35	34·7	·01] ·05	
Firm but Kindly	160	49·8		

TABLE D-11. LOW VERBAL INTELLIGENCE
(Wechsler Verbal I.Q.—below 80)

Factors and Subcategories	Number of Non-delinquents	Percentages of Respective Subcategory Totals	Significance of Variations between Subcategories	Probable Nature of Relationships between Factors and Trait
B. Crowding of Home				
More than Two Occupants per Bedroom (excluding Infants)	30	24·2%	] ·05	Contributory
One or Two Occupants per Bedroom	51	13·6		
V. Conjugal Relations of Parents				
Broken Relationship	6	8·1%		Contributory
Incompatible	26	26·5	·02	
Compatible	49	15·2		
JJ. Affection of Siblings for Boy				
Indifferent or Hostile	12	37·5%	] ·05	Contributory
Warm	62	15·1		

228

TABLE D-12. HIGH PERFORMANCE INTELLIGENCE
(Wechsler Performance I.Q.—101 and Over)

Factors and Subcategories	Number of Non-delinquents	Percentages of Respective Subcategory Totals	Significance of Variations between Subcategories	Probable Nature of Relationships between Factors and Trait
C. *Cleanliness and Orderliness of Home*				
Sporadically Clean and Neat or Habitually Disorderly	55	32·2%	⎤ ·05	Contributory
Normally Clean and Neat	153	47·2	⎦	
Q. *Household Routine*				
Partially Planned or Haphazard	93	37·3%	⎤ ·05	Contributory
Well Planned	113	47·1	⎦	
LL. *Discipline of Boy by Mother*				
Lax	34	58·6%	⎤	Contributory
Overstrict	2	25·0	⎥ ·05	
Erratic	37	35·6	⎥	
Firm but Kindly	136	42·0	⎦	

TABLE D-13. ORIGINALITY

Factors and Subcategories	Number of Non-delinquents	Percentages of Respective Subcategory Totals	Significance of Variations between Subcategories	Probable Nature of Relationships between Factors and Trait
X. *Usual Occupation of Mother*				
Occasionally Employed Outside Home	28	38·9%	⎤	Contributory
Regularly Employed Outside Home	21	23·1	⎥ ·05	
Housewife	75	22·7	⎦	
Y. *Supervision of Boy by Mother*				
Unsuitable	24	38·1%	⎤	Contributory
Fair	28	26·2	⎥ ·05	
Suitable	71	22·5	⎦	
AA. *Parents' Attitude to Boy's Companions*				
Inhospitable	35	32·4%	⎤	Contributory
Indifferent	55	28·1	⎥ ·05	
Warm	36	19·3	⎦	
BB. *Recreational Facilities for Boy in Home*				
Meager	55	31·1%	⎤ ·05	Contributory
Adequate or Some	71	22·4	⎦	

TABLE D-14. BANALITY

Factors and Subcategories	Number of Non-delinquents	Percentages of Respective Subcategory Totals	Significance of Variations between Subcategories	Probable Nature of Relationships between Factors and Trait
P. *Management of Family Income*				
Partially Planned or Haphazard	77	37·4%	]·05	Contributory
Entirely Planned	69	26·4		
R. *Cultural Refinement in Home*				
None	126	33·2%	]·05	Contributory
Marked or Slight	19	22·1		
MM. *Physical Punishment of Boy by Father*				
Used	58	39·2%	]·05	Not Clear
Not Used	78	28·9		
PP. *Threatening or Scolding of Boy by Mother*				
Used	68	38·9%	]·05	Not Clear
Not Used	77	26·6		

TABLE D-15. MARKED POWER OF OBSERVATION

Factors and Subcategories	Number of Non-delinquents	Percentages of Respective Subcategory Totals	Significance of Variations between Subcategories	Probable Nature of Relationships between Factors and Trait
Y. *Supervision of Boy by Mother*				
Unsuitable	35	56·5%		Contributory
Fair	73	68·2	]·05	
Suitable	233	74·4		
AA. *Parents' Attitude to Boy's Companions*				
Inhospitable	71	67·0%		Contributory
Indifferent	129	66·2	]·05	
Warm	144	77·0		
BB. *Recreational Facilities for Boy in Home*				
Meager	113	64·6%	]·05	Contributory
Adequate or Some	233	74·0		

TABLE D-17. TENDENCY TO PHANTASY

Factors and Subcategories	Number of Non-delinquents	Percentages of Respective Subcategory Totals	Significance of Variations between Subcategories	Probable Nature of Relationships between Factors and Trait
J. *Emotional Disturbance of Father*				
Present	35	40·7%	⎤ ·10	Contributory
Absent	123	30·7	⎦	
M. *Serious Physical Ailment of Mother*				
Present	61	37·6%	⎤ ·10	Contributory
Absent	97	29·8	⎦	
Z. *Family Group Recreations*				
Never	68	37·4%	⎤ ·10	Contributory
Often or Occasional	89	29·6	⎦	
AA. *Parents' Attitude to Boy's Companions*				
Inhospitable	44	41·1%	⎤	Contributory
Indifferent	66	34·6	⎥ ·05	
Warm	48	25·9	⎦	
FF. *Age of Boy at First Breach in Family Life*				
Less than Five Years	28	35·9%	⎤	Contributory
Five to Ten Years	16	32·7	⎥ ·05	
Ten Years or Older	5	13·5	⎦	

TABLE D-18. COMMON SENSE

Factors and Subcategories	Number of Non-delinquents	Percentages of Respective Subcategory Totals	Significance of Variations between Subcategories	Probable Nature of Relationships between Factors and Trait
Y. *Supervision of Boy by Mother*				
Unsuitable	43	70·5%	⎤	Contributory
Fair	82	79·6	⎥ ·10	
Suitable	257	83·4	⎦	
BB. *Recreational Facilities for Boy in Home*				
Meager	129	75·0%	⎤ ·05	Contributory
Adequate or Some	259	84·1	⎦	
DD. *Rank of Boy among Siblings*				
Middle	194	82·9%	⎤ ·05	Contributory
Only Child	24	61·5	⎦ ⎤ ·10	
Firstborn	75	81·5	⎥	
Youngest	96	82·8	⎦	

TABLE D-19. UNMETHODICAL APPROACH TO PROBLEMS

Factor and Subcategories	Number of Non-delinquents	Percentages of Respective Subcategory Totals	Significance of Variation between Subcategories	Probable Nature of Relationship between Factor and Trait
C. Cleanliness and Orderliness of Home				
Sporadically Clean and Neat or Habitually Disorderly	116	70·3%		Contributory
Normally Clean and Neat	186	61·8	]·10	

TABLE D-20. POTENTIAL CAPACITY FOR OBJECTIVE INTERESTS

Factor and Subcategories	Number of Non-delinquents	Percentages of Respective Subcategory Totals	Significance of Variation between Subcategories	Probable Nature of Relationship between Factor and Trait
BB. Recreational Facilities for Boy in Home				
Meager	58	47·5%	]·05	Contributory
Adequate or Some	109	59·2		

TABLE D-21. SOCIAL ASSERTIVENESS

Factor and Subcategories	Number of Non-delinquents	Percentages of Respective Subcategory Totals	Significance of Variations between Subcategories	Probable Nature of Relationship between Factor and Trait
KK. Discipline of Boy by Father				
Lax	22	32·8%	]·10	Contributory
Overstrict	4	12·1		
Erratic	14	21·2	]·10	
Firm but Kindly	38	18·0		

Analysis of Trait Formation

TABLE D-22. DEFIANCE

Factor and Subcategories	Number of Non-delin-quents	Percentages of Respective Subcategory Totals	Significance of Variation between Subcategories	Probable Nature of Relationship between Factor and Trait
A. *Parents' Attitude to Boy's Companions*				
Inhospitable	15	15·5%		Contributory
Indifferent	27	14·1	] ·05	
Warm	11	6·2		

TABLE D-23. MARKED SUBMISSIVENESS TO AUTHORITY

Factors and Subcategories	Number of Non-delin-quents	Percentages of Respective Subcategory Totals	Significance of Variations between Subcategories	Probable Nature of Relationships between Factors and Trait
Emotional Disturbance of Father				
Present	76	86·4%	] ·05	Contributory
Absent	309	78·0		
H. *Affection of Father for Boy*				
Indifferent or Hostile	79	87·8%	] ·05	Contributory
Warm	290	77·3		

TABLE D-24. AMBIVALENCE TO AUTHORITY

Factor and Subcategories	Number of Non-delin-quents	Percentages of Respective Subcategory Totals	Significance of Variation between Subcategories	Probable Nature of Relationship between Factor and Trait
I. *Affection of Mother for Boy*				
Indifferent or Hostile	8	53·3%	] ·05	Not Clear
Warm	63	18·4		

TABLE D-25. ENHANCED FEELING OF INSECURITY

Factors and Subcategories		Number of Non-delinquents	Percentages of Respective Subcategory Totals	Significance of Variations between Subcategories	Probable Nature of Relationship between Factor and Trait
G.	*Delinquency of Mother*				
	Present	26	39·4%	] 10	Contributory
	Absent	102	26·9		
T.	*Ambitiousness of Family*				
	None	96	31·3%	] ·10	Contributory
	Marked or Slight	29	22·8		
Y.	*Supervision of Boy by Mother*				
	Unsuitable	24	42·1%		Contributory
	Fair	32	32·7	·05	
	Suitable	69	24·6		
BB.	*Recreational Facilities for Boy in Home*				
	Meager	58	36·0%	] ·05	Contributory
	Adequate or Some	70	24·7		
CC.	*Family Cohesiveness*				
	Some or None	59	34·1%	] ·10	Contributory
	Marked	69	25·4		
LL.	*Discipline of Boy by Mother*				
	Lax	23	45·1%		Contributory
	Overstrict	2	28·6	·05	
	Erratic	34	35·1		
	Firm but Kindly	68	23·9		

TABLE D-26. MARKED FEELING OF NOT BEING WANTED OR LOVED

Factors and Subcategories		Number of Non-delinquents	Percentages of Respective Subcategory Totals	Significance of Variations between Subcategories	Probable Nature of Relationship between Factor and Trait
B.	*Crowding of Home*				
	More than Two Occupants per Bedroom (excluding Infants)	96	92·3%	] ·10	Contributory
	One or Two Occupants per Bedroom	249	86·5		
JJ.	*Affection of Siblings for Boy*				
	Indifferent or Hostile	24	96·0%	] ·10	Contributory
	Warm	285	88·2		
KK.	*Discipline of Boy by Father*				
	Lax	56	80·0%	] ·05	Contributory
	Overstrict	28	96·6		
	Erratic	57	89·1		
	Firm but Kindly	177	91·2		

TABLE D-27. FEELING OF NOT BEING TAKEN CARE OF

Factors and Subcategories	Number of Non-delinquents	Percentages of Respective Subcategory Totals	Significance of Variations between Subcategories	Probable Nature of Relationships between Factors and Trait
B. *Crowding of Home*				
More than Two Occupants per Bedroom (excluding Infants)	28	38·4%	]·05	Contributory
One or Two Occupants per Bedroom	49	20·0		
O. *Usual Work Habits of Father*				
Poor	8	57·1%	]·05	Contributory
Fair	19	26·8		
Good	43	20·7		
P. *Management of Family Income*				
Partially Planned or Haphazard	47	32·9%	].02	Contributory
Entirely Planned	30	17·5		
Q. *Household Routine*				
Partially Planned or Haphazard	49	31·6%	]·05	Contributory
Well Planned	28	18·2		
T. *Ambitiousness of Family*				
None	59	28·1%	]·05	Contributory
Marked or Slight	17	17·0		
U. *Conduct Standards of Family*				
Poor	48	28·2%	]·10	Contributory
Good or Fair	29	19·6		
Y. *Supervision of Boy by Mother*				
Unsuitable	18	41·9%		Contributory
Fair	25	38·5	·02]·02	
Suitable	32	15·5		
Z. *Family Group Recreations*				
Never	37	29·8%	]·10	Contributory
Often or Occasional	40	20·8		
AA. *Parents' Attitude to Boy's Companions*				
Inhospitable	26	36·6%		Contributory
Indifferent	36	29·8	·02]·02	
Warm	15	12·2		
BB. *Recreational Facilities for Boy in Home*				
Meager	46	44·2%	]·01	Contributory
Adequate or Some	31	14·6		

TABLE D-27. FEELING OF NOT BEING
TAKEN CARE OF (*Continued*)

Factors and Subcategories	Number of Non-delinquents	Percentages of Respective Subcategory Totals	Significance of Variations between Subcategories	Probable Nature of Relationships between Factors and Trait
HH. *Affection of Father for Boy*				
Indifferent or Hostile	20	36·4%	] ·05	Contributory
Warm	55	21·9		
KK. *Discipline of Boy by Father*				
Lax	16	30·8%		Contributory
Overstrict	11	47·8		
Erratic	15	29·4	] ·05	
Firm but Kindly	30	17·9		
LL. *Discipline of Boy by Mother*				
Lax	18	50·0%		Contributory
Overstrict	2	40·0		
Erratic	25	38·5	·02] ·02	
Firm but Kindly	31	14·9		
MM. *Physical Punishment of Boy by Father*				
Used	32	33·3%	] ·05	Contributory
Not Used	40	21·1		
RR. *Emotional Ties of Boy to Father*				
Indifferent or Hostile or Noncommittal	36	33·6%	] ·05	Reactive
Attached	41	19·5		
SS. *Acceptability of Father to Boy for Emulation*				
Unacceptable	38	29·2%	] ·05	Reactive
Acceptable	28	18·5		
TT. *Emotional Ties of Boy to Mother*				
Indifferent or Hostile or Noncommittal	15	39·5%	] ·05	Reactive
Attached	62	22·2		

TABLE D-28. MARKED FEELING OF NOT BEING TAKEN SERIOUSLY

Factors and Subcategories	Number of Non-delinquents	Percentages of Respective Subcategory Totals	Significance of Variations between Subcategories	Probable Nature of Relationships between Factors and Trait
B. *Crowding of Home*				
More than Two Occupants per Bedroom (excluding Infants)	52	60·5%		Contributory
One or Two Occupants per Bedroom	136	48·7	] ·10	
K. *Emotional Disturbance of Mother*				
Present	43	62·3%		Contributory
Absent	146	49·2	] ·05	
X. *Usual Occupation of Mother*				
Occasionally Employed Outside Home	36	62·1%		Contributory
Regularly Employed Outside Home	38	59·4	] ·10	
Housewife	115	47·3		
AA. *Parents' Attitude to Boy's Companions*				
Inhospitable	45	58·4%		Contributory
Indifferent	90	58·1	] ·05] ·05	
Warm	53	40·5		
BB. *Recreational Facilities for Boy in Home*				
Meager	81	58·7%		Contributory
Adequate or Some	108	47·6	] ·05	
LL. *Discipline of Boy by Mother*				
Lax	33	67·3%	] ·01	Contributory
Overstrict	5	100·0	] ·05] ·01] ·01	
Erratic	47	58·8		
Firm but Kindly	103	44·6		

TABLE D-29. FEELING OF HELPLESSNESS

Factors and Subcategories	Number of Non-delinquents	Percentages of Respective Subcategory Totals	Significance of Variations between Subcategories	Probable Nature of Relationships between Factor and Trait
B. *Crowding of Home*				
More than Two Occupants per Bedroom (excluding Infants)	64	64·0%		Contributory
One or Two Occupants per Bedroom	153	51·0	] ·05	
G. *Delinquency of Mother*				
Present	39	65·0%		Contributory
Absent	179	52·5	] ·10	
P. *Management of Family Income*				
Partially Planned or Haphazard	107	60·5%		Contributory
Entirely Planned	110	50·0	] ·05	
Y. *Supervision of Boy by Mother*				
Unsuitable	37	71·2%		Contributory
Fair	53	61·6	] ·02	
Suitable	123	48·0		
AA. *Parents' Attitude to Boy's Companions*				
Inhospitable	51	56·7%		Contributory
Indifferent	105	64·8		
Warm	61	41·8	] ·01	
BB. *Recreational Facilities for Boy in Home*				
Meager	103	68·7%		Contributory
Adequate or Some	115	46·0	] ·01	
KK. *Discipline of Boy by Father*				
Lax	32	45·1%		Contributory
Overstrict	22	73·3	] ·05	
Erratic	37	56·1		
Firm but Kindly	105	53·3		
LL. *Discipline of Boy by Mother*				
Lax	39	76·5%		Contributory
Overstrict	6	75·0		
Erratic	56	66·7	] ·02] ·02	
Firm but Kindly	115	45·5		
MM. *Physical Punishment of Boy by Father*				
Used	77	64·7%		Contributory
Not Used	119	50·0	] ·05	
OO. *Physical Punishment of Boy by Mother*				
Used	85	60·3%		Contributory
Not Used	129	51·4	] ·10	

TABLE D-30. FEELING OF NOT BEING APPRECIATED

Factors and Subcategories	Number of Non-delinquents	Percentages of Respective Subcategory Totals	Significance of Variations between Subcategories	Probable Nature of Relationships between Factors and Trait
AA. *Parents' Attitude to Boy's Companions*				
Inhospitable	32	43·8%		Contributory
Indifferent	39	27·7	·01 ⎤ ·02	
Warm	14	10·4		
BB. *Recreational Facilities for Boy in Home*				
Meager	44	35·5%	⎤ ·02	Contributory
Adequate or Some	42	18·6		

TABLE D-31. FEAR OF FAILURE AND DEFEAT

Factor and Subcategories	Number of Non-delinquents	Percentages of Respective Subcategory Totals	Significance of Variations between Subcategories	Probable Nature of Relationship between Factor and Trait
LL. *Discipline of Boy by Mother*				
Lax	45	84·9%		Contributory
Overstrict	4	57·1	·05 ⎤ ·01	
Erratic	62	66·7		
Firm but Kindly	160	58·0		

TABLE D-32. FEELING OF RESENTMENT

Factors and Subcategories	Number of Non-delinquents	Percentages of Respective Subcategory Totals	Significance of Variations between Subcategories	Probable Nature of Relationships between Factors and Trait
X. *Usual Occupation of Mother*				
Occasionally Employed Outside Home	31	63·3%		Contributory
Regularly Employed Outside Home	29	52·7	·10	
Housewife	102	47·2		
II. *Affection of Mother for Boy*				
Indifferent or Hostile	13	86·7%	⎤ ·01	Contributory
Warm	148	49·0		
LL. *Discipline of Boy by Mother*				
Lax	26	66·7%		Contributory
Overstrict	4	80·0	·10	
Erratic	34	48·6		
Firm but Kindly	95	46·8		

239

TABLE D-34. HOSTILITY

Factors and Subcategories	Number of Non-delinquents	Percentages of Respective Subcategory Totals	Significance of Variations between Subcategories	Probable Nature of Relationships between Factors and Trait
H. *Alcoholism of Father*				
Present	91	63·6%	]·05	Contributory
Absent	112	50·9		
L. *Serious Physical Ailment of Father*				
Present	67	64·4%	]·05	Contributory
Absent	136	52·5		
U. *Conduct Standards of Family*				
Poor	120	60·6%	]·05	Contributory
Good or Fair	83	50·3		
X. *Usual Occupation of Mother*				
Occasionally Employed Outside Home	43	74·1%		Contributory
Regularly Employed Outside Home	36	63·2	]·02	
Housewife	123	49·8		
HH. *Affection of Father for Boy*				
Indifferent or Hostile	50	70·4%	]·05	Contributory
Warm	148	53·6		
II. *Affection of Mother for Boy*				
Indifferent or Hostile	12	75·0%	]·10	Contributory
Warm	189	55·1		
KK. *Discipline of Boy by Father*				
Lax	36	56·3%		Contributory
Overstrict	19	61·3		
Erratic	42	77·8	]·01	
Firm but Kindly	89	48·6		
LL. *Discipline of Boy by Mother*				
Lax	32	62·7%	]·01	Contributory
Overstrict	7	100·0		
Erratic	44	55·0	]·01]·01	
Firm but Kindly	117	52·9		

TABLE D-35. MARKED SUSPICIOUSNESS

Factors and Subcategories	Number of Non-delin-quents	Percentages of Respective Subcategory Totals	Significance of Variations between Subcategories	Probable Nature of Relationships between Factors and Trait
B. *Crowding of Home*				
More than Two Occupants per Bedroom (excluding Infants)	34	33·3%	} ·10	Contributory
One or Two Occupants per Bedroom	73	23·9		
E. *Nativity of Parents*				
Both Native	28	17·6%	} ·05 } ·05	Contributory
One Native, Other Foreign-Born	33	33·3		
Both Foreign-Born	44	29·9		
C. *Ambitiousness of Family*				
None	87	31·0%	} ·02	Contributory
Marked or Slight	21	17·6		
B. *Recreational Facilities for Boy in Home*				
Meager	54	35·1%	} ·05	Contributory
Adequate or Some	54	21·3		
F. *Age of Boy at First Breach in Family Life*				
Less than Five Years	22	31·9%	} ·05	Contributory
Five to Ten Years	5	11·4		
Ten Years or Older	9	29·0		

TABLE D-36. DESTRUCTIVENESS

Factors and Subcategories	Number of Non-delin-quents	Percentages of Respective Subcategory Totals	Significance of Variations between Subcategories	Probable Nature of Relationships between Factors and Trait
B. *Crowding of Home*				
More than Two Occupants per Bedroom (excluding Infants)	24	22·6%	} ·05	Contributory
One or Two Occupants per Bedroom	41	12·9		
P. *Management of Family Income*				
Partially Planned or Haphazard	36	19·7%	} ·05	Contributory
Entirely Planned	29	12·4		
Q. *Household Routine*				
Partially Planned or Haphazard	39	18·8%	} ·10	Contributory
Well Planned	26	12·6		

241

TABLE D-36. DESTRUCTIVENESS (*Continued*)

Factors and Subcategories	Number of Non-delin-quents	Percentages of Respective Subcategory Totals	Significance of Variations between Subcategories	Probable Nature of Relationship between Factor and Trait
V. *Conjugal Relations of Parents*				
Broken Relationship	4	6·7%	] ·05	Contributory
Incompatible	18	22·2		
Compatible	43	15·5		
X. *Usual Occupation of Mother*				
Occasionally Employed Outside Home	13	22·8%	] ·10	Contributory
Regularly Employed Outside Home	7	9·0		
Housewife	45	15·7		
AA. *Parents' Attitude to Boy's Companions*				
Inhospitable	22	25·3%	] ·02] ·05	Contributory
Indifferent	30	17·2		
Warm	13	8·1		
BB. *Recreational Facilities for Boy in Home*				
Meager	35	23·2%	] ·02	Contributory
Adequate or Some	30	11·1		
JJ. *Affection of Siblings for Boy*				
Indifferent or Hostile	11	40·7%	] ·05	Not Clear
Warm	46	13·0		

TABLE D-37. FEELING OF ISOLATION

Factors and Subcategories	Number of Non-delin-quents	Percentages of Respective Subcategory Totals	Significance of Variations between Subcategories	Probable Nature of Relationship between Factor and Trait
B. *Crowding of Home*				
More than Two Occupants per Bedroom (excluding Infants)	40	46·0%	] ·05	Contributory
One or two Occupants per Bedroom	87	32·8		
X. *Usual Occupation of Mother*				
Occasionally Employed Outside Home	28	52·8%	] ·05	Contributory
Regularly Employed Outside Home	20	32·3		
Housewife	80	33·8		

TABLE D-37. FEELING OF ISOLATION (*Continued*)

Factors and Subcategories	Number of Non-delinquents	Percentages of Respective Subcategory Totals	Significance of Variations between Subcategories	Probable Nature of Relationships between Factor and Trait
Y. *Supervision of Boy by Mother*				
Unsuitable	20	44·4%		Contributory
Fair	38	46·9	] ·05	
Suitable	66	30·0		
AA. *Parents' Attitude to Boys' Companions*				
Inhospitable	38	45·8%		Contributory
Indifferent	59	41·5	] ·05] ·05	
Warm	31	24·6		
BB. *Recreational Facilities for Boy in Home*				
Meager	66	49·6%	] ·02	Contributory
Adequate or Some	62	28·3		
LL. *Discipline of Boy by Mother*				
Lax	31	67·4%		Contributory
Overstrict	2	40·0	] ·05] ·01	
Erratic	31	39·2		
Firm but Kindly	62	28·3		

TABLE D-38. DEFENSIVE ATTITUDE

Factors and Subcategories	Number of Non-delinquents	Percentages of Respective Subcategory Totals	Significance of Variations between Subcategories	Probable Nature of Relationships between Factors and Trait
G. *Delinquency of Mother*				
Present	36	58·1%	] ·05	Contributory
Absent	151	42·1		
CC. *Family Cohesiveness*				
Some or None	79	50·3%	] ·10	Contributory
Marked	108	40·9		

TABLE D-39. MARKED DEPENDENCE ON OTHERS

Factors and Subcategories	Number of Non-delin-quents	Percentages of Respective Subcategory Totals	Significance of Variations between Subcategories	Probable Nature of Relationships between Factors and Trait
J. *Emotional Disturbance of Father*				
Present	80	93·0%	]·05	Contributory
Absent	329	83·9		
O. *Usual Work Habits of Father*				
Poor	24	96·0%		Contributory
Fair	89	87·3	]·05	
Good	261	83·9		
FF. *Age of Boy at First Breach in Family Life*				
Less than Five Years	72	91·1%	]·05	Contributory
Five to Ten Years	36	73·5		
Ten Years or Older	29	80·6		
LL. *Discipline of Boy by Mother*				
Lax	52	96·3%		Contributory
Overstrict	7	87·5	]·02	
Erratic	90	90·0		
Firm but Kindly	258	83·0		
MM. *Physical Punishment of Boy by Father*				
Used	139	92·7%	]·02	Contributory
Not Used	231	82·8		

TABLE D-40. FEELING OF BEING ABLE TO MANAGE OWN LIFE

Factors and Subcategories	Number of Non-delin-quents	Percentages of Respective Subcategory Totals	Significance of Variations between Subcategories	Probable Nature of Relationships between Factors and Trait
AA. *Parents' Attitude to Boy's Companions*				
Inhospitable	44	57·9%		Contributory
Indifferent	79	56·8	]·05]·05	
Warm	85	75·2		
BB. *Recreational Facilities for Boy in Home*				
Meager	62	49·6%	]·01	Contributory
Adequate or Some	148	72·2		
CC. *Family Cohesiveness*				
Some or None	71	57·7%	]·10	Contributory
Marked	140	67·3		

244

TABLE D-40. FEELING OF BEING ABLE TO MANAGE OWN LIFE (*Continued*)

Factors and Subcategories	Number of Non-delinquents	Percentages of Respective Subcategory Totals	Significance of Variations between Subcategories	Probable Nature of Relationships between Factors and Trait
L. Discipline of Boy by Mother				
Lax	16	41·0%		Contributory
Overstrict	5	83·3	·02	
Erratic	41	53·2	·05	
Firm but Kindly	147	71·7		

TABLE D-41. NARCISSISTIC TRENDS

Factors and Subcategories	Number of Non-delinquents	Percentages of Respective Subcategory Totals	Significance of Variations between Subcategories	Probable Nature of Relationships between Factors and Trait
Family Group Recreations				
Never	33	19·1%	·05	Contributory
Often or Occasional	32	11·4		
A. Parents' Attitude to Boy's Companions				
Inhospitable	23	23·5%		Contributory
Indifferent	28	15·6	·02 ·05	
Warm	13	7·4		

TABLE D-42. RECEPTIVE TRENDS

Factors and Subcategories	Number of Non-delinquents	Percentages of Respective Subcategory Totals	Significance of Variations between Subcategories	Probable Nature of Relationships between Factors and Trait
Management of Family Income				
Partially Planned or Haphazard	40	20·5%	·02	Contributory
Entirely Planned	20	8·3		
Supervision of Boy by Mother				
Unsuitable	16	29·1%		Contributory
Fair	16	16·5	·05	
Suitable	27	9·5		
Family Group Recreations				
Never	37	21·5%	·02	Contributory
Often or Occasional	23	8·6		
F.E.D.—R	245			

TABLE D-42. RECEPTIVE TRENDS (*Continued*)

Factors and Subcategories	Number of Non-delinquents	Percentages of Respective Subcategory Totals	Significance of Variations between Subcategories	Probable Nature of Relationships between Factors and Trait
AA. *Parents' Attitude to Boy's Companions*				
Inhospitable	21	22·3%	} ·02 } ·05	Contributory
Indifferent	28	16·0		
Warm	11	6·5		
BB. *Recreational Facilities for Boy in Home*				
Meager	32	20·9%	} ·02	Contributory
Adequate or Some	28	9·7		

TABLE D-43. MASOCHISTIC TRENDS

Factors and Subcategories	Number of Non-delinquents	Percentages of Respective Subcategory Totals	Significance of Variations between Subcategories	Probable Nature of Relationships between Factors and Trait
B. *Crowding of Home*				
More than Two Occupants per Bedroom (excluding Infants)	46	46·9%	} ·05	Contributory
One or Two Occupants per Bedroom	97	33·3		
T. *Ambitiousness of Family*				
None	106	39·7%	} ·10	Contributory
Marked or Slight	34	29·8		
Y. *Supervision of Boy by Mother*				
Unsuitable	18	39·1%		Contributory
Fair	43	50·0	} ·05	
Suitable	77	30·7		
Z. *Family Group Recreations*				
Never	65	43·6%	} ·05	Contributory
Often or Occasional	77	32·5		
AA. *Parents' Attitude to Boy's Companions*				
Inhospitable	30	36·1%		Contributory
Indifferent	72	45·3	} ·05	
Warm	41	28·3		
BB. *Recreational Facilities for Boy in Home*				
Meager	73	50·7%	} ·01	Contributory
Adequate or Some	70	28·6		
LL. *Discipline of Boy by Mother*				
Lax	26	65·0%	} ·10 } ·01	Contributory
Overstrict	4	57·1		
Erratic	36	42·4		
Firm but Kindly	76	30·0		

TABLE D-44. DESTRUCTIVE-SADISTIC TRENDS

Factors and Subcategories	*Number of Non-delinquents*	*Percentages of Respective Subcategory Totals*	*Significance of Variations between Subcategories*	*Probable Nature of Relationships between Factors and Trait*
B. *Crowding of Home*				
More than Two Occupants per Bedroom (excluding Infants)	24	22·6%		Contributory
One or Two Occupants per Bedroom	43	13·6	·05	
C. *Cleanliness and Orderliness of Home*				
Sporadically Clean and Neat or Habitually Disorderly	29	20·3%		Contributory
Normally Clean and Neat	38	13·8	·10	
P. *Management of Family Income*				
Partially Planned or Haphazard	37	20·2%		Contributory
Entirely Planned	30	12·8	·05	
Q. *Household Routine*				
Partially Planned or Haphazard	41	19·8%		Contributory
Well Planned	26	12·6	·05	
. *Conjugal Relations of Parents*				
Broken Relationship	5	8·3%		Contributory
Incompatible	18	22·2	·05	
Compatible	44	15·8		
. *Usual Occupation of Mother*				
Occasionally Employed Outside Home	14	24·6%		Contributory
Regularly Employed Outside Home	7	9·0	·05	
Housewife	46	16·1		
A. *Parents' Attitude to Boy's Companions*				
Inhospitable	23	26·4%		Contributory
Indifferent	30	17·2	·02	
Warm	14	8·8		
B. *Recreational Facilities for Boy in Home*				
Meager	36	23·8%		Contributory
Adequate or Some	31	11·4	·02	
J. *Affection of Siblings for Boy*				
Indifferent or Hostile	11	40·7%		Not Clear
Warm	48	13·6	·05	

TABLE D-47. VIVACITY

Factor and Subcategories	Number of Non-delinquents	Percentages of Respective Subcategory Totals	Significance of Variation between Subcategories	Probable Nature of Relationship between Factor and Trait
PP. *Threatening or Scolding of Boy by Mother*				
Used	22	31·4%	] ·05	Reactive
Not Used	20	17·9		

TABLE D-48. COMPULSORY TRENDS

Factors and Subcategories	Number of Non-delinquents	Percentages of Respective Subcategory Totals	Significance of Variations between Subcategories	Probable Nature of Relationship between Factor and Trait
C. *Cleanliness and Orderliness of Home*				
Sporadically Clean and Neat or Habitually Disorderly	55	35·7%	] ·10	Contributory
Normally Clean and Neat	82	27·6		
P. *Management of Family Income*				
Partially Planned or Haphazard	69	35·6%	] ·05	Contributory
Entirely Planned	66	25·9		
Q. *Household Routine*				
Partially Planned or Haphazard	82	36·1%	] ·05	Contributory
Well Planned	52	24·0		
S. *Self-Respect of Family*				
None	18	40·9%	] ·05	Contributory
Marked	53	24·2		
T. *Ambitiousness of Family*				
None	105	34·3%	] ·02	Contributory
Marked or Slight	29	21·0		
Y. *Supervision of Boy by Mother*				
Unsuitable	22	40·0%		Contributory
Fair	40	38·8	] ·05	
Suitable	73	25·3		
BB. *Recreational Facilities for Boy in Home*				
Meager	72	42·6%	] ·01	Contributory
Adequate or Some	65	22·8		
LL. *Discipline of Boy by Mother*				
Lax	26	47·3%		Contributory
Overstrict	4	50·0	] ·05] ·05	
Erratic	38	40·4		
Firm but Kindly	69	23·5		

TABLE D-49. PREPONDERANCE OF EXTROVERSIVE TRENDS

Factors and Subcategories	Number of Non-delin-quents	Percentages of Respective Subcategory Totals	Significance of Variations between Subcategories	Probable Nature of Relationships between Factors and Trait
K. *Emotional Disturbance of Mother*				
Present	13	20·3%	⎤ ·02	Contributory
Absent	112	38·4	⎦	
W. *Dominant Parent in Family Affairs*				
Father	69	41·1%	⎤ ·05	Contributory
Mother	48	29·4	⎦	
HH. *Affection of Father for Boy*				
Indifferent or Hostile	19	25·7%	⎤ ·05	Contributory
Warm	104	37·8	⎦	

TABLE D-50. PREPONDERANCE OF INTROVERSIVE TRENDS

Factors and Subcategories	Number of Non-delin-quents	Percentages of Respective Subcategory Totals	Significance of Variations between Subcategories	Probable Nature of Relationships between Factors and Trait
J. *Emotional Disturbance of Father*				
Present	21	34·4%	⎤ ·10	Contributory
Absent	68	22·5	⎦	
K. *Emotional Disturbance of Mother*				
Present	24	37·5%	⎤ ·05	Contributory
Absent	65	21·7	⎦	
M. *Serious Physical Ailment of Mother*				
Present	36	31·0%	⎤ ·10	Contributory
Absent	53	21·5	⎦	
AA. *Parents' Attitude to Boy's Companions*				
Inhospitable	28	33·3%	⎤	Contributory
Indifferent	39	26·9	⎟ ·05	
Warm	22	16·5	⎦	
KK. *Discipline of Boy by Father*				
Lax	9	14·5%	⎤ ·05	Contributory
Overstrict	16	47·1	⎟	
Erratic	13	22·0	⎦	
Firm but Kindly	43	24·2		

Appendix D

TABLE D-51. SENSITIVITY

Factors and Subcategories	Number of Non-delin-quents	Percentages of Respective Subcategory Totals	Significance of Variations between Subcategories	Probable Nature of Relationships between Factors and Trait
K. *Emotional Disturbance of Mother*				
Present	42	47·7%	]·05	Not Clear
Absent	136	33·1		
S. *Self-Respect of Family*				
None	9	18·4%	]·05	Not Clear
Marked	84	35·9		

TABLE D-52. SUGGESTIBILITY

Factors and Subcategories	Number of Non-delin-quents	Percentages of Respective Subcategory Totals	Significance of Variations between Subcategories	Probable Nature of Relationships between Factors and Trait
FF. *Age of Boy at First Breach in Family Life*				
Less than Five Years	26	32·1%	]·05	Contributory
Five to Ten Years	6	11·5		
Ten Years or Older	9	23·7		
KK. *Discipline of Boy by Father*				
Lax	25	30·5%		Contributory
Overstrict	7	17·5		
Erratic	30	36·6	]·05	
Firm but Kindly	53	20·9		
SS. *Acceptability of Father to Boy for Emulation*				
Unacceptable	64	30·3%	]·05	Reactive
Acceptable	47	20·5		

TABLE D-53. FEELING OF INADEQUACY

Factors and Subcategories	Number of Non-delinquents	Percentages of Respective Subcategory Totals	Significance of Variations between Subcategories	Probable Nature of Relationships between Factors and Trait
G. *Delinquency of Mother*				
Present	58	77·3%	⎤ ·10	Contributory
Absent	288	67·9	⎦	
T. *Ambitiousness of Family*				
None	244	71·6%	⎤ ·10	Contributory
Marked or Slight	93	63·7	⎦	
DD. *Rank of Boy among Siblings*				
Middle	151	63·2%	⎤	Contributory
Only Child	33	76·7	⎥ ·05	
Firstborn	67	69·1	⎥	
Youngest	95	79·2	⎦	

TABLE D-54. STUBBORNNESS

Factors and Subcategories	Number of Non-delinquents	Percentages of Respective Subcategory Totals	Significance of Variations between Subcategories	Probable Nature of Relationships between Factors and Trait
RR. *Emotional Ties of Boy to Father*				
Indifferent or Hostile or Noncommittal	24	13·8%	⎤ ·05	Reactive
Attached	17	5·2	⎦	
TT. *Emotional Ties of Boy to Mother*				
Indifferent or Hostile or Noncommittal	10	19·6%	⎤ ·05	Reactive
Attached	31	6·9	⎦	

TABLE D-55. ADVENTUROUSNESS

Factor and Subcategories	Number of Non-delinquents	Percentages of Respective Subcategory Totals	Significance of Variation between Subcategories	Probable Nature of Relationship between Factor and Trait
T. *Ambitiousness of Family*				
None	70	20·5%	⎤ ·05	Contributory
Marked or Slight	18	12·3	⎦	

251

Appendix D

TABLE D-56. UNINHIBITED MOTOR RESPONSES TO STIMULI

Factors and Subcategories	Number of Non-delinquents	Percentages of Respective Subcategory Totals	Significance of Variations between Subcategories	Probable Nature of Relationships between Factors and Trait
C. Cleanliness and Orderliness of Home				
Sporadically Clean and Neat or Habitually Disorderly	60	35·1%	⎤ ·05	Contributory
Normally Clean and Neat	79	24·5	⎦	
P. Management of Family Income				
Partially Planned or Haphazard	73	33·8%	⎤ ·05	Contributory
Entirely Planned	66	23·9	⎦	
DD. Rank of Boy among Siblings				
Middle	90	37·7%	⎤ ·05 ⎤ ·01	Contributory
Only Child	9	20·9		
Firstborn	23	23·7	⎦	
Youngest	20	16·7		
EE. Rearing in Broken Home				
Yes	57	33·3%	⎤ ·10	Contributory
No	85	25·9	⎦	

TABLE D-57. EMOTIONAL INSTABILITY

Factors and Subcategories	Number of Non-delinquents	Percentages of Respective Subcategory Totals	Significance of Variations between Subcategories	Probable Nature of Relationships between Factors and Trait
DD Rank of Boy among Siblings				
Middle	105	43·9%	⎤ ·05	Contributory
Only Child	27	62·8		
Firstborn	60	61·9	⎦	
Youngest	58	48·3		
RR. Emotional Ties of Boy to Father				
Indifferent or Hostile or Noncommittal	106	60·9%	⎤ ·02	Reactive
Attached	144	44·3	⎦	
SS. Acceptability of Father to Boy for Emulation				
Unacceptable	122	57·8%	⎤ ·02	Reactive
Acceptable	98	42·8	⎦	
TT. Emotional Ties of Boy to Mother				
Indifferent or Hostile or Noncommittal	39	76·5%	⎤ ·01	Reactive
Attached	211	47·1	⎦	

TABLE D-58. AESTHETICISM

Factors and Subcategories	Number of Non-delinquents	Percentages of Respective Subcategory Totals	Significance of Variations between Subcategories	Probable Nature of Relationships between Factors and Trait
C. *Cleanliness and Orderliness of Home*				
Sporadically Clean and Neat or Habitually Disorderly	53	31·0%	⎤ ·05	Not Clear
Normally Clean and Neat	138	42·7	⎦	
N. *Usual Economic Condition of Family*				
Usually Dependent	19	26·0%	⎤ ·05	Not Clear
Marginal or Sporadically Dependent	171	40·9	⎦	
P. *Management of Family Income*				
Partially Planned or Haphazard	66	30·6%	⎤ ·02	Not Clear
Entirely Planned	123	44·6	⎦	
Q. *Household Routine*				
Partially Planned or Haphazard	81	32·5%	⎤ ·05	Not Clear
Well Planned	109	45·6	⎦	
S. *Self-Respect of Family*				
None	11	22·4%	⎤ ·05	Not Clear
Marked	97	41·5	⎦	
Y. *Supervision of Boy by Mother*				
Unsuitable	18	28·1%		Not Clear
Fair	26	24·3	⎤ ·05 ⎤ ·01	
Suitable	143	44·8	⎦ ⎦	
Z. *Family Group Recreations*				
Never	59	31·4%	⎤ ·05	Not Clear
Often or Occasional	131	42·7	⎦	
AA. *Parents' Attitude to Boy's Companions*				
Inhospitable	34	31·2%		Not Clear
Indifferent	71	35·9	⎤ ·05	
Warm	86	45·7	⎦	
BB. *Recreational Facilities for Boy in Home*				
Meager	54	30·2%	⎤ ·05	Not Clear
Adequate or Some	138	43·3	⎦	
KK. *Discipline of Boy by Father*				
Lax	26	31·7%		Not Clear
Overstrict	11	27·5		
Erratic	24	29·3	⎤ ·05	
Firm but Kindly	114	44·9	⎦	
RR. *Emotional Ties of Boy to Father*				
Indifferent or Hostile or Noncommittal	56	32·2%	⎤ ·05	Not Clear
Attached	136	41·8	⎦	

Appendix D

TABLE D-60. ACQUISITIVENESS

Factors and Subcategories		Number of Non-delin-quents	Percentages of Respective Subcategory Totals	Significance of Variations between Subcategories	Probable Nature of Relationships between Factors and Trait
B.	Crowding of Home				
	More than Two Occupants per Bedroom (excluding Infants)	25	20·2%	]·05	Contributory
	One or Two Occupants per Bedroom	45	12·0		
BB.	Recreational Facilities for Boy in Home				
	Meager	33	18·4%	]·05	Contributory
	Adequate or Some	37	11·6		
DD.	Rank of Boy among Siblings				
	Middle	42	17·6%		Contributory
	Only Child	4	9·3	]·10	
	Firstborn	13	13·4		
	Youngest	11	9·2		

TABLE D-61. UNCONVENTIONALITY

Factors and Subcategories		Number of Non-delin-quents	Percentages of Respective Subcategory Totals	Significance of Variations between Subcategories	Probable Nature of Relationships between Factors and Trait
H.	Alcoholism of Father				
	Present	112	52·4%	]·05	Contributory
	Absent	145	47·7		
I.	Alcoholism of Mother				
	Present	25	71·4%	]·05	Contributory
	Absent	232	50·0		
CC.	Family Cohesiveness				
	Some or None	108	56·5%	]·10	Contributory
	Marked	149	48·4		
HH.	Affection of Father for Boy				
	Indifferent or Hostile	57	61·3%	]·05	Not Clear
	Warm	191	49·5		
II.	Affection of Mother for Boy				
	Indifferent or Hostile	20	90·9%	]·01	Not Clear
	Warm	236	50·2		
JJ.	Affection of Siblings for Boy				
	Indifferent or Hostile	22	68·7%	]·05	Not Clear
	Warm	202	49·3		
RR.	Emotional Ties of Boy to Father				
	Indifferent or Hostile or Noncommittal	104	59·8%	]·05	Not Clear
	Attached	153	47·1		

TABLE D-62. LACK OF SELF-CRITICISM

Factors and Subcategories	Number of Non-delinquents	Percentages of Respective Subcategory Totals	Significance of Variations between Subcategories	Probable Nature of Relationships between Factors and Trait
C. Delinquency of Mother				
Present	13	17·3%	} ·10	Contributory
Absent	40	9·4		
S. Self-Respect of Family				
None	10	20·4%	} ·10	Contributory
Marked	22	9·4		
QQ. Number of Moves				
8 or More Times	15	16·1%		Contributory
5–7 Times	14	12·1		
2–4 Times	18	9·7	} ·10	
None or One Time	6	5·7		

TABLE D-63. CONSCIENTIOUSNESS

Factors and Subcategories	Number of Non-delinquents	Percentages of Respective Subcategory Totals	Significance of Variations between Subcategories	Probable Nature of Relationships between Factors and Trait
L. Serious Physical Ailment of Father				
Present	69	48·3%	} ·10	Contributory
Absent	202	56·7		
P. Management of Family Income				
Partially Planned or Haphazard	98	45·4%	} ·02	Contributory
Entirely Planned	168	60·9		
T. Ambitiousness of Family				
None	173	50·7%	} ·05	Contributory
Marked or Slight	91	62·3		
Y. Supervision of Boy by Mother				
Unsuitable	27	42·2%		Contributory
Fair	46	43·0	} ·05 } ·02	
Suitable	195	61·1		
AA. Parents' Attitude to Boy's Companions				
Inhospitable	61	56·0%		Contributory
Indifferent	94	47·5	} ·05	
Warm	113	60·1		
BB. Recreational Facilities for Boy in Home				
Meager	84	46·9%	} ·05	Contributory
Adequate or Some	186	58·3		

TABLE D-63. CONSCIENTIOUSNESS (*Continued*)

Factors and Subcategories	Number of Non-delin-quents	Percentages of Respective Subcategory Totals	Significance of Variations between Subcategories	Probable Nature of Relationships between Factors and Trait
LL. *Discipline of Boy by Mother*				
Lax	27	46·6%		Contributory
Overstrict	5	62·5		
Erratic	47	45·2	]·10	
Firm but Kindly	189	58·5		
RR. *Emotional Ties of Boy to Father*				
Indifferent or Hostile or Noncommittal	78	44·8%	]·02	Reactive
Attached	193	59·4		
SS. *Acceptability of Father to Boy for Emulation*				
Unacceptable	106	50·2%	].05	Reactive
Acceptable	138	60·3		

TABLE D-64. IMPRACTICALITY

Factors and Subcategories	Number of Non-delin-quents	Percentages of Respective Subcategory Totals	Significance of Variations between Subcategories	Probable Nature of Relationships between Factors and Trait
K. *Emotional Disturbance of Mother*				
Present	64	72·7%	]·10	Contributory
Absent	261	63·5		
S. *Self-Respect of Family*				
None	38	77·6%	]·05	Contributory
Marked	146	62·4		
Y. *Supervision of Boy by Mother*				
Unsuitable	48	75·0%	]·10	Contributory
Fair	63	58·9		
Suitable	208	65·2		
CC. *Family Cohesiveness*				
Some or None	135	70·7%	]·05	Contributory
Marked	190	61·7		
DD. *Rank of Boy among Siblings*				
Middle	141	59·0%	]·05	Contributory
Only Child	34	79·1		
Firstborn	64	66·0		
Youngest	86	71·7		
KK. *Discipline of Boy by Father*				
Lax	57	69·5%		Not Clear
Overstrict	29	72·5		
Erratic	60	73·2	]·05	
Firm but Kindly	147	57·9		

256

TABLE D-64. IMPRACTICALITY (*Continued*)

Factors and Subcategories	Number of Non-delinquents	Percentages of Respective Subcategory Totals	Significance of Variations between Subcategories	Probable Nature of Relationships between Factors and Trait
LL. *Discipline of Boy by Mother*				
Lax	41	70·7%		Not Clear
Overstrict	5	62·5		
Erratic	79	76·0	]·05	
Firm but Kindly	195	60·4		
RR. *Emotional Ties of Boy to Father*				
Indifferent or Hostile or Noncommittal	129	74·1%	]·02	Not Clear
Attached	196	60·3		
SS. *Acceptability of Father to Boy for Emulation*				
Unacceptable	148	70·1%	]·05	Not Clear
Acceptable	132	57·6		
TT. *Emotional Ties of Boy to Mother*				
Indifferent or Hostile or Noncommittal	39	76·5%	]·05	Not Clear
Attached	286	63·8		

TABLE D-65. EMOTIONAL CONFLICTS

Factors and Subcategories	Number of Non-delinquents	Percentages of Respective Subcategory Totals	Significance of Variations between Subcategories	Probable Nature of Relationships between Factors and Trait
CC. *Family Cohesiveness*				
Some or None	69	43·9%	]·05	Contributory
Marked	94	34·1		
JJ. *Affection of Siblings for Boy*				
Indifferent or Hostile	15	55·6%	]·05	Reactive
Warm	123	34·8		
RR. *Emotional Ties of Boy to Father*				
Indifferent or Hostile or Noncommittal	74	50·3%	]·02	Reactive
Attached	89	31·0		
SS. *Acceptability of Father to Boy for Emulation*				
Unacceptable	86	48·6%	]·02	Reactive
Acceptable	62	30·1		
TT. *Emotional Ties of Boy to Mother*				
Indifferent or Hostile or Noncommittal	26	65·0%	]·02	Reactive
Attached	137	34·8		

TABLE D-66. NEUROTICISM

Factors and Subcategories	Number of Non-delin-quents	Percentages of Respective Subcategory Totals	Significance of Variations between Subcategories	Probable Nature of Relationships between Factors and Trait
G. *Delinquency of Mother*				
Present	33	44·6%	]·10	Contributory
Absent	143	34·0		
X. *Usual Occupation of Mother*				
Occasionally Employed Outside Home	33	45·8%		Contributory
Regularly Employed Outside Home	37	41·1	]·10	
Housewife	106	32·7		
CC. *Family Cohesiveness*				
Some or None	78	41·5%	]·05	Contributory
Marked	98	32·0		
LL. *Discipline of Boy by Mother*				
Lax	27	47·4%	]·05	Contributory
Overstrict	7	87·5	]·10]·02]·01	
Erratic	43	41·7		
Firm but Kindly	98	30·6		

TABLE D-67. PSYCHOPATHY

Factor and Subcategories	Number of Non-delin-quents	Percentages of Respective Subcategory Totals	Significance of Variation between Subcategories	Probable Nature of Relationship between Factor and Trait
FF. *Age of Boy at First Breach in Family Life*				
Less than Five Years	0	0·0%	]·05	Not Clear
Five to Ten Years	2	3·9		
Ten Years or Older	6	16·2		

APPENDIX E

DATA FOR ANALYSIS OF SELECTIVE IMPACT OF FACTORS ON PHYSIQUE TYPES CHARACTERIZED BY INDICATED TRAIT

TABLE E-6. CYANOSIS

Physique Type	All Nondelinquents with Indicated Trait	Percentage of Nondelinquents with Trait and Factors	
		Physical Punishment of Boy by Father	Indifference or Hostility of Boy to Mother

Percentages of the Respective Physique Type Totals for the Particular Social Factor Categories and/or the Trait

Mesomorph	39·6%	46·0%	68·8%
Endomorph	30·5	22·2	25·0
Ectomorph	49·5	61·9	62·5
Balanced	45·9	47·8	80·0

Significance of Variations between Physique Types

Mesomorph–Endomorph	—	—	—
Mesomorph–Ectomorph	—	—	—
Mesomorph–Balanced	—	—	—
Endomorph–Ectomorph	·05	·02	—
Endomorph–Balanced	—	—	—
Ectomorph–Balanced	—	—	—

TABLE E-9. GENITAL UNDERDEVELOPMENT

Physique Type	All Nondelinquents with Indicated Trait	Nondelinquents with Trait and Factor Boy Attached to Father

Percentages of the Respective Physique Type Totals for the Particular Social Factor Category and/or the Trait

Mesomorph	4·7%	5·2%
Endomorph	27·7	30·0
Ectomorph	16·5	18·9
Balanced	9·7	9·3

Significance of Variations between Physique Types

Mesomorph–Endomorph	·02	·02
Mesomorph–Ectomorph	·02	·05
Mesomorph–Balanced	—	—
Endomorph–Ectomorph	—	—
Endomorph–Balanced	·05	·05
Ectomorph–Balanced	—	—

TABLE E-10. STRENGTH OF HAND GRIP
(Dynamometric Strength—75 Kilograms and Over)

Physique Type	All Nondelinquents with Indicated Trait	Nondelinquents with Indicated Trait and Factors				
		Compatibility of Parents	Suitable Supervision of Boy by Mother	Adequate Recreational Facilities for Boy in Home	Boy Ten Years or Older at First Breach in Family Life	Firm Discipline of Boy by Mother
			Percentages of the Respective Physique Type Totals for the Particular Social Factor Categories and/or the Trait			
Mesomorph	73·6%	76·2%	81·1%	75·8%	86·7%	78·8%
Endomorph	38·1	41·7	43·7	42·6	50·0	44·2
Ectomorph	23·9	28·6	25·8	27·0	28·6	26·2
Balanced	30·3	43·2	40·0	46·8	71·4	45·3
			Significance of Variations between Physique Types			
Mesomorph–Endomorph	·01	·02	·01	·02	—	·02
Mesomorph–Ectomorph	·01	·01	·01	·01	·02	·01
Mesomorph–Balanced	·01	·02	·01	·05	—	·02
Endomorph–Ectomorph	—	—	—	—	—	—
Endomorph–Balanced	—	—	—	·10	—	—
Ectomorph–Balanced	—	—	—	—	—	·10

TABLE E-17. TENDENCY TO PHANTASY

Physique Type	All Nondelinquents with Indicated Trait	Nondelinquents with Indicated Trait and Factors				
		Emotional Disturbance of Father	Serious Physical Aliment of Mother	Lack of Family Group Recreations	Parents Inhospitable to Boy's Companions	Boy less than Five Years of Age at First Breach in Family Life
Percentages of the Respective Physique Type Totals for the Particular Social Factor Categories and/or the Trait						
Mesomorph	24·4%	10·0%	29·8%	21·3%	30·8%	16·7%
Endomorph	28·6	47·1	34·8	37·5	46·7	30·8
Ectomorph	36·8	48·6	42·9	45·3	34·9	37·5
Balanced	42·0	50·0	42·9	53·3	68·4	60·0
Significance of Variations between Physique Types						
Mesomorph–Endomorph	—	·05	—	—	—	—
Mesomorph–Ectomorph	·10	·02	—	·05	—	—
Mesomorph–Balanced	·10	·10	—	·05	·05	·05
Endomorph–Ectomorph	—	—	—	—	—	—
Endomorph–Balanced	—	—	—	—	—	—
Ectomorph–Balanced	—	—	—	—	·05	—

TABLE E-21. SOCIAL ASSERTIVENESS

Physique Type	All Nondelinquents with Indicated Trait	Nondelinquents with Indicated Trait and Factor Lax Discipline of Boy by Father
Percentages of the Respective Physique Type Totals for the Particular Social Factor Category and/or the Trait		
Mesomorph	21·1%	35·0%
Endomorph	8·0	14·3
Ectomorph	22·0	39·1
Balanced	26·9	44·4
Significance of Variations between Physique Types		
Mesomorph–Endomorph	·05	—
Mesomorph–Ectomorph	—	—
Mesomorph–Balanced	—	—
Endomorph–Ectomorph	·05	—
Endomorph–Balanced	·05	—
Ectomorph–Balanced	—	—

TABLE E-23. MARKED SUBMISSIVENESS TO AUTHORITY

Physique Type	All Nondelinquents with Indicated Trait	Nondelinquents with Indicated Trait and Factors	
		Emotional Disturbance of Father	Indifference or Hostility of Father to Boy
Percentages of the Respective Physique Type Totals for the Particular Social Factor Categories and/or the Trait			
Mesomorph	77·4%	81·0%	84·0%
Endomorph	90·0	100·0	100·0
Ectomorph	78·4	86·1	91·7
Balanced	79·1	83·3	75·0
Significance of Variations between Physique Types			
Mesomorph–Endomorph	·10	—	—
Mesomorph–Ectomorph	—	—	—
Mesomorph–Balanced	—	—	—
Endomorph–Ectomorph	·10	·10	—
Endomorph–Balanced	—	—	—
Ectomorph–Balanced	—	—	—

TABLE E-31. FEAR OF FAILURE AND DEFEAT

Physique Type	All Nondelinquents with Indicated Trait	Nondelinquents with Indicated Trait and Factor — Lax Discipline of Boy by Mother
Percentages of the Respective Physique Type Totals for the Particular Social Factor Category and/or the Trait		
Mesomorph	67·7%	64·7%
Endomorph	75·8	91·7
Ectomorph	62·7	100·0
Balanced	45·0	75·0
Significance of Variations between Physique Types		
Mesomorph–Endomorph	—	—
Mesomorph–Ectomorph	—	·02
Mesomorph–Balanced	·05	—
Endomorph–Ectomorph	—	—
Endomorph–Balanced	·02	—
Ectomorph–Balanced	·10	—

265

TABLE E-36. DESTRUCTIVENESS

Physique Type	All Nondelinquents with Indicated Trait	Nondelinquents with Indicated Trait and Factors							
		Crowded Home	Poor Management of Family Income	Careless Household Routine	Incompatibility of Parents	Mother Occasionally Employed Outside Home	Parents Inhospitable to Boy's Companions	Meager Recreational Facilities for Boy in Home	Indifference or Hostility of Siblings to Boy
		Percentages of the Respective Physique Type Totals for the Particular Social Factor Categories and/or the Trait							
Mesomorph	11·1%	18·4%	15·3%	8·6%	12·5%	22·2%	13·0%	19·0%	16·7%
Endomorph	7·8	0·0	4·0	11·1	12·5	0·0	28·6	19·0	25·0
Ectomorph	21·8	30·2	25·4	17·1	29·7	35·0	28·1	29·7	54·5
Balanced	17·2	20·0	28·0	14·3	30·0	22·2	31·3	13·6	60·0
		Significance of Variations between Physique Types							
Mesomorph–Endomorph	—	·05	—	—	—	—	—	—	—
Mesomorph–Ectomorph	·10	—	—	—	—	—	—	—	—
Mesomorph–Balanced	—	—	—	—	—	—	—	—	—
Endomorph–Ectomorph	·05	·01	—	—	—	·05	—	—	—
Endomorph–Balanced	—	—	—	—	—	—	—	—	—
Ectomorph–Balanced	—	—	—	—	—	—	—	—	—

TABLE E-39. MARKED DEPENDENCE ON OTHERS

Physique Types	All Nondelinquents with Indicated Trait	Nondelinquents with Indicated Trait and Factors				
		Emotional Disturbance of Father	Poor Work Habits of Father	Boy less than Five Years of Age at First Breach in Family Life	Lax Discipline of Boy by Mother	Physical Punishment of Boy by Father
Percentages of the Respective Physique Type Totals for the Particular Social Factor Categories and/or the Trait						
Mesomorph	85·8%	100·0%	100·0%	83·3%	100·0%	93·9%
Endomorph	92·8	100·0	100·0	100·0	91·7	87·5
Ectomorph	87·5	88·6	100·0	87·9	96·0	93·3
Balanced	77·6	90·9	50·0	100·0	100·0	91·3
Significance of Variations between Physique Types						
Mesomorph–Endomorph	—	—	—	—	—	—
Mesomorph–Ectomorph	—	—	—	—	—	—
Mesomorph–Balanced	—	—	—	—	—	—
Endomorph–Ectomorph	—	—	—	—	—	—
Endomorph–Balanced	·10	—	—	—	—	—
Ectomorph–Balanced	—	—	—	—	—	—

TABLE E-43. MASOCHISTIC TRENDS

Physique Type	All Nondelinquents with Indicated Trait	Nondelinquents with Indicated Trait and Factors						
		Crowded Home	Lack of Family Ambition	Fair Supervision of Boy by Mother	Lack of Family Group Recreations	Parents Indifferent to Boy's Companions	Meager Recreational Facilities for Boy in Home	Lax Discipline of Boy by Mother
Percentages of the Respective Physique Type Totals for the Particular Social Factor Categories and/or the Trait								
Mesomorph	38·9%	48·6%	44·3%	48·4%	50·0%	58·1%	57·1	77·8%
Endomorph	45·9	50·0	43·9	53·8	36·4	51·6	43·5	54·5
Ectomorph	38·6	51·3	41·2	53·6	46·0	44·1	54·2	66·7
Balanced	22·8	33·3	27·8	50·0	34·6	20·0	38·9	50·0
Significance of Variations between Physique Types								
Mesomorph–Endomorph	—	—	—	—	—	—	—	—
Mesomorph–Ectomorph	—	—	—	—	—	—	—	—
Mesomorph–Balanced	—	—	—	—	—	—	—	—
Endomorph–Ectomorph	—	—	—	—	—	·05	—	—
Endomorph–Balanced	·05	—	—	—	—	·10	—	—
Ectomorph–Balanced	—	—	—	—	—	—	—	—

TABLE E-44. DESTRUCTIVE-SADISTIC TRENDS

Physique Type	All Nondelinquents with Indicated Trait	Nondelinquents with Indicated Trait and Factors								
		Crowded Home	Unclean and Disorderly Home	Poor Management of Family Income	Careless Household Routine	Incompatibility of Parents	Mother Occasionally Employed Outside Home	Parents Inhospitable to Boy's Companions	Meager Recreational Facilities for Boy in Home	Indifference or Hostility of Siblings to Boy
Percentages of the Respective Physique Type Totals for the Particular Social Factor Categories and/or the Trait										
Mesomorph	11·9%	18·4%	14·6%	15·3%	15·2%	12·5%	22·2%	13·0%	19·0%	16·7%
Endomorph	7·8	0·0	7·7	4·0	3·6	12·5	0·0	28·6	19·0	25·0
Ectomorph	22·4	30·2	32·7	26·8	29·1	29·7	40·0	31·3	31·3	54·5
Balanced	17·2	20·0	18·2	28·0	20·0	30·0	22·2	31·3	13·6	60·0
Significance of Variations between Physique Types										
Mesomorph–Endomorph	—	·05	—	—	—	—	—	—	—	—
Mesomorph–Ectomorph	·10	—	—	—	—	—	—	—	—	—
Mesomorph–Balanced	—	—	·05	·02	·02	—	·02	—	—	—
Endomorph–Ectomorph	·05	·01	—	·10	—	—	—	—	—	—
Endomorph–Balanced	—	—	—	—	—	—	—	—	—	—
Ectomorph–Balanced	—	—	—	—	—	—	—	—	—	—

TABLE E-47. VIVACITY

Physique Type	All Nondelinquents with Indicated Trait	Nondelinquents with Indicated Trait and Factor
		Threatening or Scolding of Boy by Mother

Percentages of the Respective Physique Type Totals for the Particular Social Factor Category and/or the Trait

Mesomorph	20·4%	25·0%
Endomorph	9·1	25·0
Ectomorph	29·0	34·6
Balanced	34·6	45·5

Significance of Variations between Physique Types

Mesomorph–Endomorph	—	—
Mesomorph–Ectomorph	—	—
Mesomorph–Balanced	—	—
Endomorph–Ectomorph	·05	—
Endomorph–Balanced	·10	—
Ectomorph–Balanced	—	—

TABLE E-51. SENSITIVITY

Physique Type	All Nondelinquents with Indicated Trait	Nondelinquents with Indicated Trait and Factor	
		Emotional Disturbance of Mother	Marked Family Self-Respect

Percentages of the Respective Physique Type Totals for the Particular Social Factor Category and/or the Trait

Mesomorph	20·8%	36·4%	17·4%
Endomorph	22·2	35·7	25·6
Ectomorph	50·5	51·4	58·2
Balanced	44·4	66·7	40·0

Significance of Variations between Physique Types

Mesomorph–Endomorph	—	—	—
Mesomorph–Ectomorph	·01	—	·01
Mesomorph–Balanced	·05	—	·10
Endomorph–Ectomorph	·02	—	·02
Endomorph–Balanced	·05	—	—
Ectomorph–Balanced	—	—	—

Selective Impact of Factors on Physique Types

TABLE E-53. FEELING OF INADEQUACY

Physique Type	All Nondelinquents with Indicated Trait	Nondelinquents with Indicated Trait and Factors		
		Delinquency of Mother	Lack of Family Ambition	Rank of Boy among Siblings (Youngest)
	Percentages of the Respective Physique Type Totals for the Particular Social Factor Categories and/or the Trait			
Mesomorph	54·4%	70·0%	57·5%	63·3%
Endomorph	66·7	88·9	71·7	73·7
Ectomorph	80·0	82·6	80·6	84·6
Balanced	75·0	76·9	75·6	92·9
Significance of Variations between Physique Types				
Mesomorph–Endomorph	—	—	—	—
Mesomorph–Ectomorph	·01	—	·02	—
Mesomorph–Balanced	·05	—	—	·05
Endomorph–Ectomorph	—	—	—	—
Endomorph–Balanced	—	—	—	—
Ectomorph–Balanced	—	—	—	—

TABLE E-56. UNINHIBITED MOTOR RESPONSES TO STIMULI

Physique Type	All Nondelinquents with Indicated Trait	Nondelinquents with Indicated Trait and Factors			
		Unclean and Disorderly Home	Poor Management of Family Income	Rank of Boy among Siblings (Middle)	Rearing in Broken Home
	Percentages of the Respective Physique Type Totals for the Particular Social Factor Categories and/or the Trait				
Mesomorph	45·0%	56·0%	50·8%	48·3%	50·0%
Endomorph	19·4	21·4	18·5	24·0	16·7
Ectomorph	20·5	30·8	27·3	30·0	27·4
Balanced	26·4	29·2	35·5	42·1	33·3
Significance of Variations between Physique Types					
Mesomorph–Endomorph	·02	·05	·05	·10	·05
Mesomorph–Ectomorph	·02	·05	·05	·10	·10
Mesomorph–Balanced	·05	—	—	—	—
Endomorph–Ectomorph	—	—	—	—	—
Endomorph–Balanced	—	—	—	—	—
Ectomorph–Balanced	—	—	—	—	—

TABLE E-57. EMOTIONAL INSTABILITY

Physique Type	All Nondelinquents with Indicated Trait	Nondelinquents with Indicated Trait and Factors			
		Rank of Boy among Siblings (Firstborn)	Indifference or Hostility of Boy to Father	Unaccept- ability of Father to Boy for Emulation	Indifference or Hostility of Boy to Mother
		Percentages of the Respective Physique Type Totals for the Particular Social Factor Categories and/or the Trait			
Mesomorph	35·6%	50·0%	43·4%	40·0%	68·8%
Endomorph	45·8	64·7	50·0	44·1	75·0
Ectomorph	63·7	65·1	78·8	77·2	83·3
Balanced	47·2	66·7	58·6	54·3	60·0

Significance of Variations between Physique Types

Mesomorph–Endomorph	—	—	—	—	—
Mesomorph–Ectomorph	·01	—	·02	·02	—
Mesomorph–Balanced	—	—	—	—	—
Endomorph–Ectomorph	·05	—	·10	·05	—
Endomorph–Balanced	—	—	—	—	—
Ectomorph–Balanced	·10	—	—	—	—

TABLE E-58. AESTHETICISM

Physique Type	All Nondelinquents with Indicated Trait	Nondelinquents with Indicated Trait and Factors										
		Clean and Neat Home	Marginal or Sporadically Dependent Family	Good Management of Family Income	Well Planned Household Routine	Marked Family Self-Respect	Suitable Supervision of Boy by Mother	Some Family Group Recreations	Parents Interested in Boy's Companions	Adequate Recreational Facilities for Boy in Home	Firm Discipline of Boy by Father	Boy Attached to Father

Percentages of the Respective Physique Type Totals for the Particular Social Factor Categories and/or the Trait

Physique Type	All	Clean	Marginal	Good Mgmt	Well Planned	Marked	Suitable	Some Family	Parents	Adequate	Firm Disc.	Boy Attached
Mesomorph	27·5%	32·3%	28·6%	34·6%	32·4%	34·8%	32·2%	32·6%	41·8%	31·3%	30·6%	27·1%
Endomorph	29·2	31·8	30·6	28·9	35·0	27·9	36·7	26·1	33·3	34·0	35·1	34·0
Ectomorph	48·9	54·5	51·9	58·0	62·1	57·0	57·9	55·4	55·2	57·1	57·7	54·0
Balanced	37·5	40·4	41·3	45·0	41·7	37·1	41·3	39·0	37·0	40·4	41·7	41·9

Significance of Variations between Physique Types

Physique Type	All	Clean	Marginal	Good Mgmt	Well Planned	Marked	Suitable	Some Family	Parents	Adequate	Firm Disc.	Boy Attached
Mesomorph–Endomorph	—	—	—	—	—	—	—	—	—	—	—	—
Mesomorph–Ectomorph	·02	·05	·02	·05	·02	·05	·02	·05	—	·02	·02	·01
Mesomorph–Balanced	—	—	—	—	—	—	—	—	—	—	—	—
Endomorph–Ectomorph	·05	·05	·05	·02	·05	·05	·10	·02	—	·05	·10	·10
Endomorph–Balanced	—	—	—	—	—	—	—	—	—	—	—	—
Ectomorph–Balanced	—	—	—	—	—	—	—	—	—	—	—	—

TABLE E-60. ACQUISITIVENESS

		Nondelinquents with Indicated Trait and Factors		
Physique Type	*All Nondelinquents with Indicated Trait*	*Crowded Home*	*Meager Recreational Facilities for Boy in Home*	*Rank of Boy among Siblings (Middle)*

Percentages of the Respective Physique Type Totals for the Particular Social Factor Categories and/or the Trait

Mesomorph	14·1%	23·8%	22·1%	19·1%
Endomorph	5·6	0·0	8·0	8·0
Ectomorph	20·0	29·4	23·4	22·5
Balanced	5·6	0·0	8·0	5·3

Significance of Variations between Physique Types

Mesomorph–Endomorph	—	·02	—	—
Mesomorph–Ectomorph	—	—	—	—
Mesomorph–Balanced	—	·02	—	·10
Endomorph–Ectomorph	·02	·01	—	—
Endomorph–Balanced	—	—	—	—
Ectomorph–Balanced	02	·01	—	·05

274

TABLE E-61. UNCONVENTIONALITY

Physique Type	All Nondelinquents with Indicated Trait	Nondelinquents with Indicated Trait and Factors						
		Alcoholism of Father	Alcoholism of Mother	Lack of Family Cohesiveness	Indifference or Hostility of Father to Boy	Indifference or Hostility of Mother to Boy	Indifference or Hostility of Siblings to Boy	Indifference or Hostility of Boy to Father
Percentages of the Respective Physique Type Totals for the Particular Social Factor Categories and/or the Trait								
Mesomorph	48·3%	63·0%	80·0%	41·2%	64·0%	100·0%	62·5%	50·9%
Endomorph	25·0	24·0	66·7	70·8	33·7	0·0	75·0	40·9
Ectomorph	63·7	69·7	70·6	36·3	73·0	100·0	84·6	74·2
Balanced	52·8	50·0	60·0	43·3	61·5	100·0	50·0	58·6
Significance of Variations between Physique Types								
Mesomorph–Endomorph	·02	·02	—	·10	—	—	—	—
Mesomorph–Ectomorph	·05	—	—	—	—	—	—	·05
Mesomorph–Balanced	—	—	—	—	—	—	—	—
Endomorph–Ectomorph	·01	·01	—	·05	·05	—	—	·05
Endomorph–Balanced	·02	—	—	—	—	—	—	—
Ectomorph–Balanced	—	—	—	—	—	—	—	—

TABLE E-64. IMPRACTICALITY

Physique Type	All Nondelinquents with Indicated Trait	Nondelinquents with Indicated Trait and Factors									
		Emotional Disturbance of Mother	Lack of Family Self-Respect	Unsuitable Supervision of Boy by Mother	Lack of Family Cohesiveness	Rank of Boy among Siblings (Only Child)	Erratic Discipline of Boy by Father	Erratic Discipline of Boy by Mother	Indifference or Hostility of Boy to Father	Unacceptability of Father to Boy for Emulation	Indifference or Hostility of Boy to Mother

Percentages of the Respective Physique Type Totals for the Particular Social Factor Categories and/or the Trait

Physique Type	All	Emotional	Self-Respect	Supervision	Cohesiveness	Rank	Discipline Father	Discipline Mother	Indiff. Father	Unaccept.	Indiff. Mother
Mesomorph	57·0%	54·5%	66·7%	64·7%	60·8%	70·0%	66·7%	62·1%	66·0%	65·5%	75·0%
Endomorph	66·7	64·3	100·0	90·0	75·0	90·9	66·7	75·0	81·8	64·7	100·0
Ectomorph	70·5	83·8	85·0	72·0	71·2	80·0	74·2	83·0	75·8	73·4	75·0
Balanced	66·7	83·3	83·3	91·0	76·7	80·0	90·9	81·8	79·3	77·1	80·0

Significance of Variations between Physique Types

Physique Type	All	Emotional	Self-Respect	Supervision	Cohesiveness	Rank	Discipline Father	Discipline Mother	Indiff. Father	Unaccept.	Indiff. Mother
Mesomorph–Endomorph	—	—	·05	—	—	—	—	—	—	—	—
Mesomorph–Ectomorph	·10	·10	—	—	—	—	—	—	—	—	—
Mesomorph–Balanced	—	—	—	—	—	—	—	—	—	—	—
Endomorph–Ectomorph	—	—	—	—	—	—	—	—	—	·05	—
Endomorph–Balanced	—	—	—	—	—	—	—	—	—	—	—
Ectomorph–Balanced	—	—	—	—	—	—	—	—	—	—	—

TABLE E-65. EMOTIONAL CONFLICTS

Physique Type	All Nondelinquents with Indicated Trait	Nondelinquents with Indicated Trait and Factors				
		Lack of Family Cohesiveness	Indifference or Hostility of Siblings to Boy	Indifference or Hostility of Boy to Father	Unacceptability of Father to Boy for Emulation	Indifference or Hostility of Boy to Mother

Percentages of the Respective Physique Type Totals for the Particular Social Factor Categories and/or the Trait

Physique Type	All Nondelinquents with Indicated Trait	Lack of Family Cohesiveness	Indifference or Hostility of Siblings to Boy	Indifference or Hostility of Boy to Father	Unacceptability of Father to Boy for Emulation	Indifference or Hostility of Boy to Mother
Mesomorph	22·7%	20·0%	50·0%	24·4%	28·6%	33·3%
Endomorph	36·8	28·6	100·0	44·4	45·2	33·3
Ectomorph	52·5	56·7	50·0	70·7	66·2	90·0
Balanced	31·7	52·0	50·0	54·2	50·0	50·0

Significance of Variations between Physique Types

	All Nondelinquents with Indicated Trait	Lack of Family Cohesiveness	Indifference or Hostility of Siblings to Boy	Indifference or Hostility of Boy to Father	Unacceptability of Father to Boy for Emulation	Indifference or Hostility of Boy to Mother
Mesomorph–Endomorph	·01	—	—	—	—	—
Mesomorph–Ectomorph	—	·01	—	·01	·02	·02
Mesomorph–Balanced	—	·05	—	·10	—	—
Endomorph–Ectomorph	—	·10	—	—	—	—
Endomorph–Balanced	—	—	—	—	—	—
Ectomorph–Balanced	·05	—	—	—	—	—

F.E.D.—T

APPENDIX F

DATA FOR ANALYSIS OF SELECTIVE IMPACT OF FACTORS OF FAMILY EN- VIRONMENT ON DELINQUENTS CHAR- ACTERIZED BY INDICATED TRAITS

TABLE F-3. EXTREME RESTLESSNESS IN EARLY CHILDHOOD

Factors and Subcategories	Delinquents		Differences between Delinquents and Nondelinquents in Each Subcategory	
	Percentages of the Respective Subcategory Totals	Significance of Variations between Subcategories	Percentages of the Respective Subcategory Totals	Significance of Variations between Subcategories
Conjugal Relations of Parents				
Broken Relationship	66·2%	⎤	44·6%	⎤
Incompatible	65·2	⎥·02 ⎤·05	22·3	⎥·05 ⎤·05
Compatible	48·4	⎦ ⎦	20·5	⎦ ⎦
Affection of Mother for Boy				
Indifferent or Hostile	70·3%	⎤	47·6%	⎤
Warm	55·2	⎦·02	24·6	⎦·05

TABLE F-4. ENURESIS IN EARLY CHILDHOOD

Factors and Subcategories	Delinquents		Differences between Delinquents and Nondelinquents in Each Subcategory	
	Percentages of the Respective Subcategory Totals	Significance of Variations between Subcategories	Percentages of the Respective Subcategory Totals	Significance of Variations between Subcategories
Cleanliness and Orderliness of Home				
Sporadically Clean and Neat or Habitually Disorderly	32·5%	⎤	20·2%	⎤
Normally Clean and Neat	24·0	⎦·05	9·5	⎦·05
Management of Family Income				
Partially Planned or Haphazard	31·6%	⎤	19·6%	⎤
Entirely Planned	21·6	⎦·05	6·8	⎦·05
Family Cohesiveness				
Some or None	30·3%	⎤	15·1%	⎤
Marked	17·5	⎦·05	4·9	⎦·10
Threatening or Scolding of Boy by Mother				
Used	36·7%	⎤	23·4%	⎤
Not Used	19·9	⎦·01	5·6	⎦·02

TABLE F-7. ABSENCE OF DERMOGRAPHIA

		Delinquents		Differences between Delinquents and Nondelinquents in Each Subcategory	
Factor and Subcategories		*Percentages of the Respective Subcategory Totals*	*Significance of Variation between Subcategories*	*Percentages of the Respective Subcategory Totals*	*Significance of Variation between Subcategories*
Q.	*Household Routine*				
	Partially Planned or				
	Haphazard	58·8%	]·05	16·6%	]·05
	Well Planned	45·0		3·0	

TABLE F-9. GENITAL UNDERDEVELOPMENT

		Delinquents		Differences between Delinquents and Nondelinquents in Each Subcategory	
Factors and Subcategories		*Percentages of the Respective Subcategory Totals*	*Significance of Variations between Subcategories*	*Percentages of the Respective Subcategory Totals*	*Significance of Variations between Subcategories*
R.	*Cultural Refinement in Home*				
	None	12·2%	]·05	0·2%	]·05
	Marked or Slight	4·9		−11·0	
CC.	*Family Cohesiveness*				
	Some or None	12·7%	]·05	2·8%	]·05
	Marked	6·3		−9·1	

TABLE F-11. LOW VERBAL INTELLIGENCE
(Wechsler Verbal I.Q.—below 80)

Factors and Subcategories	Delinquents — Percentages of the Respective Subcategory Totals	Delinquents — Significance of Variations between Subcategories	Differences between Delinquents and Nondelinquents in Each Subcategory — Percentages of the Respective Subcategory Totals	Differences between Delinquents and Nondelinquents in Each Subcategory — Significance of Variations between Subcategories
Usual Economic Condition of Family				
Usually Dependent	34·8%	⎤	19·7%	⎤
Marginal or Sporadically Dependent	24·9	⎦ ·05	8·4	⎦ ·10
Management of Family Income				
Partially Planned or Haphazard	32·2%	⎤	14·6%	⎤
Entirely Planned	20·4	⎦ ·05	5·2	⎦ ·10
Household Routine				
Partially Planned or Haphazard	31·7%	⎤	13·6%	⎤
Well Planned	18·3	⎦ ·02	3·7	⎦ ·10
Ambitiousness of Family				
None	30·3%	⎤	12·7%	⎤
Marked or Slight	13·2	⎦ ·02	−0·4	⎦ ·05
Family Group Recreations				
Never	31·8%	⎤	15·3%	⎤
Often or Occasional	21·1	⎦ ·05	4·9	⎦ ·10
A. *Parents' Attitude to Boy's Companions*				
Inhospitable	33·5%	⎤	16·1%	⎤
Indifferent	29·3	⎦ ·05 ⎤	18·2	⎦ ·02 ⎤
Warm	18·0	⎦ ·10	−2·6	⎦ ·05
B. *Recreational Facilities for Boy in Home*				
Meager	36·4%	⎤	22·4%	⎤
Adequate or Some	19·5	⎦ ·01	2·0	⎦ ·02
H. *Affection of Father for Boy*				
Indifferent or Hostile	32·3%	⎤	17·2%	⎤
Warm	21·7	⎦ ·05	4·9	⎦ ·05

TABLE F-12. LOW PERFORMANCE INTELLIGENCE
(Wechsler Performance I.Q.—less than 101)

Factor and Subcategories	Delinquents		Differences between Delinquents and Nondelinquents in Each Subcategory	
	Percentages of the Respective Subcategory Totals	Significance of Variations between Subcategories	Percentages of the Respective Subcategory Totals	Significance of Variation between Subcategories
X. *Usual Occupation of Mother*				
Occasionally Employed Outside Home	69·7%		13·5%	
Regularly Employed Outside Home	43·6	⎤·01 ⎤·02	−8·0	⎤·10
Housewife	62·4		2·6	

HIGH PERFORMANCE INTELLIGENCE
(Wechsler Performance I.Q.—101 and Over)

Factor and Subcategories	Delinquents		Differences between Delinquents and Nondelinquents in Each Subcategory	
	Percentages of the Respective Subcategory Totals	Significance of Variations between Subcategories	Percentages of the Respective Subcategory Totals	Significance of Variation between Subcategories
KK. *Discipline of Boy by Father*				
Lax	44·3%		1·6%	
Overstrict	35·0	⎤·02 ⎤·10 ⎤·02	2·5	⎤·05 ⎤·10
Erratic	43·5		2·0	
Firm but Kindly	15·4		−26·2	

TABLE F-15. POOR POWER OF OBSERVATION

Factor and Subcategories	Delinquents		Differences between Delinquents and Nondelinquents in Each Subcategory	
	Percentages of the Respective Subcategory Totals	Significance of Variation between Subcategories	Percentages of the Respective Subcategory Totals	Significance of Variation between Subcategories
GG. *Rearing by Parent Substitutes*				
Yes	42·4%	⎤·05	16·5%	⎤·05
No	31·2		1·4	

TABLE F-16. INTUITION

	Delinquents		Differences between Delinquents and Nondelinquents in Each Subcategory	
Factors and Subcategories	*Percentages of the Respective Subcategory Totals*	*Significance of Variations between Subcategories*	*Percentages of the Respective Subcategory Totals*	*Significance of Variations between Subcategories*
Alcoholism of Mother				
Present	23·0%	]·10	11·2%	]·10
Absent	14·6		−1·1	
)D. *Rank of Boy among Siblings*				
Middle	14·9%	]·01	0·5%	
Only Child	0·0	]·02]·01	−10·0	
Firstborn	17·3		−2·5	]·05
Youngest	25·0		9·2	

TABLE F-17. TENDENCY TO PHANTASY

	Delinquents		Differences between Delinquents and Nondelinquents in Each Subcategory	
Factor and Subcategories	*Percentages of the Respective Subcategory Totals*	*Significance of Variation between Subcategories*	*Percentages of the Respective Subcategory Totals*	*Significance of Variation between Subcategories*
G. *Delinquency of Mother*				
Present	44·3%	]·05	15·5%	]·10
Absent	34·8		1·7	

TABLE F-18. LACK OF COMMON SENSE

	Delinquents		Differences between Delinquents and Nondelinquents in Each Subcategory	
Factor and Subcategories	*Percentages of the Respective Subcategory Totals*	*Significance of Variation between Subcategories*	*Percentages of the Respective Subcategory Totals*	*Significance of Variations between Subcategories*
)D. *Rank of Boy among Siblings*				
Middle	24·2%		7·1%	]·02
Only Child	9·1	]·05	−29·4	]·02]·05
Firstborn	32·9		14·4	
Youngest	24·7		7·5	

285

TABLE F-19. UNMETHODICAL APPROACH TO PROBLEMS

	Delinquents		Differences between Delinquents and Nondelinquents in Each Subcategory	
Factors and Subcategories	*Percentages of the Respective Subcategory Totals*	*Significance of Variations between Subcategories*	*Percentages of the Respective Subcategory Totals*	*Significance of Variations between Subcategories*
R. *Cultural Refinement in Home*				
None	80·7%	] ·05	15·6%	] ·05
Marked or Slight	57·5		−6·0	
LL. *Discipline of Boy by Mother*				
Lax	83·0%		15·7%	
Overstrict	90·5	] ·05] ·10	53·0	
Erratic	72·1		3·7	] ·10] ·10
Firm but Kindly	66·7		3·3	

TABLE F-20. LACK OF POTENTIAL CAPACITY FOR OBJECTIVE INTERESTS

	Delinquents		Differences between Delinquents and Nondelinquents in Each Subcategory	
Factor and Subcategories	*Percentages of the Respective Subcategory Totals*	*Significance of Variation between Subcategories*	*Percentages of the Respective Subcategory Totals*	*Significance of Variation between Subcategories*
HH. *Affection of Father for Boy*				
Indifferent or Hostile	59·1%	] ·10	19·1%	] ·10
Warm	50·3		4·0	

TABLE F-21. SOCIAL ASSERTIVENESS

	Delinquents		Differences between Delinquents and Nondelinquents in Each Subcategory	
Factor and Subcategories	*Percentages of the Respective Subcategory Totals*	*Significance of Variations between Subcategories*	*Percentages of the Respective Subcategory Totals*	*Significance of Variations between Subcategories*
LL. *Discipline of Boy by Mother*				
Lax	46·6%		28·2%	
Overstrict	47·4	] ·02] ·10] ·02	18·8	
Erratic	47·1		26·9	] ·05] ·05
Firm but Kindly	15·0		−5·8	

TABLE F-23. NONSUBMISSIVENESS TO AUTHORITY

Factor and Subcategories	Delinquents		Differences between Delinquents and Nondelinquents in Each Subcategory	
	Percentages of the Respective Subcategory Totals	Significance of Variations between Subcategories	Percentages of the Respective Subcategory Totals	Significance of Variations between Subcategories
Discipline of Boy by Mother				
Lax	76·8%		66·3%	
Overstrict	90·0	·02 ·10	77·5	·10 ·01
Erratic	70·6	·01 ·05	48·1	·02 ·05
Firm but Kindly	35·0		13·8	

TABLE F-24. AMBIVALENCE TO AUTHORITY

Factor and Subcategories	Delinquents		Differences between Delinquents and Nondelinquents in Each Subcategory	
	Percentages of the Respective Subcategory Totals	Significance of Variation between Subcategories	Percentages of the Respective Subcategory Totals	Significance of Variation between Subcategories
Serious Physical Ailment of Mother				
Present	46·5%	·05	29·8%	·05
Absent	35·6		14·6	

TABLE F-25. ABSENCE OF FEELING OF INSECURITY

Factor and Subcategories	Delinquents		Differences between Delinquents and Nondelinquents in Each Subcategory	
	Percentages of the Respective Subcategory Totals	Significance of Variations between Subcategories	Percentages of the Respective Subcategory Totals	Significance of Variations between Subcategories
Rank of Boy among Siblings				
Middle	82·4%		7·4%	
Only Child	95·8	·05 ·05	39·0	·05 ·05
Firstborn	78·9	·05	3·6	·05 ·10
Youngest	77·5		11·7	

TABLE F-27. FEELING OF NOT BEING TAKEN CARE OF

		Delinquents		*Differences between Delinquents and Nondelinquents in Each Subcategory*	
Factor and Subcategories		*Percentages of the Respective Subcategory Totals*	*Significance of Variations between Subcategories*	*Percentages of the Respective Subcategory Totals*	*Significance of Variations between Subcategories*
DD.	*Rank of Boy among Siblings*				
	Middle	27·3%	]·05	3·1%	]·05
	Only Child	6·3		−35·4	
	Firstborn	26·5	]·02	6·9	]·05
	Youngest	40·0		17·9	

TABLE F-28. ABSENCE OF FEELING OF NOT BEING TAKEN SERIOUSLY

		Delinquents		*Differences between Delinquents and Nondelinquents in Each Subcategory*	
Factor and Subcategories		*Percentages of the Respective Subcategory Totals*	*Significance of Variation between Subcategories*	*Percentages of the Respective Subcategory Totals*	*Significance of Variation between Subcategories*
K.	*Emotional Disturbance of Mother*				
	Present	61·4%	]·10	23·7%	]·05
	Absent	51·8		1·0	

288

TABLE F-29. ABSENCE OF FEELING OF HELPLESSNESS

	Delinquents		Differences between Delinquents and Nondelinquents in Each Subcategory	
Factors and Subcategories	*Percentages of the Respective Subcategory Totals*	*Significance of Variations between Subcategories*	*Percentages of the Respective Subcategory Totals*	*Significance of Variations between Subcategories*
D. *Rank of Boy among Siblings*				
Middle	59·4%		12·6%	
Only Child	80·0	]·10]·05	49·4	]·05]·05]·02
Firstborn	54·5		11·3	
Youngest	51·2		0·7	
L. *Discipline of Boy by Mother*				
Lax	61·9%		38·4%	
Overstrict	73·7	]·02]·02]·05	48·7	]·01]·02]·01
Erratic	54·1		20·8	
Firm but Kindly	22·2		−32·3	

TABLE F-30. FEELING OF NOT BEING APPRECIATED

	Delinquents		Differences between Delinquents and Nondelinquents in Each Subcategory	
Factors and Subcategories	*Percentages of the Respective Subcategory Totals*	*Significance of Variations between Subcategories*	*Percentages of the Respective Subcategory Totals*	*Significance of Variations between Subcategories*
Delinquency of Father				
Present	40·2%	]·05	15·9%	]·10
Absent	28·4		3·8	
I. *Alcoholism of Father*				
Present	40·2%	]·05	17·4%	]·05
Absent	29·8		4·2	
Usual Economic Condition of Family				
Usually Dependent	47·9%	]·02	35·4%	]·01
Marginal and Sporadically Dependent	29·3		3·4	
Dominant Parent in Family Affairs				
Mother	41·7%	]·05	20·2%	]·05
Father	29·4		1·8	

TABLE F-31. ABSENCE OF FEAR OF FAILURE AND DEFEAT

	Delinquents		Differences between Delinquents and Nondelinquents in Each Subcategory	
Factors and Subcategories	*Percentages of the Respective Subcategory Totals*	*Significance of Variations between Subcategories*	*Percentages of the Respective Subcategory Totals*	*Significance of Variations between Subcategories*
GG. *Rearing by Parent Substitutes*				
Yes	61·2%	]·05	29·2%	]·10
No	51·8		14·2	
LL. *Discipline of Boy by Mother*				
Lax	56·4%	]·10]·05]·10	41·3%	]·01]·05
Overstrict	73·3		30·4	
Erratic	57·6		24·3	
Firm but Kindly	30·0		−12·0	

TABLE F-33. POOR SURFACE CONTACT WITH OTHERS

	Delinquents		Differences between Delinquents and Nondelinquents in Each Subcategory	
Factors and Subcategories	*Percentages of the Respective Subcategory Totals*	*Significance of Variations between Subcategories*	*Percentages of the Respective Subcategory Totals*	*Significance of Variations between Subcategories*
B. *Crowding of Home*				
More than Two Occupants per Bedroom	12·6%	]·05	10·9%	]·05
One or Two Occupants per Bedroom	6·4		2·8	
F. *Delinquency of Father*				
Present	10·0%	]·05	8·1%	]·05
Absent	4·9		0·9	
U. *Conduct Standards of Family*				
Poor	8·9%	]·05	7·4%	]·02
Good or Fair	2·2		−3·2	
BB. *Recreational Facilities for Boy in Home*				
Meager	11·5%	]·05	8·6%	]·05
Adequate or Some	4·5		1·0	
RR. *Emotional Ties of Boy to Father*				
Indifferent or Hostile or Noncommittal	9·9%	]·05	6·9%	]·10
Attached	5·1		1·6	

TABLE F-36. DESTRUCTIVENESS

	Delinquents		Differences between Delinquents and Nondelinquents in Each Subcategory	
Factor and Subcategories	*Percentages of the Respective Subcategory Totals*	*Significance of Variation between Subcategories*	*Percentages of the Respective Subcategory Totals*	*Significance of Variation between Subcategories*
J. Rearing by Parent Substitutes				
Yes	53·5%	]·10	41·0%	]·10
No	44·4		28·7	

TABLE F-37. FEELING OF ISOLATION

	Delinquents		Differences between Delinquents and Nondelinquents in Each Subcategory	
Factors and Subcategories	*Percentages of the Respective Subcategory Totals*	*Significance of Variations between Subcategories*	*Percentages of the Respective Subcategory Totals*	*Significance of Variations between Subcategories*
Alcoholism of Father				
Present	52·0%	]·02	16·6%	]·05
Absent	33·8		−2·9	
O. Rank of Boy among Siblings				
Middle	44·3%		12·0%	
Only Child	22·2	]·10	−22·2	]·10
Firstborn	52·9		9·8	
Youngest	47·9		11·7	
R. Emotional Ties of Boy to Father				
Indifferent or Hostile or Noncommittal	50·0%	]·05	12·2%	]·10
Attached	34·2		−1·4	

TABLE F-39. LACK OF DEPENDENCE ON OTHERS

	Delinquents		Differences between Delinquents and Nondelinquents in Each Subcategory	
Factor and Subcategories	*Percentages of the Respective Subcategory Totals*	*Significance of Variation between Subcategories*	*Percentages of the Respective Subcategory Totals*	*Significance of Variation between Subcategories*
M. Physical Punishment of Boy by Father				
Used	34·1%	]·05	26·8%	]·02
Not Used	23·3		6·1	

TABLE F-40. FEELING OF BEING ABLE TO MANAGE OWN LIFE

	Delinquents		*Differences between Delinquents and Nondelinquents in Each Subcategory*	
Factors and Subcategories	*Percentages of the Respective Subcategory Totals*	*Significance of Variations between Subcategories*	*Percentages of the Respective Subcategory Totals*	*Significance of Variations between Subcategories*
K. *Emotional Disturbance of Mother*				
Present	78·8%	]·10	20·0%	]·10
Absent	69·4		4·4	
Y. *Supervision of Boy by Mother*				
Unsuitable	78·9%	]·10	26·1%	
Fair	66·0		10·9	]·05
Suitable	65·5		−4·2	
DD. *Rank of Boy among Siblings*				
Middle	71·9%	]·01]·01]·10	5·6%	]·01]·02
Only Child	100·0		57·1	
Firstborn	71·2		4·5	
Youngest	72·3		8·5	

TABLE F-41. NARCISSISTIC TRENDS

	Delinquents		*Differences between Delinquents and Nondelinquents in Each Subcategory*	
Factor and Subcategories	*Percentages of the Respective Subcategory Totals*	*Significance of Variation between Subcategories*	*Percentages of the Respective Subcategory Totals*	*Significance of Variations between Subcategories*
DD. *Rank of Boy among Siblings*				
Middle	21·7%		9·8%	]·10
Only Child	8·3	]·05	−12·3	]·10
Firstborn	24·3		7·3	
Youngest	29·8		15·1	

Selective Impact of Environmental Factors on Delinquency

TABLE F-42. RECEPTIVE TRENDS

Factors and Subcategories	Delinquents — Percentages of the Respective Subcategory Totals	Delinquents — Significance of Variations between Subcategories	Differences between Delinquents and Nondelinquents in Each Subcategory — Percentages of the Respective Subcategory Totals	Differences between Delinquents and Nondelinquents in Each Subcategory — Significance of Variations between Subcategories
Delinquency of Father				
Present	34·5%	⎤	19·5%	⎤
Absent	21·6	⎦ ·05	8·7	⎦ ·10
Delinquency of Mother				
Present	35·5%	⎤	23·6%	⎤
Absent	25·5	⎦ ·05	11·6	⎦ ·10
M. *Physical Punishment of Boy by Father*				
Used	31·9%	⎤	17·4%	⎤
Not Used	19·2	⎦ ·05	5·2	⎦ ·05

TABLE F-43. ABSENCE OF MASOCHISTIC TRENDS

Factors and Subcategories	Delinquents — Percentages of the Respective Subcategory Totals	Delinquents — Significance of Variations between Subcategories	Differences between Delinquents and Nondelinquents in Each Subcategory — Percentages of the Respective Subcategory Totals	Differences between Delinquents and Nondelinquents in Each Subcategory — Significance of Variations between Subcategories
Management of Family Income				
Partially Planned or Haphazard	88·4%	⎤	27·9%	⎤
Entirely Planned	78·9	⎦ ·05	13·3	⎦ ·05
Supervision of Boy by Mother				
Unsuitable	89·1%	⎤	28·2%	
Fair	78·8	⎦ ·05	28·8	⎤
Suitable	75·0		5·7	⎦ ·10
A. *Parents' Attitude to Boy's Companions*				
Inhospitable	78·2%	⎤	14·3%	⎤
Indifferent	88·5	⎦ ·05 ⎤ ·05	33·8	⎦ ·05 ⎤ ·10
Warm	90·5		18·8	
B. *Recreational Facilities for Boy in Home*				
Meager	81·7%	⎤	32·4%	⎤
Adequate or Some	88·0	⎦ ·10	16·6	⎦ ·05
L. *Discipline of Boy by Mother*				
Lax	86·9%	⎤	51·9%	⎤
Overstrict	90·5	⎦ ·05 ⎤ ·05 ⎤ ·10	47·6	⎦ ·10 ⎤ ·01 ⎤ ·05
Erratic	83·9		26·3	
Firm but Kindly	52·9	⎦ ·05	−17·1	⎦ ·05

TABLE F-45. EMOTIONAL LABILITY

	Factors and Subcategories	Delinquents		Differences between Delinquents and Nondelinquents in Each Subcategory	
		Percentages of the Respective Subcategory Totals	Significance of Variations between Subcategories	Percentages of the Respective Subcategory Totals	Significance of Variation between Subcategories
B.	*Crowding of Home*				
	More than Two Occupants per Bedroom	49·3%	⎤ ·10	33·4%	⎤ ·10
	One or Two Occupants per Bedroom	40·7	⎦	21·2	⎦
K.	*Emotional Disturbance of Mother*				
	Present	53·1%	⎤ ·02	33·6%	⎤ ·05
	Absent	37·1	⎦	18·7	⎦
X.	*Usual Occupation of Mother*				
	Occasionally Employed Outside Home	51·7%	⎤	36·3%	⎤
	Regularly Employed Outside Home	42·5	·10	23·7	·10
	Housewife	39·7	⎦	20·4	⎦
EE.	*Rearing in Broken Home*				
	Yes	47·6%	⎤ ·05	32·1%	⎤ ·05
	No	37·2	⎦	17·1	⎦
HH.	*Affection of Father for Boy*				
	Indifferent or Hostile	49·0%	⎤ ·05	30·9%	⎤ ·05
	Warm	34·8	⎦	15·5	⎦

TABLE F-47. VIVACITY

	Factor and Subcategories	Delinquents		Differences between Delinquents and Nondelinquents in Each Subcategory	
		Percentages of the Respective Subcategory Totals	Significance of Variation between Subcategories	Percentages of the Respective Subcategory Totals	Significance of Variation between Subcategories
K.	*Emotional Disturbance of Mother*				
	Present	60·0%	⎤ ·05	39·4%	⎤ ·10
	Absent	44·5	⎦	20·7	⎦

TABLE F-49. PREPONDERANCE OF EXTROVERSIVE TRENDS

Factors and Subcategories	Delinquents		Differences between Delinquents and Nondelinquents in Each Subcategory	
	Percentages of the Respective Subcategory Totals	Significance of Variations between Subcategories	Percentages of the Respective Subcategory Totals	Significance of Variations between Subcategories
Emotional Disturbance of Mother				
Present	61·7%	]·05	41·4%	]·02
Absent	49·5		11·1	
H. *Affection of Father for Boy*				
Indifferent or Hostile	58·5%	]·05	32·8%	]·05
Warm	47·6		9·8	

TABLE F-50. PREPONDERANCE OF INTROVERSIVE TRENDS

Factors and Subcategories	Delinquents		Differences between Delinquents and Nondelinquents in Each Subcategory	
	Percentages of the Respective Subcategory Totals	Significance of Variations between Subcategories	Percentages of the Respective Subcategory Totals	Significance of Variations between Subcategories
Alcoholism of Father				
Present	33·5%	]·02	6·9%	]·10
Absent	18·1		−5·1	
Dominant Parent in Family Affairs				
Mother	36·4%	]·01	13·0%	]·02
Father	16·7		−8·3	
B. *Recreational Facilities for Boy in Home*				
Meager	34·5%	]·02	7·5%	]·10
Adequate or Some	18·9		−4·1	
K. *Discipline of Boy by Father*				
Lax	31·5%		17·0%]·02	
Overstrict	21·3	]·10	−25·8	·05]·05
Erratic	28·1		6·1]·05	
Firm but Kindly	10·5		−13·7	

Appendix F

TABLE F-53. FEELING OF INADEQUACY

Factors and Subcategories	Delinquents		Differences between Delinquents and Nondelinquents in Each Subcategory	
	Percentages of the Respective Subcategory Totals	Significance of Variations between Subcategories	Percentages of the Respective Subcategory Totals	Significance of Variations between Subcategorie
J. *Emotional Disturbance of Father*				
Present	88·5%	⎤ ·10	24·5%	⎤ ·05
Absent	82·4	⎦	11·9	⎦
EE. *Rearing in Broken Home*				
Yes	87·7%	⎤ ·10	24·0%	⎤ ·05
No	81·2	⎦	8·9	⎦

TABLE F-54. STUBBORNNESS

Factors and Subcategories	Delinquents		Differences between Delinquents and Nondelinquents in Each Subcategory	
	Percentages of the Respective Subcategory Totals	Significance of Variations between Subcategories	Percentages of the Respective Subcategory Totals	Significance of Variations between Subcategories
DD. *Rank of Boy among Siblings*				
Middle	43·3%	⎤	35·8%	⎤
Only Child	50·0	⎥ ·05 ⎤	33·7	⎥ ·10 ⎤
Firstborn	47·4	⎥ ⎦ ·10	40·2	⎥ ⎦ ·10
Youngest	28·9	⎦	21·4	⎦
JJ. *Affection of Siblings for Boy*				
Indifferent or Hostile	49·6%	⎤ ·05	43·3%	⎤ ·10
Warm	38·1	⎦	30·5	⎦
SS. *Acceptability of Father to Boy for Emulation*				
Unacceptable	45·8%	⎤ ·01	36·3%	⎤ ·05
Acceptable	21·7	⎦	16·0	⎦

TABLE F-56. UNINHIBITED MOTOR RESPONSES TO STIMULI

		Delinquents		Differences between Delinquents and Nondelinquents in Each Subcategory	
Factors and Subcategories		*Percentages of the Respective Subcategory Totals*	*Significance of Variations between Subcategories*	*Percentages of the Respective Subcategory Totals*	*Significance of Variations between Subcategories*
LL.	*Discipline of Boy by Mother*				
	Lax	60·7%	]·05	41·7%	
	Overstrict	27·3		14·8	]·05
	Erratic	57·3	]·10]·05	22·7	
	Firm but Kindly	33·3		4·5	
NN.	*Threatening or Scolding of Boy by Father*				
	Used	63·6%	]·10	39·5%	]·05
	Not Used	54·0		22·5	
SS.	*Acceptability of Father to Boy for Emulation*				
	Unacceptable	59·5%	]·05	29·6%	]·05
	Acceptable	42·0		12·3	

TABLE F-59. SENSUOUSNESS

		Delinquents		Differences between Delinquents and Nondelinquents in Each Subcategory	
Factors and Subcategories		*Percentages of the Respective Subcategory Totals*	*Significance of Variations between Subcategories*	*Percentages of the Respective Subcategory Totals*	*Significance of Variations between Subcategories*
L.	*Serious Physical Ailment of Father*				
	Present	24·9%	]·10	18·6%	]·10
	Absent	16·7		10·8	
R.	*Cultural Refinement in Home*				
	None	21·1%	]·05	14·9%	]·10
	Marked or Slight	9·8		4·1	
CC.	*Family Cohesiveness*				
	Some or None	21·3%	]·05	15·0%	]·10
	Marked	12·7		6·9	

TABLE F-60. ACQUISITIVENESS

		Delinquents		Differences between Delinquents and Nondelinquents in Each Subcategory	
Factors and Subcategories		*Percentages of the Respective Subcategory Totals*	*Significance of Variation between Subcategories*	*Percentages of the Respective Subcategory Totals*	*Significance of Variation between Subcategories*
SS.	*Acceptability of Father to Boy for Emulation*				
	Unacceptable	24·4%	⎤ ·05	12·1%	⎤ ·05
	Acceptable	14·5	⎦	0·1	⎦

TABLE F-61. UNCONVENTIONALITY

		Delinquents		Differences between Delinquents and Nondelinquents in Each Subcategory	
Factors and Subcategories		*Percentages of the Respective Subcategory Totals*	*Significance of Variations between Subcategories*	*Percentages of the Respective Subcategory Totals*	*Significance of Variations between Subcategories*
M.	*Serious Physical Ailment of Mother*				
	Present	79·2%	⎤ ·05	30·4%	⎤ ·10
	Absent	71·6	⎦	18·8	⎦
FF.	*Age of Boy at First Breach in Family Life*				
	Less than Five Years	81·2%	⎤ ·05	30·6%	⎤ ·05
	Five to Ten Years	66·7	⎦ ⎤ ·05	5·2	⎦ ⎤ ·05
	Ten Years or Older	84·8	⎦	40·1	⎦
LL.	*Discipline of Boy by Mother*				
	Lax	77·5%	⎤	34·4%	⎤
	Overstrict	81·8	⎦ ·05 ⎤ ·05 ⎤ ·05	6·8	⎥ ·05
	Erratic	74·9	⎦ ⎦	20·1	⎥
	Firm but Kindly	42·9		−8·2	⎦

TABLE F-62. LACK OF SELF-CRITICISM

	Delinquents		Differences between Delinquents and Nondelinquents in Each Subcategory	
Factor and Subcategories	*Percentages of the Respective Subcategory Totals*	*Significance of Variations between Subcategories*	*Percentages of the Respective Subcategory Totals*	*Significance of Variation between Subcategories*
A. *Parents' Attitude to Boy's Companions*				
Inhospitable	34·3%		27·0%	
Indifferent	30·1	]·05]·05	18·0	]·02
Warm	18·0		6·8	

TABLE F-64. IMPRACTICALITY

	Delinquents		Differences between Delinquents and Nondelinquents in Each Subcategory	
Factor and Subcategories	*Percentages of the Respective Subcategory Totals*	*Significance of Variation between Subcategories*	*Percentages of the Respective Subcategory Totals*	*Significance of Variation between Subcategories*
Affection of Siblings for Boy				
Indifferent or Hostile	88·5%	]·02	35·4%	]·05
Warm	76·4		11·5	

TABLE F-65. EMOTIONAL CONFLICTS

		Delinquents		Differences between Delinquents and Nondelinquents in Each Subcategory	
Factors and Subcategories		*Percentages of the Respective Subcategory Totals*	*Significance of Variations between Subcategories*	*Percentages of the Respective Subcategory Totals*	*Significance of Variations between Subcategories*
B.	*Crowding of Home*				
	More than Two Occupants per Bedroom	80·8%	] ·05	46·5%	] ·05
	One or Two Occupants per Bedroom	71·6		32·8	
X.	*Usual Occupation of Mother*				
	Occasionally Employed Outside Home	82·8%	] ·05	56·6%	] ·05] ·05
	Regularly Employed Outside Home	66·0		29·4	
	Housewife	74·0		33·9	

TABLE F-67. PSYCHOPATHY

		Delinquents		Differences between Delinquents and Nondelinquents in Each Subcategory	
Factors and Subcategories		*Percentages of the Respective Subcategory Totals*	*Significance of Variations between Subcategories*	*Percentages of the Respective Subcategory Totals*	*Significance of Variations between Subcategories*
Q.	*Household Routine*				
	Partially Planned or Haphazard	27·0%	] ·05	20·1%	] ·05
	Well Planned	18·1		10·2	
AA.	*Parents' Attitude to Boy's Companions*				
	Inhospitable	26·5%		19·1%	
	Indifferent	27·1	] ·05] ·05	20·9	] ·05
	Warm	14·3		8·4	
GG.	*Rearing by Parent Substitutes*				
	Yes	30·0%	] ·05	26·6%	] ·02
	No	19·2		12·5	
HH.	*Affection of Father for Boy*				
	Indifferent or Hostile	27·5%	] ·05	24·3%	] ·05
	Warm	18·8		11·5	

APPENDIX G

DATA FOR ANALYSIS OF SELECTIVE IMPACT OF FACTORS OF FAMILY ENVIRONMENT ON DELINQUENTS OF DIFFERENT PHYSIQUE TYPES

TABLE G-3. EXTREME RESTLESSNESS IN EARLY CHILDHOOD

Physique Type	Percentage Differences between Delinquents and Nondelinquents of Each Physique Type for the Indicated Trait and the Relevant Social Factors		
	Indicated Trait	Broken Relationship between Parents	Indifference or Hostility of Mother to Boy
Mesomorph	25·4%	35·8%	33·9%
Endomorph	27·4	62·5	18·4
Ectomorph	49·1	53·6	70·9
Balanced	41·8	45·3	77·8

	Significance of Variations between Physique Types		
Mesomorph–Endomorph	—	—	—
Mesomorph–Ectomorph	·05	—	—
Mesomorph–Balanced	—	—	—
Endomorph–Ectomorph	—	—	—
Endomorph–Balanced	—	—	—
Ectomorph–Balanced	—	—	—

TABLE G-4. ENURESIS IN EARLY CHILDHOOD

Physique Type	Percentage Differences between Delinquents and Nondelinquents of Each Physique Type for the Indicated Trait and the Relevant Social Factors				
	Indicated Trait	Unclean and Disorderly Home	Poor Management of Family Income	Lack of Family Cohesiveness	Threatening or Scolding of Boy by Mother
Mesomorph	13·0%	11·6%	13·6%	15·1%	23·3%
Endomorph	10·7	15·9	23·6	5·4	22·9
Ectomorph	28·0	46·8	34·4	27·0	34·4
Balanced	23·9	36·1	28·9	27·8	33·1

	Significance of Variations between Physique Types				
Mesomorph–Endomorph	—	—	—	—	—
Mesomorph–Ectomorph	—	·05	—	—	—
Mesomorph–Balanced	—	·10	—	—	—
Endomorph–Ectomorph	—	—	—	—	—
Endomorph–Balanced	—	—	—	—	—
Ectomorph–Balanced	—	—	—	—	—

TABLE G-7. ABSENCE OF DERMOGRAPHIA

Physique Type	Percentage Differences between Delinquents and Nondelinquents of Each Physique Type for the Indicated Trait and the Relevant Social Factor	
	Indicated Trait	*Careless Household Routine*
Mesomorph	21·1%	28·3%
Endomorph	3·9	6·5
Ectomorph	−2·0	−6·8
Balanced	−1·4	−0·4

Significance of Variations between Physique Types

Mesomorph–Endomorph	—	—
Mesomorph–Ectomorph	·05	·05
Mesomorph–Balanced	—	—
Endomorph–Ectomorph	—	—
Endomorph–Balanced	—	—
Ectomorph–Balanced	—	—

TABLE G-11. LOW VERBAL INTELLIGENCE
(Wechsler Verbal I.Q.—below 80)

Percentage Differences between Delinquents and Nondelinquents of Each Physique Type for the Indicated Trait and the Relevant Social Factors

Physique Type	Indicated Trait	Financial Dependence of Family	Poor Management of Family Income	Careless Household Routine	Lack of Family Ambition	Lack of Family Group Recreations	Parents Inhospitable or Indifferent to Boy's Companions	Meager Recreational Facilities for Boy in Home	Indifference or Hostility of Father to Boy
Mesomorph	18·7%	27·2%	21·4%	22·9%	22·1%	19·5%	23·7%	30·1%	27·7%
Endomorph	5·9	3·1	12·9	4·8	4·2	6·3	21·8	13·4	8·1
Ectomorph	−0·1	10·0	4·4	−1·8	−1·9	4·6	4·6	10·1	0·6
Balanced	6·6	15·0	8·3	3·4	8·4	11·5	10·0	13·3	22·7

Significance of Variations between Physique Types

Physique Type	Indicated Trait	Financial Dependence of Family	Poor Management of Family Income	Careless Household Routine	Lack of Family Ambition	Lack of Family Group Recreations	Parents Inhospitable or Indifferent to Boy's Companions	Meager Recreational Facilities for Boy in Home	Indifference or Hostility of Father to Boy
Mesomorph–Endomorph	·05	—	—	—	—	—	—	—	—
Mesomorph–Ectomorph	—	—	—	·10	·05	—	·10	—	·10
Mesomorph–Balanced	—	—	—	—	—	—	—	—	—
Endomorph–Ectomorph	—	—	—	—	—	—	—	—	—
Endomorph–Balanced	—	—	—	—	—	—	—	—	—
Ectomorph–Balanced	—	—	—	—	—	—	—	—	—

TABLE G-17. TENDENCY TO PHANTASY

Physique Type	Percentage Differences between Delinquents and Nondelinquents of Each Physique Type for the Indicated Trait and the Relevant Social Factor	
	Indicated Trait	Delinquency of Mother
Mesomorph	14·0%	34·8%
Endomorph	1·9	−11·9
Ectomorph	6·9	14·8
Balanced	3·2	−20·5

Significance of Variations between Physique Types

Mesomorph–Endomorph	—	—
Mesomorph–Ectomorph	—	—
Mesomorph–Balanced	—	·05
Endomorph–Ectomorph	—	—
Endomorph–Balanced	—	—
Ectomorph–Balanced	—	—

TABLE G-19. UNMETHODICAL APPROACH TO PROBLEMS

Physique Type	Percentage Differences between Delinquents and Nondelinquents of Each Physique Type for the Indicated Trait and the Relevant Social Factors		
	Indicated Trait	Lack of Cultural Refinement in Home	Overstrict Discipline of Boy by Mother
Mesomorph	9·8%	14·6%	90·9%
Endomorph	24·2	23·8	100·0
Ectomorph	17·9	13·4	20·0
Balanced	18·9	22·7	100·0

Significance of Variations between Physique Types

Mesomorph–Endomorph	—	—	—
Mesomorph–Ectomorph	—	—	·10
Mesomorph–Balanced	—	—	—
Endomorph–Ectomorph	—	—	·05
Endomorph–Balanced	—	—	—
Ectomorph–Balanced	—	—	·05

TABLE G-21. SOCIAL ASSERTIVENESS

| Physique Type | *Percentage Differences between Delinquents and Nondelinquents of Each Physique Type for the Indicated Trait and the Relevant Social Factor* | |
	Indicated Trait	*Lax/Erratic Discipline of Boy by Mother*
Mesomorph	30·2%	37·3%
Endomorph	32·5	36·7
Ectomorph	11·9	7·9
Balanced	8·4	9·7

Significance of Variations between Physique Types

Mesomorph–Endomorph	—	—
Mesomorph–Ectomorph	—	·05
Mesomorph–Balanced	—	—
Endomorph–Ectomorph	—	·10
Endomorph–Balanced	—	—
Ectomorph–Balanced	—	—

TABLE G-23. NONSUBMISSIVENESS TO AUTHORITY

| Physique Type | *Percentage Differences between Delinquents and Nondelinquents of Each Physique Type for the Indicated Trait and the Relevant Social Factor* | |
	Indicated Trait	*Lax/Overstrict/Erratic Discipline of Boy by Father*
Mesomorph	50·4%	53·7%
Endomorph	67·6	78·2
Ectomorph	51·9	53·0
Balanced	48·3	49·2

Significance of Variations between Physique Types

Mesomorph–Endomorph	—	·05
Mesomorph–Ectomorph	—	—
Mesomorph–Balanced	—	—
Endomorph–Ectomorph	—	·05
Endomorph–Balanced	—	—
Ectomorph–Balanced	—	—

Appendix G

TABLE G-24. AMBIVALENCE TO AUTHORITY

Physique Type	Percentage Differences between Delinquents and Nondelinquents of Each Physique Type for the Indicated Trait and the Relevant Social Factor	
	Indicated Trait	Serious Physical Ailment of Mother
Mesomorph	13·8%	16·4%
Endomorph	41·0	63·0
Ectomorph	24·5	30·0
Balanced	30·8	57·6

Significance of Variations between Physique Types

Mesomorph–Endomorph	·05	·02
Mesomorph–Ectomorph	—	—
Mesomorph–Balanced	—	·05
Endomorph–Ectomorph	—	—
Endomorph–Balanced	—	—
Ectomorph–Balanced	—	—

TABLE G-25. ABSENCE OF FEELING OF INSECURITY

Physique Type	Percentage Differences between Delinquents and Nondelinquents of Each Physique Type for the Indicated Trait and the Relevant Social Factor	
	Indicated Trait	Rank of Boy among Siblings (Only Child)
Mesomorph	7·8%	13·9%
Endomorph	20·6	55·6
Ectomorph	6·5	64·3
Balanced	4·9	0·0

Significance of Variations between Physique Types

Mesomorph–Endomorph	—	—
Mesomorph–Ectomorph	—	—
Mesomorph–Balanced	—	—
Endomorph–Ectomorph	—	—
Endomorph–Balanced	—	·05
Ectomorph–Balanced	—	·01

308

TABLE G-27. FEELING OF NOT BEING TAKEN CARE OF

Physique Type	Percentage Differences between Delinquents and Nondelinquents of Each Physique Type for the Indicated Trait and the Relevant Social Factor	
	Indicated Trait	Rank of Boy among Siblings (Middle/First-born/Youngest)
Mesomorph	17·7%	16·9%
Endomorph	−13·5	−10·1
Ectomorph	−4·3	−1·6
Balanced	−16·8	−9·7

Significance of Variations between Physique Types

Mesomorph–Endomorph	·05	·10
Mesomorph–Ectomorph	·10	—
Mesomorph–Balanced	·05	·05
Endomorph–Ectomorph	—	—
Endomorph–Balanced	—	—
Ectomorph–Balanced	—	—

TABLE G-29. ABSENCE OF FEELING OF HELPLESSNESS

Physique Type	Percentage Differences between Delinquents and Nondelinquents of Each Physique Type for the Indicated Trait and the Relevant Social Factors		
	Indicated Trait	Rank of Boy among Siblings (Only Child)	Lax/Overstrict/Erratic Discipline of Boy by Mother
Mesomorph	7·3%	7·1%	34·1%
Endomorph	32·2	80·0	40·4
Ectomorph	13·7	71·4	30·0
Balanced	16·9	66·7	24·2

Significance of Variations between Physique Types

Mesomorph–Endomorph	—	·10	—
Mesomorph–Ectomorph	—	—	—
Mesomorph–Balanced	—	—	—
Endomorph–Ectomorph	—	—	—
Endomorph–Balanced	—	—	—
Ectomorph–Balanced	—	—	—

TABLE G-30. FEELING OF NOT BEING APPRECIATED

Physique Type	Percentage Differences between Delinquents and Nondelinquents of Each Physique Type for the Indicated Trait and the Relevant Social Factors				
	Indicated Trait	Delinquency of Father	Alcoholism of Father	Financial Dependence of Family	Dominance of Mother in Family Affairs
Mesomorph	20·7%	32·7%	29·8%	45·8%	29·1%
Endomorph	3·6	7·1	12·9	−28·6	17·2
Ectomorph	5·6	5·7	12·7	30·4	23·2
Balanced	−2·8	−6·9	−4·7	44·4	7·7

Significance of Variations between Physique Types

Mesomorph–Endomorph	—	—	—	·10	—
Mesomorph–Ectomorph	—	—	—	—	—
Mesomorph–Balanced	—	·10	—	—	—
Endomorph–Ectomorph	—	—	—	—	—
Endomorph–Balanced	—	—	—	—	—
Ectomorph–Balanced	—	—	—	—	—

TABLE G-31. ABSENCE OF FEAR OF FAILURE AND DEFEAT

Physique Type	Percentage Differences between Delinquents and Nondelinquents of Each Physique Type for the Indicated Trait and the Relevant Social Factors		
	Indicated Trait	Rearing by Parent Substitutes	Lax/Erratic Discipline of Boy by Mother
Mesomorph	23·0%	10·9%	27·3%
Endomorph	30·5	54·8	24·1
Ectomorph	20·8	26·7	16·8
Balanced	1·2	21·1	4·8

Significance of Variations between Physique Types

Mesomorph–Endomorph	—	—	—
Mesomorph–Ectomorph	—	—	—
Mesomorph–Balanced	—	—	—
Endomorph–Ectomorph	—	—	—
Endomorph–Balanced	·10	—	—
Ectomorph–Balanced	—	—	—

TABLE G-33. POOR SURFACE CONTACT WITH OTHERS

Physique Type	Percentage Differences between Delinquents and Nondelinquents of Each Physique Type for the Indicated Trait and the Relevant Social Factors					
	Indicated Trait	Crowded Home	Delinquency of Father	Poor Conduct Standards of Family	Meager Recreational Facilities for Boy in Home	Indifference or Hostility of Boy to Father
Mesomorph	6·6%	13·7%	7·5%	7·9%	11·6%	9·3%
Endomorph	−5·4	−5·2	0·3	−0·1	−4·0	−9·4
Ectomorph	14·2	22·9	18·4	16·6	17·5	19·5
Balanced	1·8	0·0	2·8	1·2	5·7	4·3

Significance of Variations between Physique Types

Mesomorph–Endomorph	·05	—	—	—	—	—
Mesomorph–Ectomorph	—	—	—	—	—	—
Mesomorph–Balanced	—	·02	—	—	—	—
Endomorph–Ectomorph	·05	—	—	·10	—	·05
Endomorph–Balanced	—	—	—	—	—	—
Ectomorph–Balanced	—	·10	—	·05	—	—

TABLE G-36. DESTRUCTIVENESS

Physique Type	Percentage Differences between Delinquents and Nondelinquents of Each Physique Type for the Indicated Trait and the Relevant Social Factor	
	Indicated Trait	Rearing by Parent Substitutes
Mesomorph	40·8%	38·6%
Endomorph	30·9	51·8
Ectomorph	17·8	16·3
Balanced	32·8	44·2

Significance of Variations between Physique Types

Mesomorph–Endomorph	—	—
Mesomorph–Ectomorph	·05	—
Mesomorph–Balanced	—	—
Endomorph–Ectomorph	—	—
Endomorph–Balanced	—	—
Ectomorph–Balanced	—	—

TABLE G-39. LACK OF DEPENDENCE ON OTHERS

Physique Type	Percentage Differences between Delinquents and Nondelinquents of Each Physique Type for the Indicated Trait and the Relevant Social Factor	
	Indicated Trait	*Physical Punishment of Boy by Father*
Mesomorph	17·9%	29·7%
Endomorph	24·4	19·2
Ectomorph	22·6	32·1
Balanced	0·6	15·5

Significance of Variations between Physique Types

Mesomorph–Endomorph	—	—
Mesomorph–Ectomorph	—	—
Mesomorph–Balanced	—	—
Endomorph–Ectomorph	—	—
Endomorph–Balanced	·10	—
Ectomorph–Balanced	—	—

TABLE G-40. FEELING OF BEING ABLE TO MANAGE OWN LIFE

Physique Type	Percentage Differences between Delinquents and Nondelinquents of Each Physique Type for the Indicated Trait and the Relevant Social Factors			
	Indicated Trait	*Emotional Disturbance of Mother*	*Unsuitable Supervision of Boy by Mother*	*Rank of Boy among Siblings (Only Child)*
Mesomorph	3·7%	23·5%	35·0%	25·0%
Endomorph	30·5	29·0	43·5	66·7
Ectomorph	2·4	2·1	10·9	75·0
Balanced	15·4	23·3	22·2	0·0

Significance of Variations between Physique Types

Mesomorph–Endomorph	·10	—	—	—
Mesomorph–Ectomorph	—	—	—	—
Mesomorph–Balanced	—	—	—	—
Endomorph–Ectomorph	—	—	—	—
Endomorph–Balanced	—	—	—	—
Ectomorph–Balanced	—	—	—	—

TABLE G-42. RECEPTIVE TRENDS

Physique Type	Percentage Differences between Delinquents and Nondelinquents of Each Physique Type for the Indicated Trait and the Relevant Social Factors			
	Indicated Trait	Delinquency of Father	Delinquency of Mother	Physical Punishment of Boy by Father
Mesomorph	18·7%	21·2%	33·9%	18·2%
Endomorph	11·9	32·5	13·8	14·3
Ectomorph	15·6	19·6	20·3	14·9
Balanced	−6·1	−17·3	−5·0	−4·4

Significance of Variations between Physique Types

Mesomorph–Endomorph	—	—	—	—
Mesomorph–Ectomorph	—	—	—	—
Mesomorph–Balanced	·05	·05	·10	—
Endomorph–Ectomorph	—	—	—	—
Endomorph–Balanced	—	·05	—	—
Ectomorph–Balanced	·10	·10	—	—

TABLE G-43. ABSENCE OF MASOCHISTIC TRENDS

Physique Type	Percentage Differences between Delinquents and Nondelinquents of Each Physique Type for the Indicated Trait and the Relevant Social Factors					
	Indicated Trait	Poor Management of Family Income	Fair Supervision of Boy by Mother	Parents Indifferent to Boy's Companions	Meager Recreational Facilities for Boy in Home	Lax/ Overstrict/ Erratic Discipline of Boy by Mother
Mesomorph	20·5%	33·5%	25·1%	43·5%	34·2%	43·8%
Endomorph	32·9	29·7	35·1	44·2	24·5	40·2
Ectomorph	30·4	34·9	39·3	40·4	42·1	36·5
Balanced	10·9	13·7	28·6	7·5	33·0	36·0

Significance of Variations between Physique Types

Mesomorph–Endomorph	—	—	—	—	—	—
Mesomorph–Ectomorph	—	—	—	—	—	—
Mesomorph–Balanced	—	—	—	·10	—	—
Endomorph–Ectomorph	—	—	—	—	—	—
Endomorph–Balanced	—	—	—	·10	—	—
Ectomorph–Balanced	—	—	—	·10	—	—

TABLE G-45. EMOTIONAL LABILITY

Percentage Differences between Delinquents and Nondelinquents of Each Physique Type for the Indicated Trait and the Relevant Social Factors

Physique Type	Indicated Trait	Crowded Home	Emotional Disturbance of Mother	Mother Occasionally Employed Outside Home	Rearing in Broken Home	Indifference or Hostility of Father to Boy
Mesomorph	29·8%	36·5%	43·0%	49·4%	43·4%	35·3%
Endomorph	25·1	8·9	37·7	24·7	38·6	36·4
Ectomorph	13·4	32·2	14·1	16·8	17·6	27·6
Balanced	12·4	32·4	27·6	32·0	10·0	4·3

Significance of Variations between Physique Types

Mesomorph–Endomorph	—	—	—	—	—	—
Mesomorph–Ectomorph	—	—	—	—	—	—
Mesomorph–Balanced	—	—	—	—	·10	—
Endomorph–Ectomorph	—	—	—	—	—	—
Endomorph–Balanced	—	—	—	—	—	—
Ectomorph–Balanced	—	—	—	—	—	—

TABLE G-49. PREPONDERANCE OF EXTROVERSIVE TRENDS

Percentage Differences between Delinquents and Nondelinquents of Each Physique Type for the Indicated Trait and the Relevant Social Factors

Physique Type	Indicated Trait	Emotional Disturbance of Mother	Indifference or Hostility of Father to Boy
Mesomorph	24·9%	55·8%	42·7%
Enlomorph	15·0	46·8	8·3
Ectomorph	6·7	16·6	32·2
Badanced	12·3	55·0	20·8

Significance of Variations between Physique Types

Mesomorph–Endomorph	—	—	—
Mesomorph–Ectomorph	—	·10	—
Mesomorph–Balanced	—	—	—
Endomorph–Ectomorph	—	—	—
Endomorph–Balanced	—	—	—
Ectomorph–Balanced	—	—	—

314

TABLE G-53. FEELING OF INADEQUACY

Physique Type	Percentage Differences between Delinquents and Nondelinquents of Each Physique Type for the Indicated Trait and the Relevant Social Factors		
	Indicated Trait	Emotional Disturbance of Father	Rearing in Broken Home
Mesomorph	26·5%	41·8%	36·0%
Endomorph	26·3	23·8	30·9
Ectomorph	10·1	14·1	11·7
Balanced	17·4	35·8	30·3

Significance of Variations between Physique Types

Mesomorph–Endomorph	—	—	—
Mesomorph–Ectomorph	·10	—	·10
Mesomorph–Balanced	—	—	—
Endomorph–Ectomorph	—	—	—
Endomorph–Balanced	—	—	—
Ectomorph–Balanced	—	—	—

TABLE G-59. SENSUOUSNESS

Physique Type	Percentage Differences between Delinquents and Nondelinquents of Each Physique Type for the Indicated Trait and the Relevant Social Factors			
	Indicated Trait	Serious Physical Ailment of Father	Lack of Cultural Refinement in Home	Lack of Family Cohesiveness
Mesomorph	15·4%	19·5%	17·1%	15·3%
Endomorph	19·6	15·0	18·3	20·4
Ectomorph	5·7	8·9	6·4	6·6
Balanced	22·7	38·5	23·8	26·8

Significance of Variations between Physique Types

Mesomorph–Endomorph	—	—	—	—
Mesomorph–Ectomorph	—	—	—	—
Mesomorph–Balanced	—	—	—	—
Endomorph–Ectomorph	—	—	—	—
Endomorph–Balanced	—	—	—	—
Ectomorph–Balanced	·05	·10	·05	·05

Appendix G

TABLE G-65. EMOTIONAL CONFLICTS

Physique Type	Percentage Differences between Delinquents and Nondelinquents of Each Physique Type for the Indicated Trait and the Relevant Social Factors		
	Indicated Trait	Crowded Home	Mother Occasionally Employed Outside Home
Mesomorph	48·4%	67·4%	59·9%
Endomorph	48·1	45·1	76·6
Ectomorph	28·4	40·5	55·0
Balanced	45·5	26·0	40·4

Significance of Variations between Physique Types			
Mesomorph–Endomorph	—	—	—
Mesomorph–Ectomorph	·05	—	—
Mesomorph–Balanced	—	—	—
Endomorph–Ectomorph	—	—	—
Endomorph–Balanced	—	—	—
Ectomorph–Balanced	—	—	—

INDEX

Acquisitiveness, 56, 68, 69, 73, 77, 89, 101, 102, 117, 126, 131, 139, 159, 254, 274, 298
   definition of, 211
Adventurousness, 6, 26, 29, 31, 32, 76, 87, 88, 100, 120, 143, 145, 154, 251
   definition of, 211
Aestheticism, 37, 56, 59, 67-8, 72, 76, 88, 89, 142, 145, 253, 273
   definition of, 211
Affect starvation, 67
Affection in home, 6
   of father for boy, 43, 51, 61, 69, 81, 82, 84, 87, 98, 102, 103, 139, 143, 144, 145, 148, 158
   of mother for boy, 15 n, 31, 44, 69, 83, 84, 92, 98, 126, 145
   definition of, 220
Age, matching delinquents and non-delinquents by, 4
   of boy at first breach in family life, 48, 56, 60, 61, 62, 79, 80, 81, 83, 85, 88, 102, 124, 139
   definition of, 219
Aggressiveness, 6
Alcoholism
   of father, 47, 69, 84, 89, 107, 108, 138, 144, 145, 158, 160
   of mother, 69, 100, 110, 138, 142
   definition of, 217
Alexander, L., 10 n
Allport, G. W., 9 n, 19 n
Ambition, family, 27, 31, 42, 47, 66, 82, 84, 86, 87, 88, 90, 98, 100, 120, 138, 144, 148
Ambivalence to authority, 20, 26, 29, 30, 31, 32, 44, 76, 81, 111, 138, 143, 147, 233, 287, 308
   definition of, 208
Antisocial behavior, weakening of defenses against, 114
Anxiety, enhanced feeling of, 26, 35, 41, 54, 58, 82, 98
Appetitive-aesthetic tendencies, 88-9, 211
   definition of, 211
Appreciated, feeling of not being, 26, 35, 41, 44, 83, 101, 107, 113, 116, 123, 131, 137, 138, 139, 145, 146, 148, 160, 239, 289, 310
   definition, of 209

Assertiveness, social, 6, 30, 31, 56, 58, 72, 76, 81, 134, 140, 142, 147, 232, 264, 286, 307
   definition of, 208
Association and causation, 20
Atchley, V., 167
Atlas of Men, 8
Attitude of delinquents and non-delinquents, 6
Authority, ambivalence to, 20, 26, 29, 30, 31, 32, 44, 76, 81, 111, 138, 143, 147, 233, 287, 308
   definition of, 208
   basic attitudes to, 26, 81, 208
   nonsubmissiveness (or submissiveness) to, 6, 14 n, 30, 56, 61, 72, 76, 86, 140, 142, 147, 233, 264, 287, 307
   definition of, 208

Background of inquiry, 3
Balanced physique, 5, 61, 63, 65, 68, 69, 70, 71, 147, 157
Banality, 25, 35, 37, 40, 80, 98, 230
   definition of, 207
Basic research, 4
Behaviorists, xi
Biosocial (biocultural) continuum, 9, 18, 20, 28, 30, 31, 32, 33, 34, 46, 53, 55, 59, 65, 71, 72, 73, 74, 75, 76, 77, 81, 83, 85, 86, 88, 89, 91, 99, 141, 155, 160, 162
Bleuler, E., 31
Body, human, xi
   structure and delinquency, 4, 5, 103 *et seq. See* also *Physique and Delinquency* and Physique types
'Born criminal,' 37 n
Boy, age of, at first breach in family, 60, 62, 79, 80, 81, 83, 85, 88, 102, 124, 139
   definition of, 219
   attachment (or lack of attachment) of,
   to father, 43, 53, 54, 57, 67, 68, 69, 70, 71, 102, 125-6, 139, 145, 147
   to mother, 53, 67, 70, 71, 126-7
   definition of, 220
   discipline of, by parents 39, 40, 41 42, 43, 45, 58, 98
   definition of, 220

Index

Physical (*continued*)
    types, *see* Balanced, Ectomorphs,
    Endomorphs, Mesomorphs
Physique and Delinquency, 3, 4, 5, 6, 7,
    8, 11, 13, 14, 15, 16, 17, 18, 20, 28,
    30, 31, 34, 38 *n*, 45, 46, 56, 57, 58,
    59, 63, 64, 65, 66, 67, 68, 69, 70,
    71, 72, 73, 74, 75, 76, 79, 80, 81, 83,
    85, 88, 89, 90, 91, 103, 105 *n*, 118,
    141, 146, 147, 149, 153, 157, 158 *n*,
    161
Physique–trait relationships, 162, 303–
    316
    types, incidence of traits among, 11,
      14, 28, 32, 303–16
    variation in delinquency potential
      of, 14, 146–9, 157, 159
Pin-pointing of therapy, 163
Planlessness in household, 29, 42, 44,
    51, 53, 62, 63, 64, 66, 67, 80, 82,
    84, 86, 87, 88, 90, 100, 116
    definition of, 218
Potential capacity for objective inter-
    ests, 26, 28, 29, 32, 76, 80, 101,
    131, 139, 143, 232, 286
    definition of, 208
Potential delinquency, 13, 14 *n*, 107,
    113, 118, 119, 131, 142, 159, 160,
    162, 232
    definition of, 207
Poverty, 115
Practicability of findings, 158
Practicality (practical sense,), 70, 135
Prediction table based on certain as-
    pects of family life, 4
Predictive power, 91
Prevention, 3
Privacy, 42, 48
Probability, statistical, 164
Problems, methodical approach to, 26,
    28, 29, 32, 76, 80, 81, 100, 115,
    138, 140, 142, 147, 232, 286,
    306
    definition of, 208
Pseudo-delinquents, 4
Psychologists, xi
Psychology, 75
Psychopathy, 26, 29, 31, 32, 76, 90, 118,
    124, 132, 138, 139, 140, 143, 258,
    300
    definition of, 211

Qualitative and quantitative distinc-
    tions in trait-factor analysis, 91

Rank of boy among siblings, 66, 68,
    70, 88, 102, 127, 139, 143, 144,
    145, 148
    definition of, 219
'Reactive' (responsive) association of

trait and factor, 19, 57, 59, 60, 62,
    64, 67, 68, 69, 71, 72, 92
'Reading in,' absence of, in *Unraveling
    Juvenile Delinquency*, 6, 47 *n*
Reality and phantasy, 60
Rearing by substitute parents, 102, 103,
    105, 124, 139, 142, 143, 144
    definition of, 219
Receptive (oral) trends, 26, 35, 50, 78,
    86, 101, 107, 109, 116, 131, 132,
    133, 135, 137, 140, 145, 147, 148,
    245–6, 293, 313
    definition of, 210
Reciprocal influences (dynamisms) of
    trait and factor, 19, 57, 59, 60, 62,
    64, 67, 68, 69, 71, 72, 92, 97
Reconditioning, 157, 161
Recreational facilities
    in home, 27, 30, 36, 37, 40, 41, 42,
      43, 44, 48, 49–50, 51, 59, 60,
      61, 63, 67, 68, 69, 80, 81, 83,
      84, 85, 86, 87, 90, 98, 101, 130,
      131, 132, 140, 143, 144, 145
      definition of, 219
    outside home, 40, 118
Reflexes, irregular, 25, 28, 32, 76, 78,
    79, 142
    definition of, 207
Rejection, feeling of, 42
Resentment, feeling of, 6, 26, 35, 44,
    78, 82, 83, 98, 101, 102, 111, 126,
    133, 144, 145, 208, 239
    definition of, 209
Restlessness in early childhood, ex-
    treme, 25, 35–6, 78, 79, 97, 100,
    101, 110, 122, 126, 128, 134, 135,
    136, 139, 145, 225–6, 281, 303
    definition of, 207
Rorschach Test, 5

Sadism, 6
Samples, matched, compared in *Un-
    raveling Juvenile Delinquency*, 3, 4
Schachtel, E. G., 32 *n*
Science, steps of, xi
Selectivity of social factors on various
    body types and traits, 63, 105, 108,
    112, 115, 117, 120, 121, 130, 136,
    147, 148, 155, 162, 281–300
Self-control, lack of, 26, 28, 32, 76, 87,
    143, 145
    definition of, 210
Self-criticism, lack of, 26, 35, 53, 78,
    89, 100, 102, 109, 120, 125, 132,
    140, 145, 255, 299
    definition of, 211
Self-respect (pride), family, 37, 51, 53,
    65, 67, 70, 87, 89, 90, 100, 120, 139
    definition of, 218